THE HUG
OF THE
BEAR

THE HUG OF THE BEAR

by MISCHA JAC FELD

with IVAN H. PETERMAN

HOLT, RINEHART AND WINSTON • NEW YORK

D
811
F435

Dedication

To the memory of my loved ones and
those companions who did not survive.

THE HUG
OF THE
BEAR

1

SPRINGTIME on the Baltic arrived late, but it was lovely. The ice moved out of the harbors and rivers, the buds opened and songbirds returned while the snow still covered the ground. When June came the season was assured and serene, and our town's inhabitants made their way each weekend to the seaside, there to regenerate the friendships and simple pleasures which may have languished during winter's cold and competitive living.

The residents of Mitau, some forty kilometers from the Latvian capital of Riga, were a mixture of business and professional people who annually followed this routine. They would buy or rent a house in Dubbell, or perhaps stop in the Majorenhof, one of the better resorts favored by those with money. Mitau was a prosperous town whose families could afford a summer home.

Sometimes they would entertain friends or relatives from Germany, and there was great curiosity whenever a flaxen-haired Fräulein appeared on the beach, adding a new and pretty face to the summer's cast. This too, was part of spring's enchantment, for there were occasions when the visitors did not just come and go like ships on the distant horizon. Their charm remained long after they left and, this June when I was twenty, one in particular became a lasting impression, emerging often in a later and unhappier period.

My entries here are like those in a boyhood diary, found in a dusty trunk, and grown tattered and blurred with the years. It is a record of violence and wandering, in which the last pages are suddenly torn and illegible, as if the entries were urgent and fragmentary, and then interrupted altogether by the harsh hand whose red fingerprints stain the final notation.

The year was 1940, among the blackest in the history of Europe. Brave Finland had made peace on Russia's terms, Red garrisons held new outposts across the Baltic, and the phony war had grown real and grim as the Nazis overran Denmark, Norway, and the Lowlands.

"They have forced the Dutch to surrender. Rotterdam is bombed to ashes!"

Such were the exclamations as my parents and I listened to radio broadcasts that told of heaped tragedy across the borders of Germany's frightened neighbors. Then the Belgian King and his army gave up, and France collapsed. We heard the BBC describe the events at Dunkirk, and next the Germans had entered Paris.

That June everyone in Mitau stayed home. There was no movement to the seashore and not many bothered to go into the country as an alternative. Our island town huddled in the river, tense and worried. The refugees from Poland whispered and exchanged meaningful glances as week by week the war spread. Spring had come again, but our world was sad.

One Sunday morning I hitched the horses and drove into the country to see some Latvian friends. I had planned a few days with them, but no more had I been joyfully received than an inexplicable fear took hold of me. All the pleasure I had anticipated disappeared and I could do nothing but turn back. Above me were the same blue skies as when I had left the town, the green fields, the winding road, the peasant cottages—all the same. But the horse's hoofs clopping along the dirt road seemed to urge, "Hurry up, hurry up."

I found the town as I had left it, only sleepier. Night had fallen and the people were preparing for bed. From ancient Trinity Church the deep-throated bells struck ten. They were the same bells that proclaimed births and marriages, feasts and triumphs, but also death and defeat and sorrow.

Witness of the past, you ancient church, what will your gray walls yet behold? And ye bells, what will your voices still proclaim?

I unharnessed the horses, full of thought and wondering that made me, a lad of twenty, feel much older. I entered the house, still not knowing what impulse had led me to return.

Nothing special had happened at home. Another dull day in Mitau. After a few questions about my trip and quick return, we went to bed and I immediately fell asleep.

At the first light of morning I awakened to harsh sounds: a grinding rumble with a high overtone of running motors, the rattle of chains, and blaring of auto horns.

Was this a bad dream, or was I actually awake? Fears of the last month welled up in me. Were these mechanical ghosts, or something real and present? I jumped from bed and ran downstairs, not stopping to get dressed.

My mother stood behind a curtain, weeping quietly. I saw my father spit and go angrily into another room. My sister, silent with fear, clung to my mother. The only one with a light heart was my younger brother. He was laughing. I wanted to box his ears, if only because he laughed while my mother wept.

I looked out the window and there were great gray giants crawling down our street. Broad caterpillar tracks rolling over grinding wheels were raising the clamor. Dusty creatures in strange caps stood half exposed in the open turrets. They waved and laughed at the few who had ventured outside. Peculiar-looking fellows. They were neither brown nor black, just gray, gray as the dust of the roads. Pointing from each vehicle was a long, artillery gun. Tanks!

Why, this was invasion! These were foreign tanks with foreign soldiers on them. The thought was like an iron glove across the face.

I assumed at once that they were Nazis. We had been hearing right along how one country after another had fallen before them. Now our turn had come. It was a terrifying thought for my family and the hundreds of others in Mitau.

Just then a new column with a Red flag appeared—the Hammer and Sickle!

5

"Russians, thank God!"

I said it aloud and my mother turned, surprised. In that moment I had expressed what many of us felt: the Communists were the lesser of two evils. But that conveyed no admiration or illusions about the Soviets or their system.

The tanks kept coming. There were truckloads of soldiers, too. Hundreds of them. I stayed in the house until ten o'clock, watching them rumble through the normally quiet street. Except for these horrible machines pulverizing the cobblestones and coating lawns and houses with dust, Mitau's streets were deserted. It was Monday morning and a new week, but nobody ventured out to work.

By noon the people, hearing no shooting, decided there was no imminent danger and began to show themselves. First came the young boys and neighborhood dogs. The youngsters appeared everywhere, marveling at the steel monsters. The soldiers tossed them sugar squares. When a tank stopped for repairs, the boys immediately surrounded it, offering the crewmen suggestions.

"Can't I go out?" my brother demanded, when I prepared to leave the house.

"Stay inside," father advised. But I went.

At the main intersection I came upon an unusual tableau: Our old police chief (we call him a prefect) was standing on the sidewalk; people I had never particularly admired were shaking their fists at him and cursing. This to me was a rude and senseless thing.

"What ails them?" I asked another bystander, but he looked at me strangely and said nothing.

Near the police chief was indolent Karl, a chubby fellow whose allergy to work left him ragged, dirty, and whenever possible, drunk. The chief was as red as a turkey gobbler. And with reason.

"Watch this," someone murmured as another tank approached.

Immediately Karl took the police chief's club and rubbed it roughly across his fat neck. At the same time this upstart of the streets muttered into the law's ear: *"Buh, Muh,"* an expression of contempt that altered the prefect's complexion like a chameleon's. When the chief sought to leave, the crowd would not allow him to pass, boldly defying this symbol of authority. They made plain they had no respect for him. I watched for a while, but it made me sick.

One event tumbled upon another, as the days passed. The populace was plainly in shock. There was no organization of thought or ac-

6

tion. Existing authorities quite obviously had lost status. The tanks and soldiers, without saying a word, had taken over. But nobody knew precisely what was going on.

With the resilience of youth I acquired a temporary philosophy: "If we have to be saved, it's better by the Russians than by the Germans. But who is actually being saved, and from what?"

I said this the second evening, but had little response from my family. Later I would remember the incident and understand their reluctance.

We soon learned exactly who was being freed, from a practical standpoint. Things were happening in the town's government. A temporary City Council was established and quickly decided to have a demonstration at which all prisoners would be released. The prison warden had already run away, knowing what the people's revenge would be against him. Only a few turnkeys remained on duty. They were the sort who would work for God or the devil, depending on which sat in the main office and paid the quickest wage.

Under the direction of the Politruks (propagandists) the crowd gathered behind the town near the powder tower. All with socialistic inclinations were welcome. How quickly political sentiment shifts when it becomes a question of survival.

The scream of sirens proclaimed the closing of all factories in Mitau. Workmen turned out in droves, arranging themselves in neat and orderly rows. Red fabrics appeared and the more enthusiastic waved them above their heads. It was obvious that some of the faithful had been unprepared, and their identifying banners were homemade for the emergency. Placards also were raised on high.

Among the marchers I noticed some whose presence surprised me very much. Well in front was a Czech who for years had worked as a bookkeeper for a friend of my father's. His eyes shone as though this were actually an ovation just for him. I wondered if his "liberators" also knew that twenty years before he had been in jail—for political reasons.

"There is the opulent Mr. Fulk, our grain merchant," I whispered to my companion.

"Yes, and perhaps he goes to declare bankruptcy again," my friend replied, for everyone knew Mr. Fulk had three times been judged insolvent, and hoped privately someday to achieve a bankruptcy that would net him a profit. On his shoulders he bore a sign on which was written in bold letters: "Bread for mothers and children."

I studied Mr. Fulk, unconvinced. I felt that a man who fattened pigs and chickens on wheat might himself have done something for the mothers and children.

The mass pushed on, a few women having joined but not for political reasons. Rather, they seemed to enjoy being pushed back and forth among the stalwart males.

Gradually the column approached the Red rendezvous. Numerous inquisitive peasants and workers were already there from nearby villages. They welcomed Mitau's contingent with raised arms and hurrahs, to the tune of the "Marseillaise." Napoleon's armies had played it during another invasion of these lands.

The prison wardens had slipped red arm bands around the sleeves of their uniforms. Thus they joined the people's democracy. From a platform quickly constructed of planks and covered with red bunting the freedom demonstration of the prisoners began.

First to step forward was Comrade Tocek. He was greeted by stormy applause and shouts of approval. He had only one problem: Which language would he choose for his freedom speech? He could not speak Latvian, and Latvians did not understand Czech. So it would be in Russian. Neither he nor the Latvians understood much Russian, but he realized that was the tongue in which to reap ovations. Sure enough, all he had to do was mention the name of "our great leader," and there were roars of approval.

Here is the way Comrade Tocek opened the era of new freedom for Mitau:

"Comrades, fighters! Above us shines the sun of Stalin. Our serfhood by capitalist bloodsuckers has come to an end. Look around, Comrades! Do you see one of your tormentors? They are at home, figuring how much of their wealth they will lose because nobody is working today, wealth they owe to your work and diligence. Now the time has come for us; we no longer need capitalism, and as we grab the cat by the tail, it screams."

A few hurrahs were heard, but not until the cheerleaders started did the majority join, for Tocek's Russian was almost unintelligible to them and even if they had understood his words they would not have known what he was talking about.

The program quickly warmed up. One particular enthusiast pushed

8

toward the tribune through a wall of listeners: "Comrades, fighters," he cried, "I am but a poor man."

The crowd began to laugh, for on this there could be no argument. He was definitely a poor man, and so were all those about him.

"Comrades, the capitalists have heaped enough dung on our heads. It is time, it is time . . ."

Before he could finish the sentence a character in the back yelled, "Open your mouth," a suggestion that brought a howl of laughter.

What the poor workman said next I never heard, for there was a terrific commotion as the heckler was set upon, mercilessly beaten by the people's democrats, and finally dragged away to jail, half dead.

The iron-barred prison stood nearby, and from its windows calls and whistles were now heard. The gentlemen inside were getting tired of the program and plainly meant: "Comrades, cut the preliminaries and open up. You can give your speeches after we are out. We have been here long enough."

Their noisy supplication shook Comrade Tocek into action. He remembered the primary purpose of the meeting and exhorted the crowds: "Comrades, open the iron gates and free your brethren who have suffered long enough. They gave their liberty for your liberty; let us thank them with a cheer."

With a great shout the workers rushed to unlock the portals, poured in, and began opening the cells. In the process, another metamorphosis took place. All prisoners became political cases or underground fighters and heroes, although several hardened criminals had never heard those terms. In any event, their sentences now bore dividends. Some were lifted on the people's shoulders and carried homeward, while others, less notorious, roamed through the crowd receiving congratulations. A few who had been erroneously included among the heroes discreetly lost themselves in the mob.

Once the prisoners had been released and the cells emptied of all except the poor fellow who wisecracked, the great peoples' feast began, with all the trimmings. It continued far into the night, and naturally such an occasion called for proper wassail. It would be unfair to say the lower classes failed to meet accepted standards in this department. The only difficulty was an eventual shortage of liquid refreshments.

The historic occasion closed with an impressive fireworks' display, in honor of "the great father and teacher of the People's Proletariat."

2

WHEN ONE is a boy and not yet experienced in this world, time and distance seem long and without meaning. But once matured and removed from boyhood scenes, their imprint seems the deeper if the change has been abrupt.

The town in which my story begins exists today only in the memories of a few survivors. They are mostly the youths who were able to endure the subsequent hardships and who, now scattered all over the world, meet occasionally and exchange reminiscences of the chaotic 1930's. We are not many.

I have watched strangers at the mention of my native town stare in surprise and repeat the name: "Mitau . . . Mitau . . . ?" A shake of the head and a blank expression. They never heard of it. And that, as it is now, may be just as well. Often I envied them; it would have been better for me, too, had I not known that lovely town.

Mitau was actually a small green island in a river which the Latvians, with that disregard for geography so common in small countries, called "the great stream." Although it embraced our town with silvery arms, at some points I could wade across without taking off my shirt.

The streets and scenes along the waterways were typical of the economic life: fishmongers shouted the qualities of freshly smoked herrings, and the compelling "bouquet" of these goods appealed quite as strongly. Farmers' carts stood in long rows, laden with wheat, fruits, and meat. Brokers argued with producers, dealers haggled with housewives, and the latter were insulted when a farmer brusquely warned them not to paw over his stock. Pervading all, was the pleasant amalgam of smoked fish, horse manure, and freshly mown hay. How could a boy ever forget?

"Good morning, Mrs. Schoenfeldt; and how are you, Mrs. Stein? Your horse seems sleepy this morning; did you keep him up all night?"

For a young fellow, I had plenty to say to everyone—farmers, real estate dealers, or merchants, who in turn called me by my first name. I was especially fond of stranded soldiers and fishermen who drifted to our island town. They supplied me with stories of their adventures.

Patting the horses, teasing the housewives, watching the genial drunkards who sought with a cheery "Good Morning" to soften a passer-by into contributing a few cents, it was a pleasant life for a boy without serious pursuits.

Of course, I might have spent some time across the river, where amid enormous oaks and a splendid park stood the castle of Duke Jacob, no longer the reigning house, its sway having ended with the passing of the Duke two centuries before. The castle, built in the 1700's by the Italian architect Rastrelli, was lavishly rococo, having many columns, balconies, façades, and crescent windows. Proud, forbidding, and connected to the outer world by drawbridge only, it linked the past to the present, for it had become the Academie Petrina, a private school.

As such, Duke Jacob's castle was a brief restriction on my self-education in the produce marts of Mitau, but since I gave it as much trouble as it caused me, Rastrelli's influence left little imprint.

The town actually began behind the bridge at the Grosse Strasse,

12

Mitau's boulevard. It consisted of a hotel (with view of the river and castle) to which few local citizens dared go because next morning the whole town would talk about it, a "skyscraper" of four stories, two motion-picture houses and a legitimate theater, a few sizable stores, and a stand for droshkies with a trough in which to feed the horses.

Finally, at the end of the street, were some dilapidated houses with a red lantern marking each. They were not mentioned in polite circles.

Our town was certainly religious too, for we had six churches, two cathedrals, and one synagogue. On Sundays, when the bells called the pious to prayers, carriages of farmers and city dwellers stood in orderly rows. There were no preferences. The only qualification was that you have a carriage—or be able to borrow one—in order to line up. From outside, I liked to hear the choirs singing with organ accompaniment: sometimes conciliatory, sometimes gay like the rippling brook, sometimes deep and growling, like thunder and the rising hurricane. It was a warning of the Judgment before which we all would one day stand.

Latvia, like almost all European countries, mixed its politics and social life, and our little town was no exception. It was a question only of where politics left off and sociability began. All political parties were included; all philosophies had their turn.

We observed the standard rules in such matters; the optimists learned English, the pessimists studied Russian, and the opportunists, with an ear to daily news dispatches, also took up German. The fatalists mostly spoke Yiddish.

Because heated political discussions often ended in fights, I found it less arduous to join a sports club. At least there the fights were refereed, and one didn't ruin a suit of clothing. Such sports activities also prepared a young fellow for later exercises, grim and necessary.

One of our biggest economic problems in those days concerned the German Jewish immigrants who came in constantly increasing numbers, seeking refuge. Over and over we listened to their stories, gave them the best of advice free of charge, with a share of our thin-spread sympathies. Usually the conversations ended: "Why don't you try America? It's a free country."

This because there were among the immigrants many sharp businessmen, scientists, professional workers, and skilled laborers who might have the notion of establishing themselves in Latvia, thus in-

13

creasing the competition. Especially with so much pity involved.

We liked best the helpless and the lazy ones who sold from door to door pencils with the trade name "Johann Faber." With these every magnanimous Mitau burgher could demonstrate his generosity for five cents, and be qualified to say, "Yes, I also have helped."

One individual, an elderly lady whom I remember well, brought her protégé to a card party, a popular social event. He was a shy, neatly dressed young man with large horn-rimmed spectacles, who gallantly kissed each lady's hand upon being introduced. One of his shoulders drooped lower than the other and when I asked about this circumstance, he whispered confidentially, "That is from so much patting on the shoulder by my friends. Each adds the same consolation: 'Don't worry.' "

Whereupon he would sip a cognac, smoke a cigarette, and perhaps make some light comment on the poker game. This pose continued, ever gallant, ever smiling, ever understanding. He who holds the high cards smiles, he who holds the losers, smiles also. And when the strange young man with the horn-rimmed spectacles appears with another elderly lady, at the next party, everyone smiles—and understands.

As time passed, every family according to its standing, had its protégé. The butcher, Meyer, now risen to estate of sausage manufacturer, took a refugee professor. The department-store owner, Mr. Hirsch, took a lawyer; and the tailor, Markus, who had little more than a large family and small apartment, took in three immigrants who, however, had to earn their own livelihood.

"They sell pencils. Johann Faber," Mr. Markus explained.

Had we been prophets, we might have enjoyed even more the cynical aspect of Johann Faber's product. But who could foretell in 1939 that six years later in Johann Faber's private *Schloss* near Nuremberg, Germany, the free world's correspondents would be housed, using Faber pencils to take notes on the Nazis' War Crimes trial? But of that coincidence few in Mitau would ever hear. . . .

At home, the developments in world politics made little impression. Such matters stimulated discussion and conjecture, but there was no spoken suggestion. War between Germany and Poland had begun, but even that was 300 kilometers distant. After all, Latvia was not Poland. We continued to feel rather safe.

So our social life continued and the war's progress created no

14

panic. It has been said, and I must now agree, that the closer one is to terror, the more quiet is its acceptance. Groups met as usual. The women played bridge, the men poker, and all ate at midnight before cheerful good nights and leave-taking.

One evening an embarrassing situation came up when the radio, always on to keep us in touch, suddenly gave out howling, growling sounds, interspersed with what seemed like heavy blows being exchanged. The set was about to burst with the conflict when Mrs. Hirsch flounced across the room and turned it low.

"What nerve!" she cried, only by that time the set was playing *"Monika, du bist die schoenste frau in der welt für mich."* It was a totally new program in a completey different language, so suddenly could entertainment switch with the fortunes of next-door governments.

"Uwaga, uwaga!" the card players chorused, hoping thus to get the name of the new announcer.

"Uwaga," sniffed Mrs. Schoenfeldt in disgust, turning the radio off altogether. She was winning, and this uncouth interruption spoiled the fun.

But the group, knowing *uwaga,* the equivalent of Germany's *Achtung,* meant "attention," were disturbed for other reasons; what we had just heard was the announcement of the Nazi air attack on Warsaw.

"But why at this moment should anyone wish to drop bombs on Warsaw?" a lady demanded.

"Yes, why?" exclaimed Mrs. Schoenfeldt, who had game in hand and would take the rubber.

But nobody looked up from his cards, if indeed there was one who felt like justifying any attack on Warsaw. The poker players upon drawing a good card amused themselves repeating sotto voce, *"Uwaga, uwaga,"* and when someone turned on the radio again, it gave no sound at all. Warsaw stations would be silent a long time.

It was daylight when the party broke up, the men still muttering *Uwaga,* instead of the more customary *Auf Wiedersehen.* Some pondered their losses, while others thought gloomily of greater reverses in friendly Poland.

That was in September, 1939. To the joy and pride of my parents and the relief of the whole Feld family, I, Mischa Jac Feld, usually called Jac, had passed the final preparatory-school examinations and

15

was now an example to my brother. All my friends were happy for me. Only my private tutor was sad, because he had lost a well-paying numskull.

Life in Mitau continued as before, except more immigrants appeared. This time they came from Poland. Our town was getting crowded.

Originally I had intended to become a physician. My mother and father so wished, and I did not object. My brother already was calling me "Doctor." Everyone was in accord, except the faculty at the university. They rejected me in spite of my connections.

"Why don't you take up law?" my principal suggested. Why not? Young, gay, and without misgivings, I was accepted for law. Anyway, a man studying for a law career was more respected than one who failed to make the grade in medicine. It was a college degree, above all, and the course leading to it made little difference.

My mother quickly made this clear at the next tea.

"Mischa is studying law. All my life I have wished to see him as a defense attorney," she confided.

While Mrs. Meyer, whose son had failed both medical and legal preliminaries, announced with what pleasure he was preparing for a military career.

The term began, the refugees increased, the card parties continued, but the broadcasts now from Oslo, Copenhagen, from Paris, and London, too, were filled with disquieting surprises. The people of Mitau might resist change, but life on the island, so green in the great river, had drifted into a swifter, more treacherous current. Within months, harsh eddies from without and within would sweep that life away, never to return.

16

NEARLY a year had passed. A period that changed our city as if a political glacier had swept through it. The buildings were still standing, but they looked upon depressed people. Gone was the cheerful, neighborly spirit and the Sunday-go-to-meeting anticipation. The joy of living had left Mitau.

At first it had been barely noticeable. Except for the loutish behavior of a few and the bravado of the ignorant when the Reds arrived, the flip-flop of the social order took place gradually, or so it seemed.

"Maybe it is better," my mother would console us when, after a frustrating day, Father returned to speak of trends he could no longer ignore.

Then came the visit of Comrade Eidus. He arrived early one morning with a power of attorney from the new City Council. This, with

17

his credentials, he presented to Father in the office of the firm. Above all, he had a requisition.

"I am, beginning today, appointed the responsible head of this undertaking," he announced briskly, to remove any doubts we might have. He was a small, meager man who seemed anxious to convey the idea of confiscation without stating it in specific terms.

I watched my father's expression as Comrade Eidus continued, "I will be glad to keep you as my assistant. The salary is six hundred rubles—for as long as I will need you."

I dared not speak, but stood at one side, my throat tight. My father's eyes said all too plainly: Are these to be my heirs? Have I worked and saved all these years for these strangers? Is this God's justice, the equality of man . . . ?

Comrade Eidus looked coldly at my father and said stiffly, "I shall come in the evening for confirmation."

Then he added that tomorrow neither my father nor anyone else would be permitted to enter the establishment. However, if it should later be discovered that any merchandise was missing, Father would be taken before the People's Tribunal. Comrade Eidus slammed the door as he left.

For a moment my father looked after him, repeating, "Tribunal!" He laughed sadly and turned to me.

"I know, Jac. I have gone through all this before. In 1917 the same thing took place in Moscow."

When it was time to go home, Father took me by the arm and commanded, "Jac, Mother must not hear of this. Not yet."

At that moment, as he clutched me, I felt my father had suddenly aged. He walked that slowly from our store.

Nevertheless, family life had to change, and it did—from the bottom up. Father, who was the soul of energy and never idle, usually leaving the house by seven o'clock every morning, now slept until ten, sometimes longer. There were days when I did not see him at all. My mother worried a great deal, as what mother does not who knows the happiness of her family is imperiled?

Life at the university, where I was wading into the law, also changed, as the auditoriums filled with hundreds of new students from the working classes. Their matriculation qualifications were merely certificates that asserted a proletarian background. They required no tuition, no credits, no personal maintenance fees. But the former stu-

18

dent body was now asked to pay double. It was already difficult to get up the money.

New subjects suddenly appeared on the curriculum. The elements of materialism became the basis of our scientific instruction. There was a combing out of what might be considered bourgeois subjects in favor of those more in keeping with the new order. This realignment extended into all courses. To many on the faculty teaching had become an unhappy profession.

We students also had the pleasure of writing one essay after another. The usual subjects were: What was your grandfather? Who and what is your father? Does your family have a bank account? Do you own houses, country estates, and how many people do you employ?

We sought to answer as evasively as possible, but we knew that our days at the university were numbered.

Overnight the attitude of our rulers left our town without nationalities and classes. Once the new "democrats" were established, other things were disestablished. Standards of the past, traditions by which Mitau and all Latvia lived, were obsolete. They had no influence on the authorities. Now we had categories.

Men were rated "dangerous," "productive," or "unreliable." I was grouped with the "dangerous." I had committed no felonies, had no record of arrests, was not even regarded as delinquent, but I was "dangerous." The reason was that my family owned property and shared their daily bread with the less fortunate. My father, if anyone inquired, was a highly dangerous man because of this, and it was lucky my grandfather had died in time to avoid a similar stigma.

Thus the economic reshuffling was set in motion. All business firms which employed as many as one person were declared "people's property." Large establishments were confiscated out-of-hand, and from the day of seizure the janitor of each respective place became a superintendent for the State. As an external sign of his new power he received a nice red arm band.

Our personal lives were soon touched by this topsy-turvy procedure. My father once had taken on a poor out-of-work lad, who was going about with nothing more in his pockets than holes. Berl was called "the Dirty One" by his companions because, among his allergies, was one for water, which he abhorred more than fire. He was a redheaded, silent, yet sentimental young man, who spent his weekends on a bench before the stables, watching the flies and the sunsets.

Berl had worked for Father many years, and finally he discovered a girl who fitted him as a lid the proper pot. Her name was Betty and together they appeared before my father to confide their plans and hopes.

"You should become an independent merchant, but in what line?" my father mused.

The bride-to-be instantly had a suggestion: Give Berl a horse and cart and he could buy scrap iron, rags, bones, and other trash. He would have an assured income and their wedded bliss could begin at once.

Father happily advanced the money to finance horse and cart, wished them luck, and promised to be godfather for their first-born. That was in 1934. By 1941, Berl and Betty had six children, including twins. Then, when the scavenger's income lagged, Mrs. Betty chiseled a few lat from steadier jobholders and disappeared.

But the situation chez Berl changed astonishingly when the new Democratic Republic was proclaimed. Berl at once became head of the "Sojustil," that is to say the Rag Pickers' Union, and presently appeared in an elegant horse-drawn vehicle, large yellow portfolio in hand, conducting his business. Still more amazing Mr. Disenik, formerly among the very wealthy citizens of our town, was given the honor of working under Berl as bookkeeper. Berl was a celebrity, rich Mr. Disenik his helper, and Mrs. Betty returned to share the good fortune.

"We have an invitation to tea with Mr. and Mrs. Berl," my father announced not long afterward. "I suppose we must go."

"Yes, although it may be the NKVD at tea," Mother agreed.

They were accorded every courtesy and amid the best surroundings. Why not? The Berls now lived in Mr. Hirschmann's first-class apartment, requisitioned from this respected citizen with all his furniture, although he had been for years head of the synagogue. The furniture was declared "unjustly acquired property" and turned over to servants of the state. Hirschmann moved in with a brother, and Berl, his wife, and children, burdened with supervising the rag-picking industry, were awarded the premises.

"We were lucky," Father told us upon arriving home. "Only Berl and his wife were there, with all the children. Everyone was very noisy and happy. We shook hands all around, while Berl with pride

20

described his reorganization of the scavengers' trade on a truly socialistic basis.

"Mrs. Berl was everywhere, and had the right word at all times. She took us into Mr. Hirschmann's drawing room, where the good paintings had been removed and three new ones hung. On the left was Lenin, on the right Stalin, and in the middle—in a golden frame, smiling recognition upon us—was Berl."

"What do you think of this, Mr. Feld?" chortled Mrs. Berl. "Who could believe that in the center, between the great Lenin and Stalin, is my husband, once called the Dirty One? My portrait soon will be ready. Shall we have tea?"

At that cheery reunion with his former ward and employee, my father heard a prediction that fetched a chill when he told us.

"During the visit Berl confided to me a number of probabilities, among which was the report that all bourgeoisie ultimately will be sent far away. When he told me that, he looked off into space as you remember, Jac, he did while sunning himself by the stable."

Meanwhile Berl's wife had interjected that "the days are gone when we had to be satisfied on Friday night with herring while others ate gefüllte fish."

"But who prevented your choice in fish?" My father asked a logical question.

"What do you mean, 'prevented'? The main obstacle is having no money," Berl snapped. By this time it was evident that for a certain bribery Father could depend upon Berl's protection, which would be worth a great deal under the conditions.

One of the groups to which change came relentlessly was the Jews. Since we were the weather birds of politics, our behavior had come to guide world opinion and speculation. A certain segment could therefore warm in the reflected benefits of any politics. Most of the political posts were held by Latvians, however. After the arrival of the Russian tanks, the social life of the Jews altered. Only those with known Socialist backgrounds were allowed to hold positions of consequence. Naturally, some strange professional deviations developed.

Our chief cantor, for example, removed his robe and became director of the operatic theater. Mr. Kahn, for years a shoe-stall proprietor, blossomed as a public speaker—he discoursed at length before large public and social gatherings on the subject of world affairs.

Chaeke, who had prospered making caps, showed up as a court-of-justice underling; but when the witnesses and their friends, and sometimes the accused and accusers also, arose and put on their caps to leave, Chaeke's eye followed them fondly. He loved the old trade more than his new and elevated station.

Mrs. Lewo, wife of the director of a large American firm, became commissar in a confiscated-food store. She spoke Russian from that time on, avoiding former friends. When her husband, older than she, lost his job he also lost her. Not long thereafter she fell in love with the Marxian line of a young Soviet officer, and together they took over the well-appointed apartment of the ex-director, her discarded spouse.

Even more realistic was the watchmaker, Golofschiner, ordered into the Workmen's Guard. He rose rapidly in rank and his wife and mother-in-law watched with pride as he marched through the town, leading his troops. It never occurred to them as all eyes focused on him that his fellow townsmen were enjoying a good laugh at Soldier Golofschiner. They knew he actually remained a watchmaker, dealing now in larger quantities and through intermediaries, as became an important figure in the community's defense! All at a good Socialist profit.

Confiscations increased, restrictions piled upon limitations, and day by day private business and normal life became more entangled in the planned chaos. On top of everything were our "liberators," who swarmed in like insects, overflowing the wholly congested housing and often moving into rooms already occupied.

Officers' families were assigned to us, and only three rooms were reserved for my parents and us three grown children. The air officer and his wife were enchanted with the wallpaper in my room, and while they were exclaiming, a large military truck appeared and deposited wooden suitcases and a trunk, each with a mighty lock. We dragged them upstairs, and since I had never seen such baggage, I pulled out one of our leather cases to display it. The Russian woman flew into a rage.

"Soviet citizens do not look at the exterior of men or suitcases; they judge only by what's inside," she screamed.

I checked my question as to why such massive locks in that case, and decided against further hospitable overtures.

We had other tenants too, and the kitchen was soon subject to traffic jams. When Mother tried to prepare a meal, our official guests

22

were cooking supper. Father's friends came no more. They also had their troubles. One, a man named Macliach, became friendly with a Soviet major who often expressed the wish "to become acquainted as soon as possible with all these bourgeois." Macliach's wife, also eager to appease, taught the Soviet women the styling of clothes and gave them other hints on fashion. Yet this couple owed my father so very much. I would think of that fact many times afterward.

And why do I speak thus bitterly? Because these efforts to forestall the inevitable, to split from the group and try to achieve a special standing with the new order, these refusals to unite in our common misery helped speed the inexorable day of our undoing. But many preferred to make adjustments. The present was urgent; there was little time to consider what lay ahead. Fear and oppression in the hands of the powerful have a dissolving effect upon the resolution of every people. Those who have the most comforts and know the good life are in the end least willing of all to let them go.

Such thoughts were to recur many times when in more drastic hours I permitted myself to reflect. But during that last year in Mitau, like most of the people, I did not think seriously of the why, the how, or even the right or wrong of developments.

Living from day to day, I thought only of tomorrow and hoped it would not be unbearable. I was no longer a boy in a happy home, without fear of the future. That boy had been abandoned somewhere in the hurly-burly world that so quickly engulfed us. In his place stood a youth with the worries and guarded outlook of an adult.

4

ONCE, during a visit to the country, I picked up an apple in the yard and was intrigued at how a worm had hollowed it out, leaving the outside apparently healthy except for the borer's entrance. Mitau was to become that apple a year after the Russians' deliverance.

All houses, rooms, sheds, and spare structures were filled with soldiers, Russian overseers, and local yokels raised to eminence. Everything of importance and most of what was not important had been confiscated. Consumer goods had been grabbed, bought up regardless of price until inflation made a mockery of supply and demand.

The greatest clamor was for yard goods, shoes, and—a strange phenomenon I was to witness again and again—the Russian craze for watches. Anything that resembled a watch or clock, whether a cheap alarm model or a grandfather's clock in the corner, was grabbed

25

at any price. Stores were soon emptied, and prices out of sight.

As more troops arrived the demand became so great that watch and clock trading centers sprang up on the curbs. At some of these, specialists in the trade could peddle a potato as a watch. I was present when one such transaction took place, and I can still laugh when I recall it.

A platform had been erected in the center of town and the hucksters raised their wares for passing soldiers to see. Now some of the Soviet military were simple Mongolians, and nearsighted, but they wanted a watch more than anything. Presently a veteran in uniform edged toward a voluble young salesman.

"Does it work?" he asked in bad Russian.

"Like a race horse, and strong as a Soviet tractor," the youth replied, smiling his confidence.

As the Mongol hesitated the salesman invited him to listen, extending an imitation watch with no works at all.

"Can't you hear it?" the youth bellowed at the soldier, chattering his teeth in the upturned ear. The Mongol, unaccustomed to a watch's tick, nodded eagerly and handed over his money. The seller promptly lost himself in the crowd, and a few minutes later I saw the Mongol searching for him. In the end, he hurled the worthless toy to the pavement, jumping on it with both feet.

The watch market kept going, however, and if the Soviets lost in any of their World War II "trading deals," it might have been in the timepiece exchange.

June again, and it was 1941. The youth who once skipped school to go fishing was well prepared for his final examinations. I knew the biographies of Lenin and Stalin by heart, and I could lecture by the hour on the elements of materialism. Unfortunately, hard studying was not enough, not in the Latvia of that spring.

A new rule had come with the new rulers: "He who does not work shall not eat."

So I was also doing strenuous labor in a Riga metal factory, now under state management and called "The Red Star." After a period in the foundry, the director, out of consideration for my studies, placed me in the office. There I had prospects of becoming the weighing inspector, and if anyone is inclined to dismiss this as routine or trivial, I hasten to correct him.

In the Soviet system the weighing master is an important fellow, being directly below the managing director. Although the latter runs the entire operation, all foodstuffs and materials must pass the scales. Should Comrade the Weigher, with the help of the guards at the gate, forget to give a receipt, and also neglect to record the merchandise in the books, the director and his colleagues have done some business. Generally there are no more than four involved in such a transaction: the director, the weigher, a guard, and a silent partner in the NKVD, Soviet Russia's dread secret police.

The "business" prospers only if these four get along harmoniously; that is to say, should anything be discovered, someone who hasn't participated at all suddenly lands behind bars. This is the approved and tested system, and throughout the considerable indoctrination that lay ahead for me the rule did not alter very much. It was always better to catch someone who wasn't there than involve any of the principals. The victim was often the second guard or the driver, who actually worked the other shift and couldn't possibly know about the deal.

Aware of such affairs, I was content to keep on working in the office, though I could easily have graduated to the weighing job because the man in line was the bookkeeper, and not a Party member. At the time, however, it seemed more important to me to be only a working student, so as not to get kicked out of the university.

Returning home one evening I ran into great hubbub. The crowds in the streets, the numerous trucks, trailers, carts, and horses, were evidence of another crisis.

"What goes on?" I whispered to a guard with whom I was friendly. (By then fear and expediency had driven our normal instincts for friendship into the background.)

"They're talking of deportations," he replied in low voice.

"But surely nobody is still so well endowed as to be a candidate for deportation?"

"Much too well off," he muttered, and walked away.

I wondered at his words; his attitude, too, puzzled me. Did he suggest it was too much that we lived? Was that what he meant by "too well"?

Surely he has not done much for humanity, I thought, but now in a new blue shirt he feels superior. Assigned a uniform and high boots, people who have never felt important quickly discover authority and power.

The guard's warning, if meant as such, proved all too real. I returned home to talk with my parents, but Father had little to say. He evidently had heard the worst. Mother's distress was obvious; her every question revealing anguish over my safety. I tried to act unconcerned, but inside I was frightened. What was to happen?

Did she in her heart sense what lay ahead? Did a mother's instinct foresee the dangers? Was she aware that this would be our last conversation, that we would never again stand in each other's presence? Did Mother in some mysterious way understand that this was the end of our family, her last sight of her son?

Father interrupted to say they were going to the country to see a peasant to whom he had rented some land. "If you need us, get in touch right away," he said a little abruptly. He was taking Mother, my brother and sister along. He seemed terribly upset, and if he had spoken further, I sensed that he would have told me many things—had he believed they would do any good. Hurriedly they prepared to leave.

"Remember, look us up—out there," he repeated. I promised and those were the last words I exchanged with my loved ones.

I hurried back to Riga and went to bed early, for by going to bed one saves money when it is scarce. Lying in the darkness, I suddenly realized that by no standards could I consider myself a rich man. Our family wealth was gone.

A sudden shaking of the door awoke me. I sat up terribly frightened, a condition to which I was no longer a stranger.

"Open, in the name of the law!"

I put on the light and saw by the clock it was 3:00 A.M. From my window I saw columns of trucks and uniformed men escorting them. The trucks, piled with valises and boxes, were headed toward the main highway.

I opened the door. Two guardsmen with some people's policemen, all in uniform, faced me.

"Are you Mr. Feld?" The name was peculiarly emphasized. They scrutinized me from head to toe, as if a sleepy man in nightclothes was extraordinary.

"I am," I stammered.

Whereupon one of the guardsmen, speaking with obvious relish of his powers, delivered the bad news: "You see, citizen, the great day has arrived. Today all subversives are being transported to the Soviet

28

Union. At the moment you are not included, but where are your parents?" His voice rose and he screamed the last inquiry.

"My parents?" I could scarcely speak for terror. "They are at home. Home, in Mitau."

"They are not home in Mitau. Why do you lie?" the man screeched.

"We know very well they're not here, but you must know where they are," a second guardsman added.

Then the other resumed. "We demand for the first and last time that you tell us where your parents are. If you don't, you go to Siberia in their place."

My brain raced for a reply. My knees felt weak.

"For God's sake, gentlemen, how can this be? I'm about to take the examinations. I have memorized all of Marxism. Ask me, ask me anything, gentlemen. Here are my papers; I am to enter for examinations next week."

They shoved the papers aside without looking at them. All of them began to laugh.

"You can take your examinations with the bears and the wolves, you son-of-a-bitch! Speak up! Where is your old man?"

I don't know what I would have said had they not have called me the son of a dog. But at that a dreadful fury seethed inside me. I felt on fire, and with the fire I knew what I had to do.

I, Jac Feld, son of a dog, would not tell these beasts where my parents had gone. I would tell them absolutely nothing. I would go to Siberia in place of my beloved family. I would take my examinations with the bears and the wolves. Yes, you beasts in uniform, I will pass those examinations, too! I will pass, if God gives me the strength, far better than you would like. The fury receded. I stared at them, but remained silent.

"For the last time," said the people's policeman, "speak up. 'The shirt is nearer the body than the coat.' " He quoted a familiar saying, implying that I would know better than anyone else.

"I know nothing," I said shortly.

"Then pack your rags. You can take up to a hundred kilograms. Be ready in twenty minutes. We'll wait."

I began packing. The second guardsman, formerly a high-school teacher, helped.

"Take only warm things, kid," he whispered as we bent over a case.

"Now, in the middle of summer?"

"Now. Take them, just pack. There are parts of this world where the summer is like winter," he urged. Then, saying no more, he firmly placed my woolen underwear in the valise. I could see he wasn't happy in his job; he had a conscience.

My luggage was ready. It weighed about 30 kilos. I took my money, approximately 600 rubles, and went out to the waiting vehicle.

To my surprise, most of the passengers were Jews. I noted the pale faces, eyes red from crying, small children as well as grownups, but the strangest fact of all was that not one of them was a subversive character, according to even strictest Communist standards.

They were very simple people: emigrants of the middle class, who had come from Germany or, more recently, from Poland and other areas the Nazis had overrun, and many who always had lived in Latvia. There was Mr. Cohn with his wife and children; he had been agent for a large company. I realized immediately that, had I revealed my parents' whereabouts, they, too, would have been dragged to this assemblage.

Were these really enemies of the people? My mind full of Marxian precepts, with a thorough interpolation of Lenin's lore, still prompted questions. But I reached one sorrowful conclusion: it was a misfortune to have been born a Jew.

The Latvian Communists and their informers had treacherously portrayed us to the Russians as capitalists. If one was also described as a Jew from Germany, he was finished. But the fundamental accusation went back thousands of years. We who had remained true to our faith, to our worship and traditions, were being led to destruction.

There in the morning light, I, a student who had been denied the right to take examinations, examined the events that took place about me. But even with all my preparation in the university, I did not understand them.

5

A KICK in the butt interrupted my philosophizing. I had scarcely climbed on the truck when the gate went up and we began to move. The column headed toward the freight terminal, a slow-moving cavalcade of horse-drawn vehicles, automobiles, trucks, and buses. Freight cars stood waiting in unpainted, dreary welcome.

The drivers broke ranks and noisily parked anywhere. In the confusion somebody shouted, "Watch your baggage," as if we wouldn't.

There were bags and boxes everywhere, people running, shouting, trying to keep in touch with family members. Some wore two and three coats, one over the other, although it was summer. Their sweating, distorted faces bent over crying children, then looked up startled as some almighty Red guard, bursting with authority, bellowed another order.

For some of the guards this was a dream fulfilled. Today, with a departing kick, they could thrust their former employers, to whom previously they had been accustomed to tip their hats, into a deportation train, and oblivion. It was plain they relished the task.

The choice in transportation was limited. Lucky ones landed in passenger cars, but most were packed like herrings into cattle *wagons-lits*. When no more could be wedged in, the door was slid shut and a guard locked it. He then took his place, rifle in hand.

I was fortunate. Our truck stopped opposite a passenger car, and we were quickly processed. This consisted of someone scribbling the names. Mr. Cohn was distressed at such deplorable conditions, and kept muttering, "If I had only gone on my business trip." If he had gone, he would have missed deportation, but three days later Germany attacked Soviet Russia and in the course of invasion and the fortunes of war, instead of this pilgrimage to Siberia, Mr. Cohn and his family could have expected a shorter one to a crematory.

The sun was high by the time the train was loaded, and slowly we began to move. Every face turned toward Riga in which we had spent the best years of our lives, and which held the graves of ancestors and nearer relatives and all the sweet and painful memories of youth.

The steeple of St. Peter's reflected the sunlight. Then we passed the university, that temple of knowledge from which on this day, I sardonically thought, the "will of the people" extends. I felt very bitter.

Next came the factories, built "through betrayal by capitalists of the working classes"; and then the central prison behind whose gray stone walls must languish, if this Communist denunciation was to be accepted, "the evil patrons and directors" who had committed the "crime" of private ownership. I stared through the dirty window, trying to make sense of the nightmare. The rhythm of the wheels increased, the city's outskirts disappeared, the countryside began. Farewell, beloved parents; good-bye, dear family. God grant that we may meet again. . . .

It was suffocating inside the car. With such a congestion, the air was soon heated by the overclad passengers, most of whom sat silent, staring straight ahead.

A woman in one corner nursed a baby, cuddling it and trying to smile.

A small girl scrawled "Mama, Papa, Bobby" in the dust of a windowpane. Underneath she drew a little dog.

The baggage was falling off racks and getting mixed up. This became an early source of irritation. It was noticeable, too, that many were not only depressed at their own misfortune, but angry because close acquaintances were not deported. This ill feeling was contagious, especially as people knew of the stay-behinds. A sullen spirit arose.

Shrewder ones soon began to mark out sleeping quarters. I sat next to Mr. Cohn, and gradually a sense of humor was restored. After all, brooding would not help.

"Did you forget anything important?" we joked, as if anything important could be remembered.

"I wish I had taken my business trip," Mr. Cohn repeated.

The train didn't stop at any station, but once we were sidetracked to let a troop train rattle past. The soldiers looked sullenly at our penned-up cargo, as though we were the reason for their journey to Latvia.

As the first day drew to a close, I began to eat what little I had taken along. There had been no pause for food, and of course there was no provision for feeding aboard this jammed conveyance. In our car we drank cold coffee or tea and ate sparingly of our bread. We tried to guess the name of the next station, and I began to review the events of the last incredible year.

As darkness closed in people began to adjust themselves for sleep. Some rolled and curled like dogs. Old ladies drooped on the benches, old men sprawled on the floor. There was no adequate place for a full-grown human to lie down, but I found a niche under a bench and there I rested with open eyes, listening to the click-click of the wheels. They sounded like the Latvian equivalent of "Bear up, bear up." Finally, overcome by fatigue, I fell asleep.

Suddenly we were aroused by a terrible scream. I bumped my head, jumping up under the bench.

"Somebody is attacking the train," I heard. But it was nothing like that. A young man, who was apparently unable to accept the sudden change, had gone mad.

"I cannot go on. Let me die. Let me hang myself," he shouted, clawing his way toward the toilet. He struck at everyone who tried to stop him, but finally it was made clear to him that the toilet was already occupied by women and children.

"There is need for this toilet more urgent than suicide," one mother snapped.

Meanwhile someone tossed a blanket over the youth's head and

33

called the NKVD guard. At his approach, the unruly one became amazingly quiet and abandoned thoughts of self-destruction. He promised to behave. People resumed sleeping, and soon the car resounded to the snoring, sighing, and sniffling of over 140 assorted humans, suddenly cast into the same rolling, prison boudoir.

Just before dawn new military transports rolled by, and we stood aside on the track, our second stop. This time we were permitted to disembark a few moments to meet the mass demands of nature. Some of the women were embarrassed and younger ones moved off to screen themselves with bushes, but the grim guards warned them to return. The whistle tooted twice and we were hustled aboard again as the train chugged toward the land of the workingman's heaven.

Were we in Soviet Russia now? So far the woods and meadows looked like Latvia's, but after a few more hours we saw the first of many strange villages. We knew that in the night we had crossed the frontier, but nobody had stopped us to ask questions or see our papers. Indeed, nobody cared who or why or where. We were hauled like cattle, in cattle cars.

The landscape looked very different. No more white-painted rural homes with red-tiled roofs, high trees bordering lanes, and well-kept gardens; no more neat roads coming up to the tracks, with cheerful crowds at the stations; no more square, fenced cornfields from which peasants waved.

To the deportees the most notable difference was in the church steeples. Instead of the traditional cross, we now saw the onion-shaped minaret of the Byzantines. It was usually topped by the Red flag. The houses were of rough-cut lumber or logs, plastered with mud and straw. They looked miserably uncomfortable.

We reached the first large town at noon the second day. It was Pleskau, and from a distance the sun upon its golden cupola seemed to smile at us. The closer we approached, however, the sadder Pleskau became. The buildings unpainted, neglected, and dilapidated, stared at each other across rough cobbled streets. The station, in contrast to the city beyond, was somewhat newer and more inviting.

"Unload. We stop here," the guards told us. For a moment some thought it was journey's end, but not so. We had stopped to take on water and to obtain food, if we had any money. A few younger men, under guard, were selected to buy the provisions in a store near the station. I was among them.

34

The store could have accommodated a truck, it was so large, but we quickly discovered the stock was limited. We could buy champagne and canned crabs, nothing else. Naturally, we bought crabs and champagne and hurried back to the train.

"What is this?" cried Mr. Cohn.

"Crabmeat," I said, showing the cans.

"Crabs? Are you crazy? I never liked them in good times, and much less now. Didn't you have sense enough to buy bread?" He was furious.

"Sense I had, Mr. Cohn. But bread they didn't have. It was crabs or nothing. So I bought crabs."

The poor man fumed and grieved until he had satisfied himself that everyone in our car had crabmeat—and champagne.

Again the short and long whistle and off we went, through more woods, fields, and villages.

As time passed, the passengers became meaner and more cantankerous. Most of them were hungry and all were worried. As everyone prepared for the night, I crawled into my nook under the bench and opened a can of crabs. The second night began.

What were my father and mother doing? Could they guess how far away I was, that I was in a Soviet train riding into uncertainty? I wished I could send a message that I was well. Thus wrapped in thought, I slept, despite the foul air, snoring passengers, and crying babies. During the night people groped their way toward the toilets. A rotation was established permitting at least one daily visit to this haven.

With daybreak I began to philosophize again. What contradictions were all around me! Outside, the sun, blue skies, a warm and pleasant June. And just inside this train, a heap of sad, miserable people fearful of their fate. Each one complained, but thought only of himself. Not one sympathetic glance was turned toward our companions in the cattle cars, who had neither windows nor toilets.

The third day came and with it new and oppressive traveling companions. They lived with and upon us, and gave no indication of leaving. Indeed, each hour brought more of their companions. When I crawled from under my bench and put on my jacket, a woman screamed.

"A louse! A big louse!" she told the whole car.

He was taking a morning stroll across my back. Everyone craned to see what he looked like. We were to meet plenty of his kind from now on. The first one, however, was a new experience for this group, for they were all well-to-do, from the better-washed class. They watched with interest as I tore off a piece of paper, grabbed the disgusting guest, put it on the floor, and stepped on it. But when I examined the paper fragment, the louse had mysteriously escaped. It had probably leaped onto another host.

My companions, alarmed by this occurrence, diligently inspected underwear and clothing, and of course, found the cheerful little insects everywhere and in all sizes.

With that, all remaining distinctions went. Embarrassment was no more. What a sense of personal consciousness and class upbringing had maintained, even in these deplorable conditions, the common louse destroyed.

The train rolled on. Kilometers flowed into more kilometers, and nothing changed outside except perhaps the degree of village drabness. A few more military trains passed, but the trip was a monotony of the same bedraggled scenes. On June 21 we reached Ivanovo. It was neither village nor city. We did not as yet realize that most Russian cities begin many kilometers beyond the railway station. But crowds of people at the station were dashing about, excited as swarming bees.

Something must have happened, I thought. The faces of these people look as ours did when we were loaded for deportation. They must be afraid. What has happened?

High Communist Party functionaries moved among the people, trying to quiet and reassure them. Men and women, including peasants, workmen, and some soldiers, milled about the platform. I turned to our guard. "Comrade, has something happened?"

"*Nichevo*," he shrugged, the age-old Russian indifference. He continued rolling a Machorka cigarette.

"But, Comrade, what do you mean, *nichevo?* There's a demonstration going on out there!"

Each minute more people assembled. They didn't speak, but the scuffling feet made a din. Then two whispered words circulated the throng: "Molotov speaks."

A breathless silence wrapped the railroad station; the same fear was on every face. War. It was a terrible thought.

A voice over the loud-speaker: Molotov's.

"Brothers and sisters, Comrades: Today the German armies in a surprise attack crossed the Russian, Latvian, and Ukranian borders. Motorized units are not far from Kiev. It has been ruthlessly bombed. Kiev, Kharkhov, Lodz, Riga, and Schaulen were attacked. Hitler's cowardly forces have made a sneak attack on our motherland.

"Comrades, we will drive them back, for our cause is just. We shall conquer!"

A short address, but a dreadful piece of news. My mind was troubled anew with its possibilities. What of the people in Mitau, just outside Riga? What of those Soviet troops gathered there? A battle?

Outside the car window I saw Russians crying and nobody was ashamed. Some of the men, disturbed as they were, produced a bottle of vodka, but they had hardly finished a drink before government notices appeared everywhere—on telephone poles, fences, walls, even large trees. From afar I could read the top word:

"M-O-B-I-L-I-Z-A-T-I-O-N!"

I looked again at the guard who accompanied our train. He was leaning against the locomotive tender, still smoking his Machorka.

"Tovarich," I said, "we are at war! The Germans have attacked us. They have bombed your towns and mine."

He looked away and waved his cigarette. *"Nichevo, nichevo,"* he repeated.

And he had reason not to be overly excited. The train, taking us to Siberia, was also taking him East, away from the war.

6

HUMAN emotions show strange reactions under crisis. With the news of the German invasion, deportation to Siberia seemed less dreadful than before. At least we were moving away from the clutch of panzar spearheads.

It would be years before we knew it, but this train ride probably prolonged the lives of all who survived it. During the week in which we rode wearily toward the Urals, Nazi forces rolled across the Baltic countries, seizing Riga by July 1. Mitau was in the path of that assault, and overrun as the Soviet troops retreated. But we knew none of this until it came over the grapevine many months later.

The realization of war affected our guard immediately. He treated us more harshly, as enemies from outside Russia. We had become somewhat organized, however, and were better able to withstand his ill-treatment. Raw sugar cane and occasional bits of bread purchased at stations restored some energy. Nevertheless, there were numerous deaths, especially in the crowded cattle cars where people had to stand.

Brooding about the worsened military situation, I couldn't get my family out of my mind. What would happen to them? Would they be captured by the invading Hitler horde? Could they somehow escape again, as they had from this Russian deportation? We all realized no good would come of the Nazi onslaught. But how bad would it become?

"We are like all humans," Mr. Cohn said, "we look on the brighter side."

"But what is bright about either side?" I asked him.

"We could be worse off, if the Germans are in Mitau," he replied.

I forced myself to believe everything in Mitau was as we left it; man always believes what he hopes. What is the phrase? Wishful thinking? . . . So I dropped off to bumpy sleep.

Gorki, formerly called Nischnynovgorod, about 250 miles northeast of Moscow, was the first big city we saw. We approached by viaduct over the Oka into the Kuibyschev station, the railhead for embarkation to the city of that name. We were unloaded there in a small, sunny square under strict watch. Again I was struck by the changes in my train companions. Were these the same people who left from Mitau and Riga? Were these the ladies who at the Café Schwartz hesitated before acknowledging a salutation? These the Riga gentlemen who, a short time ago, walked the Latvian capital's boulevards in elegant dress and with lofty poise, although some had no more perhaps than their family name?

Here the polish had rubbed away. They were bitter and brutal. Each strove for the best seat, the first chance at food and water. They pushed and snarled, and the rule of ladies first was trampled under their selfish feet. And this was barely the beginning.

Before I completed my reappraisals of human behavior we encountered yet another species of human kind, who played a definite role in Soviet Russia. They usually belonged to no political party but were, nevertheless, well organized. They were the "Blattnoy," a special breed of scoundrels with criminal instincts that were encouraged in certain quarters.

The Blattnoy prospered through undercover liaison with the NKVD and the militia, and whatever their misdeeds, they were rarely, if ever, punished. At the time of our arrival they were doing especially well.

It should be remembered that in wartime, in addition to the involuntarily moving prisoners or deportees, hundreds of thousands of fleeing civilians also were crowding the railway centers. All were in the category of refugees, and thus fair game for the Blattnoy, who preyed on their belongings and persons, completely indifferent as to whether the victim was a Soviet citizen or a foreigner.

In roving bands, using their connections to the limit, they operated with little or no fear of reprisal, since most Russians, like all Europeans, carried no firearms or comparable weapons. As a matter of fact, householders asked nothing better than such a robber as a tenant. Then at least the owner was safe from the raids of his accomplices.

Observing the Blattnoy at the Kuibyschev station, I learned their tricks at close range. Could I, as a hungry and desperate young student, bound for his examinations with the wolves and bears, be blamed if I noted them in detail? My developing sense of survival said no.

It was simple enough for these rogues to offer their services as porters. Our group had baggage in plenty, and the first rule was to stay with it. But baggage becomes burdensome in a strange city square, particularly when the train whistle toots.

Some of the unwary accepted such overtures. Immediately a second Blattnoy would appear, snatching the valise from the other's hand to pass it to a third colleague. This continued until the horrified owner saw it no more. Meanwhile, the rest of the crowd enjoyed his loss, and laughed.

Bag snatching was only one of their arts. Some were expert pickpockets.

I watched an elderly pair who, fearing the German advance, had squeezed into the station for flight. They had with them as many of their possessions as they could carry. Several well-dressed youths approached.

"Where away in such haste, little father?"

"We move east; our two boys are at the front."

"Yes, and you fear the enemy, little father, little mother?"

"I was a prisoner of war the last time," the man explained.

"Ah, but this time the Germans won't get so far. But go with God, little father, we shall defend Gorki."

41

As they turned away, the old fellow plucked at a sleeve: "Can't you youngsters help us? Look, with all this baggage, how can we board the train? God will reward you for the deed!"

Whereupon, as if grudgingly, when in truth they had planned it, the Blattnoy picked up the bags and moved toward a crowded car. So began a sorry maneuver which I did not interrupt. In Russia it is a rule that, although you see an injustice and could be an eyewitness, you do not intervene. Nor do you call anyone's attention. Not if you value your life or health.

One of the boys thrust back the crowd and jumped up the car steps. A second stood on the running board, with the poor little father, perspiring and puffing, behind him. The second youth quickly passed the suitcases through the open door to an accomplice standing on the other side, where yet a fourth grabbed them and disappeared. Meanwhile the trusting owner waited quietly while the helpful boys settled his baggage and found space for him and his wife.

"May God reward them," he whispered again. Then, helping little mother aboard, he found neither space nor baggage.

"These Satans in human flesh! These children of hell have stolen our everything," the man shouted and he and his wife broke into sobs. I watched the train carry the despairing couple out of sight.

It was a lesson to me and my companions. We kept a hand on our stuff at all times, since the soldiers permitted numbers of such suspicious characters to wander about freely, ostensibly to bargain for watches.

Old Mr. Cohn took no chances. He was determined to balk the robbers, and sat on his most valuable suitcase.

"They won't get this," he said firmly.

Then a young chap in good-looking clothes signaled from over the intervening fence. He looked prosperous, and besides, there was that inviting wink. He shook his head when I pointed to myself; he was interested in Mr. Cohn. The latter, unable to resist a deal, rose to meet him. Again the negation, but as Mr. Cohn attempted to resume his perch, he sat on the ground. His suitcase was already being passed from hand to hand; a confederate had seized it the moment he stood up.

The horrified Cohn dashed behind the fence, yelling, "For God's sake, my suitcase is flying. Help me!"

"Your suitcase, flying?" The boy laughed heartily. "You are mistaken, dear bourgeois. That is no flying suitcase. It's a flying carpet." He grabbed and pinched Mr. Cohn's nose.

The latter wailed around the square for hours, inconsolable at the loss of his clothing, food, and money. His spirits sank lower than the gutter.

We spent that night in the open air, curled up in the public square, under wartime blackout. General mobilization had been proclaimed in Gorki as elsewhere, and passing citizens eyed us skeptically. We were well dressed, so we had money and therefore belonged to the hated bourgeoisie. Moreover, we were strangers—unpopular in Russia. From somewhere a fine voice, accompanied by a balalaika, sang the lovely "Volga, Volga."

Some of the history I had studied came back to me. The island of Jamarka, in the midst of the river Oka, had once been a great fur-trading post. Merchants from the Far East, arriving by boat or caravan, with silks and spices, had traded for furs, leather, and other products of the North. But today the great storehouses were empty; the tradesmen who had paid in gold pieces, the freight vessels, and the cheerful crowds that met them, were gone. My thoughts ran on.

The Czar, placed on the Russian throne by God—so history had it, but maybe it also involved force and intrigue?—that Czar and his descendants had also passed. The last ones liquidated like millions of other humans, just another 500 miles northeast from this island, in the Ural village of Ekaterinsburg.

And God let it happen. Now this war has happened. And I am on a weird train ride to what? Thus wondering, I slept.

Morning, and more placards met our sleepy eyes:

"To Arms, Sons of Russia!"

I read excitedly, for this was the Soviet vanguard of conscription. I noticed particularly the phrase "Mother Russia," the many references to "our soil," "your country and families," with ringing allusions to nationalistic pride. Until war struck there had been little of this in Soviet broadcasts or Communist preachments in Mitau.

"Destroy the Hitler beast in its own Hell!"

The proclamations became more vivid as we moved about the square. The Russian Bear had awakened quickly, and in a rage. He who had rolled by night into the Balkan countries resented fiercely

43

this violation of the Molotov-von Ribbentrop nonaggression agreement. Nazi double-crossers had come to Soviet Russia under the cover of surprise and darkness!

It didn't seem to matter much that we had been deported. War had also overrun our Latvian homes, and the Nazis would be even more brutal than the Reds.

Rumors, like the lice, spread everywhere. The guard said we would most likely continue our trip by boat. Trains were needed to haul troops.

"Get up, pack your stuff!"

A lot of horse-drawn vehicles arrived, the luggage was placed on them and in closed ranks we were marched behind. Mr. Cohn couldn't forget his lost suitcase and cursed without interruption. The old folks who had been permitted to ride sat on their cases. We passed along a hilly road, near the massive monument to the Russian aviator Schkalov. The three-coat wearers were soon perspiring.

"Down there is Gorki." A soldier pointed. "We're marching now through Kanawina."

Double-decked, side-wheel steamers awaited us in the harbor. They unloaded soldiers from the Volga district and took back refugees and the deported. It was a full-house one-class transportation business. The steamer we boarded was named *Volga*. Her crew looked at us curiously. Not many passengers wore so much clothing in June. Besides, none of us spoke Russian.

The baggage was stored in a freight compartment and we were told to make ourselves comfortable. Freedom of movement, however, was restricted by numbers. The boat was packed. We also received our *pajok* for the first time—our ration, a piece of bread and one dry herring. We ate it at once, although it was supposed to last two days. I actually enjoyed it.

We had an opportunity to talk with those released from the cattle cars and we consequently understood our problems better. Some had picked up a few Russian words, too. We chose a leader, a man to whom we could appeal and from whom we could obtain directions.

The loadings, meanwhile, were completed. Instead of the two whistle toots, a bell clanged three times. At the third the landing bridge came up, the paddle wheels churned, and slowly we moved into the stream.

In a short time a tremendous scene broke upon us. We had

reached the Volga River. This giant of European rivers swallowed the Oka's waters and widened to make room for the human-laden boats. Enchanted with the prospect I forgot my own troubles.

Villages, peasant houses, then the land disappeared. At times it seemed as though we sailed on a sea whose shore line one could only guess. But the river traffic was heavy. Many boats, some with seemingly endless barges, floated past. The bargemen shouted to us, but the noise of the paddle wheels drowned their voices. Dusk came on, then nightfall wrapped the Volga in black, the stars the only sparks of light.

That night we slept soundly for the first time since our journey had begun.

7

EVERY DAY is washday on the Volga. It is also washday at night when you are on a deportation voyage. The women, with that regard for cleanliness traditional among our people, laundered through the darkness, and when morning came the vessel fluttered with assorted clothing. The first objective was to try to evict the lice; by this time we were all aware of the typhus danger.

The sailors, more talkative and cheerful than our military escort on the train, played small, skin-covered accordions common to the provinces, and sang their melodious folksongs. There was a deceptive quiet not in tune with our inner feelings, for the sailors also relayed news picked up at the ports.

Kiev had fallen. Nazi tanks were approaching Leningrad. Riga was in German hands, and Latvia, with Estonia and Lithuania, had been overrun. Everyone talked of relatives left behind. What awaited them? Many huddled in small clusters, weeping.

"What use are tears?" I asked Mr. Cohn. "So many of us have gone down the river before this. Not many will come back."

The steamer anchored at Dschiboksari, which had a bazaar near the water. Rows of freighters from Astrakhan unloaded melons; kolchos women offered eggs and fruit. All one needed was money, but I no longer had any. I merely imagined what I would buy if I had 100 rubles.

At this point we became aware that the Soviet Union placed a value upon us. We were fed. Square loaves of bread, one for six persons, were issued. We sliced them with a thin cord. Moreover, we received noodle soup without the noodles, a watery dish that tasted like noodles anyway. There were also dried herrings and tea. This was supposed to last for two days.

Why had they changed toward us? Once again the sailors dropped hints.

With mobilization under way, many workers were being taken into the Red Army. But the fields and factories must still produce. We would replace some of the conscriptees.

What if we could not do the work?

"You will learn. It is not technical work you will do. Those who wish to eat will learn to work."

Later I was to hear that the Soviet Union transported populations from whole cities and provinces for this purpose. It was a mighty wartime migration, and we the human pawns upon a Russian chessboard too large and too complicated to comprehend. It certainly was beyond appreciation of the bewildered regimented thousands deported on orders from Moscow.

Some of the passengers pooled funds to buy a melon, and I went to get it. I scrambled aboard when the ship's bell rang, and we moved into midstream. As we did so, we heard from the opposite shore the wail of many voices. It was the crying of women and children in desolation and despair.

"Why do they make this sad sound?" I asked the guard.

He smiled, as an older man upon a youth, and motioned. *"Bouci,"* he said. The word meant "soldiers," and an approaching ship was jammed with them. They passed near us, but none spoke and their silent, indifferent expressions indicated they didn't expect to return.

On shore the women knelt, praying and crossing themselves. What good any attempt to be heroic? Was this something over which to

48

be proud? Here were thousands of peaceful men, taken to fight others as simple and home-loving, those from both sides leaving mothers, wives, and children at home, unprotected and unprovided for.

Are not Germans also born of women? Doesn't the German mother weep the same as the Russian, the Polish, or the Jewish?

We met more such shiploads, always with the same fatalistic expressions on board, the same weeping behind. It was as if the Volga itself wept. Mighty Russia convulsed with sadness, but responding. Her sons would die, but they obeyed. There was no choice.

We came to Kazan, then Sisran. There were orders to unload us.

"Where next? Where are we going?" The questions flew.

"Patience. Slowly, slowly. . . ." The Soviet guards never hurried. "We have time, and Mother Russia is vast," they told us. "You will get to where you are going in due time."

Once more disembarkation, counting, sorting our belongings. Some of the people sold more of their goods. A rumor said the Germans occupied the Ukraine. They were moving upon the Caucasus. They were attacking Leningrad. The Red armies had been defeated everywhere. Could it be true the Germans were unconquerable?

This suggested another peril: what would Russians eat? The captured territories provided much of their food. We observed that people no longer sang. The soldiers and guards spoke less and more sharply. We slept where we could.

It was noon when an NKVD official showed up with orders.

"You will receive rations and transportation to Kuibyschev, then to Central Asia," he said.

Central Asia. Those with ideas of someday returning home shook with fear. Strangely, I no longer felt afraid. Who would await me? Everywhere now I was on my own, a stranger in strange lands.

Kuibyschev was a large city with skyscrapers and paved streets. It made a good impression, although we saw little of it. The truck stopped before a long tunnel, and when we had gone through there was another railway station and the waiting train. We were loaded quickly, and only a few cars had benches. Guards watched us as though we were sacks of gold.

There were few formalities; the Russians were anxious to get us moving. They had many things on their mind in those days. It would be years before the world learned that one of the celebrated visitors

49

to Kuibyschev at that time was the great Lenin. He also had become a fugitive from the Germans. Of course he did not take active part in the transfer, since he was embalmed and in his Kremlin Casket. But he was also hurried to Kuibyschev, far east of the Nazi advance, to prevent desecration of the body. And presently Lenin's successor, the mighty Marshal Stalin himself, would establish headquarters in Kuibyschev. Such were the exigencies of war, when its fortunes turned against Russia in the early days.

We crossed the longest bridge in the USSR, over the Volga toward remote Tashkent. En route, we glimpsed our steamer leaving port. It had provided the best part of our journey, which now took us southeast. In two days we reached Orenburg, where we saw our first camels and carts.

A funny animal, the camel. Never content like the tired horse or well-fed cow, he lashes about when asked to pull, but in the end he responds. Once at a run he is hard to slow down and stop. And his driver, this Kazakh, he also stirred my thoughts.

So these were the "Chinese" who had entered Mitau in tanks? These slant-eyed fellows in peaked caps, the descendants of Genghis-Khan's hordes, were in reality peaceful people. Here at home they wouldn't trade one camel for ten tanks. They had their way of life staked out, working only when it was positively essential and leaving drudgery to the women.

The women, I decided with the candor of youth, left something to be desired. Maybe it was their roundish, plump faces, but surely they were lacking in style, standing in heavy boots, shawls, and half-skirts over their working breeches. Probably not one had ever heard of a hairdresser. They raised in me no carnal desires.

Leaving Orenburg, we crossed the high country of Kazakhstan. That geographical wonder, the Kirghiz Steppe, lay before us, but not many of my frightened, mile-weary companions knew. Their education had not been channeled, as had mine in the last year, to appreciate the territories and political extent of the spreading Soviet order.

It was colder on the plateau, a vast, disconsolate desert where the wind howled day and night, with only a small oasis occasionally breaking the blustery expanse. Above the rattle of the tired train, we heard the shriek of wind. It got on our nerves. The irritations and bitterness of the first days out of Latvia returned.

50

People were dying in larger numbers, too. Oh, they had been dying from the beginning, for the Reds had not troubled to give physical examinations before they seized us. Nobody had asked, "Is this journey necessary?" So the ill died early, and the well became ill, and gradually a percentage of all ages passed away.

The dead were lifted up onto the baggage shelves or placed on top of the cars. Each morning the guards, with an iron hook, dragged them down and quickly buried them near the tracks. This dreadful matutinal scene added to the general depression.

One morning there was a wild shriek when the burying detail began work. A tired traveler had crawled up on the rack to snatch some sleep. When the men jabbed the hook into his Achilles' tendon, he soon let them know he was no corpse.

During the stops at oases and villages the Kazakhs approached to trade. They offered eggs, fish, or money for whatever we had to sell, but most of all they craved tea. In that region tea, their main beverage, was rare. Black tea, which we had not often seen, brought the highest prices.

We growled with regret, for in Kuibyschev we could have bought it in plenty. But who knew? Who thought of tea? I told myself, not for the first time: We are as sheep, meek and unsuspecting, driven across a wilderness by the winds of war and oppression.

Even so, there was lively bargaining with the natives. A bright yellow evening gown went in exchange for some cooked mutton. I watched, smiling. What if the frock was only a nightgown, and the mutton in truth goat's meat? Seller and buyer were both happy, for each in his heart was convinced he had cheated the other.

This passion sometimes took bizarre turns. Old Rummel, the baker, for example, traded for the fun of it. He had nothing to swap but his cap, which he offered to a Kazakh. The customer bid only half what Rummel asked. They haggled and gestured and savored to the fullest their negotiations, although neither understood a word of the other's language.

"Well, enough of this," said Rummel. "I have enjoyed the experience. Here, friend, you can have my cap for nothing." And he gave it to the astonished Kazakh.

The man had hardly disappeared when the baker's wife came up. "And what's with your cap?"

"Sold it," said Rummel complacently.

51

"For how much?"

"For nothing. We go to Central Asia where it's warm. Who needs a cap? For that matter, who needs money where there's nothing to buy?"

The torrent of abuse from Madame Rummel was something to hear, ending in an emphatic, "You are a stupid old ass."

Days dragged by as the train rattled on its monotonous course through patches of earth that God had definitely forgotten, always, however, to come upon a new scene, a new oasis, a new bunch of tea-buying natives. High, snow-covered mountains appeared with their illusion of nearness. Hours would pass, and they seemed just as distant. This was the country of Tamerlane, the land of deserts, mountain ranges, of craggy giants and emirs and Oriental legends of splendor.

It was nearing the end of July, and the sun beat down pitilessly. The steppe had become a plain of vast fields, with enormous irrigation canals. I thought of an article describing the supposed canals on Mars, and wondered if this part of Earth looked like that to other worlds.

This was farming the hard way. Nobody pressed a button or opened a valve to send water into the canals. It came down directly from the mountains, and the artisans who regulated its flow, standing for hours in the sun-baked clay soil, were Uzbeks.

They were a fine sturdy people with slant eyes and sun-tanned skins. Some of them were handsome. The nearer we came to Tashkent the more Uzbeks we saw. They stood in long queues, digging canals in the hard soil. Women worked with the same rhythm as the men.

The mountains now converged about us, and between them we entered a wide, green plain with tall poplars and pleasant villages on the horizon. This was the gateway to Tashkent, the "city of stone." The houses of its suburbs were low and white, with high-walled gardens. Nestling in heavy shade they looked inviting to our exhausted people. These homes, called kibitkas, lined winding streets so narrow that two donkey carts could barely pass.

The donkey, we quickly discovered, was a prized possession in these parts. Not only an animal of burden, he was an object for barter, for work, for dowry, as well as a companion and friend. The Uzbek is very partial to his donkey. He often talks to him, and gets no disagreement or unkind answers.

52

The position of the Uzbek female is more difficult. She is more truly the beast of burden. She toils in the field and garden, while her lord and master rides his donkey to town to drink tea. If the wife becomes ill, she must be taken to the Polyclinic at Tashkent.

"In such case," one of the elders once told me, "the Uzbek husband mounts his donkey with great sorrow, and the sick one walks beside him. Thus he makes sure she reaches the physician without mishap."

I suggested that the Uzbeks were the only people who did not consider time as money.

"My son, what is time? What is money? He who has time also has money, and he who runs fast stumbles over small stones."

With this philosophy, I entered a world in which the men never worked hard unless someone stood over them with a gun. And never did one run fast unless a policeman was pursuing. I would remember the old Uzbek many times.

8

THE Uzbek Soviet Socialist Republic is a sprawling, sparsely popu-
lated province that curves upward around the salty Aral Sea and
reaches down to Afghanistan. In the north are the Kazakhs of what
is broadly called Turkestan, and to the south the rugged Turkmen
whose territory abuts the Caspian's waters. These, with the Tadzhiks
and Kirghiz tribesmen to the east, provide some rather tough neighbors on all sides. The Uzbeks naturally developed a certain guile.

Despite its area of 186,000 square kilometers, Uzbek SSR has to
depend upon the products of its irrigated plains and its fabulous oases
with their fruits and vegetables. The annual cotton crop helps to keep
Soviet mills running, and during the war 5,000,000 recalcitrant
Uzbeks were asked for more. To augment production, an increasing
flow of "guests," of which our trainload was only a drop in the stream,
was poured into the seasonal operations.

We had thousands of miles behind us when the train entered

Tschirschik–Sroy station, in the stone-faced city of Tashkent. There, as almost everywhere in Russia, was a great bronze statue of V. I. Lenin. With outstretched hand, he invites his people to a brighter future. At least that's what the guide will say, should you ever visit this former Khan's capital of more than a half million.

But the Uzbeks have their own explanation for Lenin's outstretched hand. And to this day they laugh at the old Scheitan, a local term meaning "Satan."

"Oh, yes," the elders told us, "before we had this statue of Lenin life in our country was quite pleasant. We had wine and plenty of it, and also fine homes and beautiful horses. We had so many sheep that we counted them by the hundreds in each herd.

"But now? Everything has been taken for the kolchos and the *sowehos,* down to the last sheep and chicken. Still the old Scheitan stands there, pointing to the mountains with his hand.

"Do you know what he really means? 'Over there, far away in the mountains, you wily Uzbeks have hidden the sheep.' And every Uzbek knows bronze Lenin speaks the truth!"

Which might explain why the Uzbeks today are the wealthiest, individually, of any people in Soviet Central Asia. Although it infuriates Russian overseers, they cannot track down the sheep that continually escape from state collectivization.

Hitler's attack on the Soviet Union, like Lenin's invitation to the good life, meant little to this people. Although a minor mobilization was begun, most Uzbek peasants found it more important to keep water flowing from the glacial ponds in the mountains and to make sure their women stayed healthy. There was no hurrying, and surely no dismay among those we watched from our smelly train.

Tschirschik was the first truly Oriental village I saw. The bazaar near the station contained enormous two-wheeled arabas, to which were hitched complacent-looking camels. The carriages stood in rows, laden with great mounds of grapes, melons, apples, and pumpkins. Bread was the most expensive item.

But there again the Uzbeks beat the market, for they were satisfied with *lipjoschki,* a cornmeal pancake that to our starved tastes seemed like Old Testament manna. Some traded their last possessions for it.

Only one thing could be had free: tobacco. Sellers of this fragrant commodity sat in lines at the bazaar, proffering Machorka in glasses.

56

Those without money would take a sample, roll a cigarette in a scrap of paper, and after smoking it, protest the grade of tobacco, proceeding to the opposite end of the line to try another brand.

After a ration of inferior food, our railway trek continued. We were disappointed that we were not to stay in Tashkent, although the unbearable heat made some wish they were already in Siberia. By now not many carried extra coats, most of them having long since been exchanged for food.

Drinking water was so scarce that we began to have more deaths. We passed Kagan and rolled toward Samarkand. This was country from the Arabian Nights, but we didn't enjoy it. They were taking out the dead in greater numbers, sprinkling them with quicklime in rapid, roadside burials. The rising sun flickered off the golden minarets of ruined castles. I saw the former residence of the Emir of Bokhara, the high Mechetas and Medressas in which the priests were trained, towering over the roof lines.

"Water. Give us water!" The cry took my thoughts from Tamerlane's architectural wonders and all interest from historic reminders. The present was more urgent.

When we asked how far and how long, the guard's answer was the same as in Ivanovo: *"Nichevo . . . nichevo . . .* you will get there . . . have patience."

Before we reached Stalinabad there were whispers that Uzbeks resenting conscription had formed guerrilla bands and fled to the mountains. They were attacking unguarded convoys.

We also heard that Soviet Russia and the captive Poles had reached an agreement. Russia pledged to free all imprisoned Poles who agreed to join General Anders and fight the Germans. There were two assembly points for the Poles: Busuluk, in Russia, and Gusar, near the Afghan border. They would be sent out by way of Iran and Egypt.

I was filled with hope at learning that there were Poles in this part of the world. What they did, where and how or why, was secondary. It was enough to know there were people within reach to whom one could speak and be understood.

The first train we met out of Stalinabad was filled with Polish volunteers. What would these punished supporters of the Nazi regime be like? we wondered.

But the train contained only Polish Jews. We could actually count

57

the non-Jewish, they were so few. Old Man Cohn nearly lost his mind.

"Are our people truly accursed? Here again the oppressed turn out to be Jewish. Polish Jews. German Jews. Baltic Jews. My God, when will this change?"

The trains halted on parallel tracks. Overjoyed, we exchanged information. There was a strange, mad camaraderie among those who had endured common hardships. We became friendly immediately. Our sympathies blended and we acted, in a sense, like long lost kinsmen and neighbors.

"Where are you from? Where were you taken?"

They brought and offered food and water, telling how they had come from a concentration camp near Stalinabad where they picked cotton and built a railroad.

"Many have been sick with malaria," they cautioned. There had been no inoculations, of course. Who cared about Poles or Jews?

The whistle tooted and all too quickly the trains pulled in opposite directions, toward unpredictable new adventures. Next day we were in Stalinabad. To our relief the baggage was unloaded and barracks awaited us. We were not permitted to leave them.

Next morning under order, the men in one group, the women in another, we took a community bath. Our clothing was thrown into a disinfecting oven, where our unpleasant tenants met well-deserved extinction. We were in far better mood, although there was nothing definite about the future.

"Maybe things aren't as bad as we've imagined," I said to Mr. Cohn. "If the liberated Poles put in two years here, it shows somebody can live through it."

I had not taken account of one fact, which he mentioned. We had met only those who survived; how many hadn't? It was a sobering thought.

The NKVD commissar inspected us next day. Young men went to one side, older ones the other. The bossman then told us our mission.

"Citizens: Our country is in danger. The Germans intend to destroy our homes and factories. They certainly shall not succeed. Each of us must do his best to save Russia. There is no time to choose a task as a kolchos worker, in the factory, or on the railroad.

"Here we are on a front, just as the soldiers ahead of us. Our task may be described as 'All for the front.'

58

"For that reason, Citizens, I wish to advise at the outset that you are under military law. You will be punished strictly according to the rules. Every mistake, every negligence weakens the army's strength. For that reason, mistakes and negligence will be considered sabotage, and for this there is only one punishment. . . ."

The NKVD leader passed his fingers across his throat, the signal for execution.

"I shall not go into more detail today. Only make sure that you come up to your quota. Prove there is in you a good spirit, and follow your superior's orders. Tomorrow you will be taken to work. If you still wish to buy anything, give your money to the guard."

He wheeled and left.

The crowd was greatly agitated. Would families be separated if the work area was divided? What was the quota? Where was the work to be?

I had other thoughts, however. I must get to the center of the city, for many Polish Jews were there, I had learned. First, a look at our detention camp. A simple barbed wire surrounded the barracks; four armed soldiers stood at each corner, slightly elevated. There were bushes about the uneven terrain. A half-destroyed hut stood nearby. In the darkness, I might sneak under that fence. I intended to return, but the great gamble was getting caught in the town without papers.

As night fell, luckily I got through the wire, crawled along the bushy hedges, and presently was on Wossenessenskajas Street. It ran through a cheerful city with white houses and landscaped yards. I paused in the park to inhale free air and feel the pulse of life.

Who can imagine what it is to stand for a moment thus? After that captive journey, under war's grinding conditions? I wanted to shout with joy, just at seeing people and vehicles going back and forth without fear of being stopped. I hid in shadow, reflecting on where this cruel journey had brought me.

Stalinabad was in an agricultural region, really a vast oasis, surrounded by several kolchos and small peasant villages. Cotton, now so vital to Moscow's war production, was the important crop. It was cleaned and processed here, then shipped by the Trans-Siberian railway branch over which we had just arrived. Keeping the line open was a project in this country.

Because shifting sands covered the rails, Soviet engineers tried planting junipers and poplars to break the dunes along the right of way. Whole rivers changed courses we were told, and the claylike soil baked so hard in the blazing sun that mud cottages were like brick. Temperatures bubbled over 100 degrees Fahrenheit, and drinking water was always insufficient.

After six months of hot weather, severe cold would set in. The plateau which grew such fine cotton, would become a bleak expanse. Although the five-year planners gradually absorbed all industry, border herdsmen continued to evade the collectives by taking themselves and their sheep to the hills. At least the caves were cooler in summer, and not much worse in winter than a hut on the plain.

With the 1917 Revolution, periodic civil wars and rebellions had shaken Uzbekistan until the fertile valleys were eventually subdued. But the irrigation systems had been destroyed. A great deal of five-year planning had gone into their restoration. When we arrived, Nazi forces had captured the Ukraine's wheat baskets, and German spearheads were reaching toward the Caucasus and Crimea. So Uzbek's production became an obsession with Soviet officials.

That was why the NKVD official had spoken so harshly about sabotage, although he used the word to cover all human failures. I shuddered at the recollection of his hanging gesture. Just then I spotted a police patrol. What if they asked for my papers?

"Keep calm. Don't act nervous," I counseled myself.

A peculiar, whimpering music came from a *tschaichana,* the local teahouse. The Tadzhiks were having a jam session of folk songs. I maneuvered until I had a view of the interior. The customers sat on straw mats, drinking from a *pjelle,* a sort of bowl. The music increased in tempo, rhythmic and gay as the audience beat time with their palms. Military police kept an eye on the crowd. . . . I made another wide circle to the main thoroughfare.

I had been anxious to find at least one of my countrymen, whether Pole or Jew. Now hundreds passed me, and I feared to approach. Arm in arm they walked the pavements, easily recognizable by their loud talk.

Finally, I moved toward a group, but when I did not greet them in Polish, they became suspicious.

"A Jake (German Jew) or Litwak (Latvian)," I heard one say.

"Whatever I am, it is the same as you," I retorted, indignation swelling within me. "I am going to the same place you have left."

60

They were startled.

"Did you commit a crime?"

"No more than you did. We have all done nothing criminal, but here we are. I have been put in the Latvian command barracks."

An older Pole interrupted. "Come with me," he said, motioning.

He took a devious route and soon we were in a small but comfortable home where his wife brewed tea. I told of Latvia's seizure by the Russians, and the sudden deportations after a year. We talked a long time.

"I don't want to remain in this camp," I told them, "because even should I survive and one day be liberated, I am sure to be classified as a bourgeois. As such a 'parasite' I would still be exterminated. I would like to join your people, and become a Pole."

The older man understood and believed me. That was my first piece of luck since the deportation. He believed my story—where I had been, where I was to go. Nobody believed anyone anymore. It was easier to lie, and, moreover, who could check? I would remember this elderly Jewish gentleman thereafter, for he promised to obtain papers and help me.

Up to that moment, except for the good God who watched over us, I felt I had not one friend left on earth. It is a terrible, lonely feeling.

Meanwhile other Jewish youths had joined the earlier group, so on my return I had additional friends. Two walked ahead to signal should a police patrol appear. I returned to the camp without incident. At the barracks door the guard stopped me.

"Stoy?" ("Where to?")

"Toilet," I replied.

"So far?"

He watched me as I walked in; I felt his eyes burning a hole in my shirt.

I couldn't sleep at all that night. "Salvation is near," I kept thinking, "if only this new friend keeps his word."

All I needed was a proper piece of paper with a stamp. Then I would again be free, a Pole, and entitled to join the Polish army.

How circumstances can change, I thought. What would have seemed a fate worse than death one year ago, suddenly was my consuming objective!

9

WE WERE awakened at sunrise. Except for shoes, there was no dressing. We slept in our clothes. The guards gave each person his *pajok* and told us to line up as before. My unit was called Jangi Bazaar, and to that place we promptly marched. I looked around helplessly, hoping for some message or signal from my new friends, but at that hour there was nobody around.

Jangi Bazaar was a dirty village 40 kilometers beyond Stalinabad. The railroad was being built through it, and clouds of smoke and blasting marked the operation as we approached. Tracks were to be laid through a small tunnel, but first the tunnel had to be driven through a rocky bridge. It was heavy, dusty labor with pick and shovel, and the mounting sun was demonstrating the truth of local heat waves.

As we joined the other crews, I noticed that while some looked well and strong, others staggered around like living skeletons. Before I could ask questions or make my own deductions, we were called to attention. The head overseer had instructions for us:

"Citizens," he said, although not one of us was really a citizen of Soviet Russia, "in our country there are neither good nor bad people. There are only good or bad citizens. The good citizen has a light and responsible duty"—obviously referring to his own authority—"while bad citizens have hard labor and quotas. For that reason, we have here simple regulations. As one works, so one eats."

He permitted himself a slight smile, but not of sympathy toward new arrivals. He was a well-fed Uzbek to whom life or death meant little, as long as it was not his own.

"This is how we do things," he continued. "The first quota entitles you to one kettle of soup, one kilo of bread, a piece of sausage, and two liters of water per day. Those who make the second quota will get half a kilo of bread, one plate of soup, one liter of water. The third-quota worker receives two hundred grams of bread, soup, and half a liter of water."

Again the flicker of a smile. "Those who can do no better than the fourth quota may as well pick out a burial place.

"There is no forced labor in the Union of Soviet Republics. I do not force you to work. But he who does not work does not eat."

With this he closed the welcoming address, and we immediately understood the starved condition of other workers. They were third-quota citizens, or worse. Moreover, there was nobody to whom they could appeal. There were also no wages, for we were regarded as prisoners who do not get paid. We worked hard for a bare subsistence. We were, to all intents and purposes, to live and endure as slaves.

It soon became plain we were in the hands of heartless underlings no happier in their duty than we. The foremen were Uzbeks or Tadzhiks. One of these by name of Birkimbaef had received orders to lay the tracks from Stalinabad to Horog. A line had been drawn and it was his responsibility to construct it. Somewhere in my feverish preparations for examinations, I had read that Peter the Great once gave a similar order. He wanted a new road from Moscow to Petersburg. So he called the head engineer and drew a straight line. It went through some of the worst swamps and bogs of all Russia and cost many lives to build. But the route today is the shortest distance between those two cities.

Down here in the desert and heat, what did the Uzbek care about tunnels and railways? He preferred his little *kischlak* in the shady grove, where his wife made pancakes and the dog watched his sheep. He cursed the orders that kept him frying in the sun, like a *shaslik* on a spit.

Now it is easier to get along with two Uzbeks than one Russian, for the latter is always looking for the most with the least effort. We soon discovered that this acquisitive trait reduced the entire quota system to a sham. The bosses were "on the take."

Water was always scarce. It took great effort to fetch it down from the mountains. The tank cars could come no closer than 15 kilometers because that was where the railroad ended. The last stretch was by donkey. Every day there was an accident, too, an excuse—the cans sprang a leak, the donkey dropped dead, the train was late. There was never enough. The grim truth was that the Uzbek foremen made money through the shortage, and if their trade in water cost human lives it did not trouble them. After all, they were the descendants of Bukhara's ancient slave dealers, to whom the spectacle of men mad with thirst was commonplace.

We did not march to and from work, but slept in tents or out in the open. Mosquitoes added nightly misery to our existence. They not only stung, but crawled into our mouths, ears, and noses, keeping us awake, so that in the morning we went to work weary as well as thirsty. I thought about ways to escape.

The nearest kolchos was about 12 kilometers distant. Collective workers always needed clothing. But where to get some? My supply was reduced to a few dirty shirts and a pair of ragged trousers. Nobody wanted to entrust anything to me to trade for fear I would not return. I was angered, and finally told my friends the ugly prospects:

"You with things to trade will die here with them. You may bribe these Uzbeks from time to time and get first-quota benefits, but once the trading articles are finished so are you." They listened but gave me nothing.

Meanwhile I never had my two liters of water although, being young and strong, I could make the first quota. There simply wasn't enough water to go around. It was a dreadful existence.

Toiling in the ceaseless heat, we dripped perspiration and dried out like wilted weeds. Everyone lost weight from the start. I realized this couldn't last long and wondered what had happened with my friends in the town. They had promised not to let me down.

One day a man named Kirsch said he would trust me with a towel if I could sell it for two *pud* of wheat. Anything above that, I could keep. Towels and shorts were highly prized in that region, and instantly salable. The Uzbeks tied Turkish towels around their heads as turbans, and the underwear made excellent summer pants. Any Uzbek thus attired was in the height of fashion.

I obtained permission from the overseer (who would sell my *pajok*), rolled the towel up, and headed for the kolchos. It was a fine, fluffy towel and reasonably clean. The work camp soon was behind me; if only I had a document besides my Latvian passport! I had contrived a peaked cap from an old newspaper and, thus protected against the sun, plodded in wooden sandals across the fields. I didn't worry about missing the quota, because I realized that as strength ebbed I would drop into a lower and lower category and gradually come to the end of everything. Judging from the graves we saw, this had been the fate of many predecessors.

As I walked I reviewed the few Uzbek words and Ukrainian phrases I had learned. *Salem alekum* (How do you do?). I could count up to ten and pronounce the words for wheat and *pud*. *Jackshi* meant "good," *jaman* "bad." *Auchat* was "eat," at that moment the most important word of all. I was absolutely famished and made up my mind that, whatever happened, I would for once get my belly full of food. I hurried as the high poplars of the Oktjaber kolchos beckoned and barking dogs announced my approach.

How I would love to be just a happy Uzbek with a cow, a few chickens, and sheep! Yes, and with one of those hard-working women. What a fine life. Really, what more could one ask?

Another fit of philosophy overtook me.

Here was I, intelligent university student, with only a towel between me and hunger. Why must I continually suffer this thirst and inner craving? Wasn't I a member of a superior European society? Was this what hard study and disciplined upbringing rated?

"Take it easy, boy. Take it easy," my good sense warned.

Yes, but what does it profit to be self-controlled? Sure, I'm civilized, but I'm starving, too. I'm slowly dying on a filthy railroad job because there isn't enough drinking water. I'm not here of my choice. I'm not even paid. And I didn't commit . . .

"Easy. Easy does it. Don't blow your top," reason urged.

But what good are Ovid and Virgil here? Who cares about Dante's Inferno when there is a hot, Asian hell all around him? Let the Devil take our European knowledge and customs to his own Hell or to Dante's, it doesn't matter. My God, I'm thirsty! Beethoven and Schubert? To hell with them, too. And their music. *Leise flehen meine Lieder*—"Softly flow my songs." I imagined I could hear them as the heat burned into my brain until I wanted to scream at the door of these complacent, leather-faced natives.

And then you must ask them to be kind and take your towel, so you can eat. The realization taunted me. What could these dark-skinned peasants know of Chopin? They didn't give a damn for all the concertos or poems ever penned. They would want a shirt, but I had none to sell.

"Maybe the towel will do the trick," hope prompted. "Whatever you do, don't go mad. Don't get hotheaded and spoil your chance. Rage and self-pity don't help much in trade."

I was talking to myself when I came to the kolchos, a sizable settlement with clay houses and attractive gardens. Nobody was stirring, and only a pair of emaciated dogs ran up, snarling and baring their teeth. It was just before noon, hottest hour of the day. At such a time only convicts worked. Everyone else was indoors; the better-class people asleep.

Fine, I thought. Everybody is at home. Here goes.

I approached the nearest kibitka. The door was open; the dog, too lazy to bark, beat his tail on the ground. Inside, the head of the house sat on the floor, drinking tea.

"Salem alekum," I greeted.

The old Uzbek glanced up and waved me off. He obviously considered me a beggar. I was disturbing him.

"Pardon, *Aka*," I stammered. The word means "uncle." *"Almaschen alamen"* (I want to trade).

"Almaschen?" He looked at me, unconvinced. *"Imne?"* (Trade? What?)

"Towel," I replied, this time in German, while unrolling the handsome article for his inspection. My feet ached from the hike. The wooden sandals didn't fit. My instep was rubbed raw, and bled. I wanted to sit, but waited.

"*Jackshi.*" I lauded the merchandise.

"*Nitchpul?*" The Old One asked how much. Curtly then, he bade me sit down, which made me his guest.

All at once I was inspired. An idea popped into my throbbing brain, perhaps the best of my life. It certainly saved that life, as things turned out.

I spoke slowly: "One good meal, and a half *pud* of wheat." I made signs to suggest a full stomach.

The old fellow knew how to deal with a hungry client and muttered "*kombat,*" meaning expensive. But he rubbed his hands, for he could see the value of the towel. His wife brought thick sour milk and a pile of pancakes with soup and dumplings. I went at them like a wolf, stuffing myself. There had been nothing like this meal since I left Mother's table in Mitau. While the Old One was returning thanks that Allah sent such a bargain, I filled my pockets with spare pancakes. Then the wife fetched a small bag of wheat.

Pointing, the man asked for the towel. I pretended not to understand.

"*Ikijarum kerek,*" I told him, indicating I wanted two and one-half *pud*.

"Two extra *pud?*" the Old One screamed. "You miserable *karaptschul!*" The word meant "thief."

"*Sen karaptschul,*" I retorted calmly. "A thief yourself." I held up two fingers and a half.

The old man all but burst with rage, but since I was under his roof at his bidding, Uzbek custom held my position inviolate.

"Out!" he managed to gurgle, red of face and pointing to the door.

I was waiting for that and, tucking the towel under my arm, left without delay. After a short walk some shady shrubbery invited rest and concealment, so I took a nap. Filled with that wonderful food and the satisfaction of an extremely good piece of business, I felt fine. I didn't awaken until late afternoon.

Should I return to the camp, or repeat my towel experiment? I decided on the latter and headed for a second kibitka, starting the same game. But this Uzbek wanted the towel first. I pretended to be insulted and left. The next one trusted me.

68

I ate almost as much as the first time, took an extra slice of bread, and was thrown out amid the same sort of screaming and uproar. Then, well pleased with my day, I proceeded leisurely back to camp. I arrived after dark and without detection.

Everything was as I had left it. Dead tired and dehydrated by the heat, my comrades sprawled on the ground, asleep. Most of them had had little food after the day long labor. Many, unconditioned for shovel duty, had blistered their hands and feet. I could hear them whimpering in sleep.

Finding Kirsch, I shook him and he sat up, frightened. He was sure I had run away. I whispered encouragement and slipped him two rolls as his percentage. He agreed I could keep the towel so long as I could provide dividends. But I told nothing of my method. The poor man must have overworked his mind, trying to figure it out.

Days passed and many good and bad incidents evolved from my trading towel. But I was never beaten or arrested, and neither did anyone dare take it from me. I always kept possession. Meanwhile, the gang boss did not report me, selling my ration as his little graft.

Once a wily and wealthy Uzbek caught onto the towel ruse and proposed his own elaboration.

First he let me eat, and when I upped my price, he laughed loudly and gave me a couple of extra loaves on condition I visit the next kibitka, where the town's miser lived. This fellow was so mean and grouchy that people enjoyed seeing him annoyed.

I went in, put on my act, and was heaved out into a circle of delighted and applauding onlookers. My recent host then went and chided his neighbor while the villagers stood outside, enjoying the fuss.

Of course the day arrived when I couldn't go near the kolchos. The man in the paper hat had become celebrated as the village crook. Peasants sicked their dogs on me and chased me with clubs, but they gave up trying to get the towel.

Should I branch out and seek a different collective? Restored in body, full of confidence, and with a remarkably improved Uzbek vocabulary—although a good portion was unsuited to polite discussion—I conferred with Kirsch, who was also faring much better on the towel profits.

A sudden change of program interrupted our further plotting.

Returning to camp one evening, I learned that two Poles had been out there with a package for me. They went around trying to find me, but departed without leaving a message. I was disappointed at missing the parcel which may have contained food. I was well fed, but some of my friends could have used it. Worse still, the overseer decided that it was time I entered a closed concentration camp. My movements and operations evidently had come to his attention.

But I didn't worry. I was too happy at the thought that my friends in Stalinabad had not forgotten. They were concerned for a perfect stranger, willing to try to avert his slave's fate.

Lying under the summer stars, I began to reappraise human relationships. These Polish Jews, for example: back in Latvia, we paid them little attention. In fact, we avoided them when possible. Was it because we thought they weren't so well educated? A bit cruder in speech and manner? Had we, in our comparative prosperity, assumed an unwarranted loftiness? Yet they had the same Jewish spirit, the binding regard for others of their faith. They certainly had proved it to me. That dreadful train ride, the Volga journey, the group action, and our existence since then had taught me much about my people.

Now these two had personally appeared at a guarded work project to aid another comrade. I stared into the canopy of heaven where God's planets and suns and whole worlds circulated without, I hoped, armed guards over those lying in slumber and dreams.

I must go to Stalinabad. At once. But how to get there?

70

10

IT WAS 50 kilometers from the labor camp to Stalinabad. Jangi Bazaar lay between, and along the entire route armed Soviet police patrolled. Worst of all, I had no papers or excuse for being on that highway. Ah, I kept brooding, if I could get possession of some official identification. It could be the difference between this living death and a return to human dignity.

The inmates of a Soviet labor camp have practically no chance to escape. The terrain, the climate—hot or cold—and the dreadful distances from centers of population provide impassable barriers. But the cunning efficiency of the NKVD required no assistance from nature.

Experience had taught the guards what to expect. Only newly arrived prisoners attempted a break. There might be a shot if several tried, but more often the poor, stupid victim was caught, dragged back, beaten, and given doubled tasks and halved rations. In short, the escapee shortened his life and added one more to the unmarked mounds that commemorate the system.

"We have no forced labor in Soviet Russia. . . . But he who does not work shall not eat." I remembered the overseer's smile. I knew the odds against flight.

Nevertheless, I had to get to town, if afoot. I had no choice. I knew I couldn't take even these conditions much longer, and they were going to get worse, for I was ticketed for the criminals' project.

I slipped away in the darkness, following the route of my towel adventures but paralleling the road where no patrols were likely. The details of that journey, made by night without much food or water, I have filed with my special nightmares. It was days before I saw the walls of Stalinabad, a sunrise prospect that, in my exhausted state, was like nearing the gates of heaven. Looking like the foulest beggar and barely able to stagger along, I mingled with the morning traffic and entered the city.

Once more fear dropped away as I lost myself in the crowds. At that hour everyone was intent on his own business. Nobody even glanced at me as I drifted along side streets and crept to the house of my friends. The old gentleman opened the door for me and I could see his shock at my appearance.

I was bewhiskered and filthy, my hair uncombed, my skin scratched and scabbed. The ill-fitting sandals had rubbed my feet raw and dried blood caked the straps. I had no shirt. My pants were shredded, barely covering the mid-section. I was indescribable, but joyous.

"I knew you would make it," he exclaimed, grabbing my hand and drawing me inside. "You know, Jac, we've thought of you so often. We're going to Gusar in a few days, and now you can join us. We wanted to send you extra food, so you'd have strength to get here. We'll find you some shoes."

Thanking him, fighting for self-control while I washed up, I explained quickly that whatever they planned I must join Anders's or some other army immediately. Anything to get away from Stalinabad. I could no longer go about as a despised criminal.

"I have committed no crimes! One is perfectly innocent, but still a criminal in this place!"

I blurted my bitterness, and then—for the first time since the Red guards seized me in Mitau—broke down and wept. My body shook and a chill rattled my teeth. Tears streaked my face, but I didn't care. I was with friends.

"Don't you know that no crime is necessary to be a criminal? Dear boy, you are in a place where crimes and accusations are made after the arrests. They are prefabricated." The old man's quiet voice went on. "The legal procedure is very cold, very simple. They need prove nothing to you, but you must prove you are not guilty. So long as you cannot prove your innocence, they will work you until you drop dead!"

It was that simple. We were seized for no reason, we were not specifically accused, but still we were treated as common criminals. If one protested he received worse treatment. If he broke the rules he went to barbed-wire camps. My host had confirmed my worst suspicions.

I was to stay with them, but not venture into the street until they obtained papers. How? I didn't ask. One learns to ask few questions in Soviet Russia. No question is better yet. But I had a wonderful feeling of being once more part of the human race.

All Polish Jews in Central Asia were to join Anders's army at once. In two days they were to report at the railway station. I had escaped just in time. But I still needed the vital papers.

Since my friends had escorted so many, they had a routine. Two Poles in front of each railway compartment checked credentials. They didn't require photographs. The name was then confirmed by the car senior. The task was to get into the compartment.

A lad named Itschu proposed that he go first, borrow the credentials of someone already registered, and slip them to me. Together we would then board the train.

The decisive hour arrived. NKVD lined the route, and everyone not Polish was suspect. That included me; I was Latvian with an accent to prove it. The patrols made spot checks, picking anyone at random. Silently I walked with the others. At a safe distance I waited, and the old terror returned. A thousand possibilities tormented me. Would they seize me? But I worried most that at the last moment my friends would reconsider this crazy effort. After all, they were sticking their necks way out.

Then someone came swiftly from the group, pressed a folded document into my hand, and motioned me to follow. In the pushing column, as name after name was called, my comrade whispered, "You're

Pan Melach. Remember!" That was my benefactor inside the compartment. I had his papers.

The train was nearly filled. The blood rushed to my neck and face. "Pan Melach."

I stepped forward, took the paper from my belt, and held it toward the trainman. Now or never!

"Melach . . . M-E-L-A-C-H." He spelled it out. Did he remember having already called the name? Perspiration trickled down my neck.

"Sachodi," he said, "Enter." He patted me on the shoulder. I felt sure he knew what was up, but I was inside that precious compartment. I could have embraced everyone.

The trains allocated to the Poles were sturdier and better equipped than the rattletraps on which we had crossed Russia. They were enormous freight cars on eight wheels, each car containing an iron stove with smoke pipe through the roof and furnished with wooden stools and clean straw. To me it was a rolling palace. Given supplies, we were in good humor as the train pulled out.

"Thank you, God. I'm now at least half Pole, on the way to join the army."

Whether for better or worse, we would soon find out, but everyone seemed to be happy at the prospects. The Russian proverb "Many heads, many opinions" was verified every mile of that chattering, expectant journey.

And what a mixed bagful we were. Rich and poor, of assorted trades, accomplishments, and character. Those considered well fixed were addressed as "Pan." Affluence was rated according to the number of suitcases. Mr. Ruwen had six large pieces of baggage, so we called him "Prosche Pan."

Elisier, an older man, was not poor by any standards, but he had a whimpering, miserly way and sat alone in a corner. His favorite observation was, "Money gets away very quickly, but it's mighty slow in returning." Which may have explained why he offered nobody a cigarette or cube of sugar, although well stocked with both.

We, the have-nothings, happily hustled wood, coal, and water. We had no wealth or possessions, but we knew from recent events that much more could be lost.

Over the rumbling of the wheels, the men sang of their home towns. "Belz, lovely city of Belz," was among them. One Jewish youth hummed the hymn "Hatikvah." Others joined. Presently the whole trainload picked up the tune, and it didn't matter if they were Jews, Gentiles, or plain irreligious Poles. It became a thunderous chorus from a thousand freedom-seeking throats.

Soon we noticed that Old Elisier had joined. He opened a suitcase and began passing out sugar and Machorkas. His eyes glowed with a new light, and a smile actually crossed his bearded face.

What had changed him? When the rest lay down to sleep, Elisier remained on his stool, humming the old hymn. I crawled over beside him and he began telling me about his life.

He had been an early colonist in Palestine, accompanying the Zionists after World War I. But he had become discouraged and had gone to America. He couldn't get started there either.

"One cannot force fortune," he whispered, for we didn't want to waken weary companions. "Fortune searches and chooses unto itself. It decides whom it wishes to protect." Old Elisier sounded for a moment like the Psalmist.

So he had returned to Poland, opened a little store and kept head above water until *they* came. Yes, the same Red columns we saw in Mitau.

That was after the Nazi-Soviet partition, when hundreds of thousands of Poles were taken to remote parts of Russia. Here he was, therefore, riding back alone, aimlessly and without family, old and broken. But with the singing of "Hatikvah" a flickering spirit was rekindled. Once more he had an objective. During the journey he kept close to the group, sharing its hopes and discussions.

We rode to Samarkand and then on to Germes, another day away. There the guards were doubled and nobody was allowed out of the cars. This sent a wave of apprehension through us. Had something gone wrong?

It was merely a border precaution, however, for Germes is only a few kilometers from Afghanistan. We chugged on toward Gusar, another twenty-four hour ride. There were large washing tanks on board; we warmed water and did our laundry. Underwear and shirts hung crisscross throughout the train, a noble array of "banners." What cavalcades the times had conjured!

We were still traveling through desert and mountains and hot winds. Sometimes we passed a station without a village anywhere visible. We saw moving dots on the horizons and were told they were camel caravans, as of old. They were going to Deshkanabad, where the camel still held preference over power-driven vehicles. Then we came to Gusar, where the station resembled a synagogue and a car-rental office stood opposite the market.

A tremendous reception committee awaited. It was really a mob of hopeful relatives. People jumped on the train seeking lost family members, friends, or home townsmen. They shouted for word of this one or that, and every now and again a shriek of joy arose above the turmoil. But for me there was no relative, no friend, nobody from Mitau on the platform.

We unloaded promptly and most of the waiting Poles retired, dis-appointed. Their kinsmen were not with us. They consoled them-selves with thoughts of the next trainload. The baggage was put on carts, but my suitcase contained little, so I carried it. We walked down the main street of Gusar.

It was a surprising place, more like what one would expect to see in Biblical Palestine rather than in Central Asia, although some an-cient Jewish tribe had migrated here. The narrow streets twisted and jogged, alive with Uzbeks, Tadzhiks, Afghans, and grizzled Bucharers. The market place was a procession of characters and costumes such as Hans Christian Andersen might have devised. Peculiar-looking fellows wearing turbans and long sheepskin outfits walked beside equally odd-looking chaps in shorts. Shorts, as I have said, were standard equipment in this region, especially in summer. But the sheepskin wearers seemed satisfied with their choice.

Into this Oriental potpourri we poured ingredients from Warsaw, Danzig, and Lodz. It didn't take them long to amalgamate. Although there was no common language, everyone had enough vocabulary for trade. Commerce, I discovered, is a universal means of communica-tion. Nowhere does it get going faster than on this ancient caravan route. Those trooping camels we saw—they moving along that trail before Marco Polo.

The Poles had a few last belongings. Uzbeks offered bread and grapes. I watched as one Uzbek proudly rode off on his donkey, robed in a Persian-lamb coat. Whatever his wares, he had made a good deal.

All non-Jewish Poles had already left Gusar and were in Tehran, or en route to Great Britain from Egypt. There had been some high-level political maneuverings meanwhile. The liberated Polish Jews

76

presented a different problem. We were shocked to hear that none of us would be taken by General Anders's army.

When I heard that I was stunned. Then I decided it might be good news. Why should Jews fight for Poland, a nation that had exterminated nearly 90 per cent of our people at one time or another? Pogroms had been a common occurrence. The misery and suffering so recently undergone had provided me with a fair taste of military transportation and war conditions. Soldiering for someone else had little appeal.

We were no cowards, and all stood ready and anxious to fight against Hitler. But we preferred to do it on our own soil. Where would that be?

For the time being, we had to remain in Soviet Russia, but nobody knew in what part. Except for Poles, no foreigners were permitted in Gusar, and since I had passed myself off as a Danzig Pole—which explained my limited grasp of the language—I could remain.

So our present circumstances as well as our future remained cloudy. It was true that we were free. But we had no money, no jobs, and no remaining resources with which to barter. Moreover, every arriving train poured out more Polish Jews who did not discover until unloaded that they could go neither forward nor back.

We were collecting in a great herd, but at the end of the world and in a desert.

11

LIFE soon grew grim in Gusar. The place was chock-full of able-bodied people, all without visible means of support. In that Old World area nobody had yet established government assistance. We discovered a slight modification of the concentration camp rule: He who has no funds may not eat.

Unfortunately, stomachs paid little attention to rules. Hunger, I found, was the same in Latvia, Poland, or the Uzbek Socialist Republic. It was particularly insistent in Gusar. We cursed the day our train left Stalinabad. There at least one might find work as a Russian Jew. But among these Uzbeks and Afghans there was nothing to do and thousands to do it.

All the volunteers were lodged in a former café, a broken-down structure we repaired after a fashion. We made ourselves as comfortable as we could on the floor. The more that crowded in, the greater the misery. A few picked up jobs; others set up their own shops. Those who had a trade or who could provide a service were in demand. For example, barbers. Uzbek barbers had a peculiar approach to their profession, which gradually encouraged outside competition. For one thing, barbershops, such as we knew in Europe, didn't exist.

The tonsorial expert carried his tools and a stool on his back like the bootblack, walking the pavements and shouting, *"Parikmacher!"* My companions tried the Uzbek barber only once. The price was reasonable, but the technique not so good.

One friend took his place on the stool to be lathered. The Uzbek pulled a sharp-edged knife from his boot and a bit of hard soap from a pocket. Since the Uzbek water shortage prevailed in Gusar, he sprinkled the customer's face from a small bottle. Then he spit lustily on the soap and prepared to rub it over my friend's face.

"Here, what're you doing?" The customer registered disgust.

"Work. Shave beard."

"With spittle? On my cheeks and chin?"

"Why you so angry?" The Uzbek was perfectly sincere. "I give special service. You are visitor here. You are foreigner; otherwise, like Gusar man, I spit not on soap but directly on face!"

Our Polish barbers, without spit, were doing rather well. So were the shoe repairmen and tailors. But the greater number, having no such skills and no time to learn during captivity, were reduced to aimless waiting.

This illustrated the monumental dislocations of Soviet war days. Perhaps such confusion couldn't be helped, but with nothing to do but complain we protested bitterly at having been hauled these dusty distances on a rare-bird chase. Hopes for freedom and a chance to join the war effort beyond Russia had been dashed. On top of it, we were left to hunger and rot in a place without work or resources.

Weeks went by, and still nothing. Not one to take starvation lying down, I grubbed a job as porter in a caravan court. I helped load and unload cotton bales, for which they gave me a few rubles or an occasional chunk of bread. It was heavy work and camels have a mean streak.

As I was hoisting a huge bale one afternoon, a well-dressed Uzbek kept watching me. He wore European clothing, was taller than average, and obviously a man of composure and confidence. My first reaction was: Secret police! They've caught up with me.

80

But what would he be doing at a native caravan court?

"The hat burns on the thief's head," runs a Russian maxim. But I'm no thief, I reminded myself, with slight reservation regarding recent trading ethics. I went right up to the Uzbek, affably inquiring whether he owned the camels or the cotton they carried.

"I don't own either," he answered, smiling. "Are you a Pole?"

"What else?" I shrugged.

"Listen. Poles aren't such bad people. But there are plenty of other bad ones around these market towns. I can spot them. Let's say I'm a speculator. For the last five years I have been a private operator. That's why I cannot go to the public bazaars."

His Russian was clumsy and his accent South Asian. I began to have a sympathetic feeling.

"I have leather goods, food supplies, money," he continued. "Here at the court there are lots of camels but few people. And only one Pole. I would like to get a gold watch for my wife, with a golden bracelet and chain. We can agree on price." He gave an address and faded away.

I quit wrestling bales and made a fast trip to the bazaar. I must find somebody with a gold watch for sale. This wasn't too easy, most of them having long since traded such valuables for food. Then who should appear but Old Elisier. He not only had a lady's gold watch, but was willing to part with it for a price.

But how does a cat cross the water? Elisier wouldn't go to the Uzbeks for fear of being set upon and robbed; this had happened to a number of Poles. On the other hand, my Uzbek client declined to be seen because of implied illegal status. Elisier and I went into "executive session," decided that two stout friends would come along, and bring clubs. They would hide near the Uzbek's residence, and if we didn't come out by a certain time they would call others we had alerted. Then they would close in.

That night the four of us set out. Back of the town, near the cotton mill, we found the house in a pretty garden surrounded by the usual clay wall. A door plate read: CHARDIROFF.

We knocked, a dog barked, and someone called, *"Kto?"* and retreated. Next came the energetic voice of the master: "Who is it?"

"I, the Pole from the court."

"Ah, so. . . ." The door opened and we walked into a comfortable hall where stood Comrade Chardiroff in yellow silk shirt, green robe, a knitted cap, and embroidered sandals. He needed only a magic wand to be Le Bon Prince.

Elisier and I were flabbergasted. What a change from the trains and work camps!—Deep-pile tasteful carpets, a luxurious divan with ottomans and cushions, two large brass chests, and a pair of silver inlaid sabers crossed upon the wall. It was Oriental splendor, Class A. If Chardiroff owned this place, we were in the presence of a wealthy man.

A warm and gracious smile, the extended hand, and immediate concern for our comfort melted the usually suspicious Elisier. All doubts dissipated, he asked me to send our bodyguards away. Then we had the inevitable tea.

Rich Uzbeks have the same innate guile as beggar Uzbeks. They are sly as merchants, and where do you find a completely honest, forthright—and successful—trader? I looked around admiringly, while conversation flowed on about politics, the cotton yield, travel conditions, the war, and so forth. But nothing about buying or selling a gold watch. Not one inquiry. Not a hint. Apparently this easygoing Uzbek had time, and the watch was not going to run away.

After two or three hours of amiable chatter, there was nothing to do but thank him and prepare to leave. We were the soul of courtesy, but by now I wished this affluent fraud would go to hell. As we were saying good night, Elisier couldn't contain himself.

"We brought a gold watch," he exclaimed as we neared the door.

"Ah, you did? Let me see it. Why didn't you tell me at the outset?" He examined the timepiece and turning to me said, "I was so happy to meet your friend I had completely forgotten about the watch."

I could tell he was impressed with it, but he casually remarked the gold was its main value. But who isn't pleased with gold? It was extremely late when we reached a mutually fair agreement and he paid us. Then he asked that we get him another watch.

When I had completed this second transaction he entrusted me with money to buy other jewelry from the starving, stranded Poles. I became a welcome guest at Chardiroff's and had tea there whenever I wished. I was also saving a few rubles. Things looked better. I had hopes for the future.

All prospects for Jews in Anders's forces had evaporated. It was imperative that we integrate into Soviet War production. The first requirement was an official identification card which I did not possess.

But in Gusar it was comparatively simple to obtain, for all the police were Uzbeks. I appeared with two witnesses and swore I was a Polish citizen, and since the police already knew me by sight I was properly accredited. I put down Bromberg as my birthplace, which allowed me to speak as much German as I needed and still be 100 per cent Polish. But I defiantly signed my own name, Mischa Jac Feld.

Living conditions had become intolerable; with no food or a place to sleep for Poles in Gusar, many took advantage of a new decree that Polish Jews could settle anywhere in Central Asia. A wholesale migration began. Trains that brought more hopefuls to Gusar took other thousands away, and when they discovered the transports were government supplied and fairly decent, the smart ones rode back and forth without purpose or compunction. I was among those who considered thus shuttling out the war. Before doing so, however, I decided to ask Chardiroff's advice.

He listened carefully, thought for a moment, and then said, "Let the others go where they may. You stay. I'm a big operator here. I run a lot of things and I've made a little mistake, but you can depend on me. If I'd known where the shoe pinched, you'd have had a job long ago. One like this." He raised a thumb to eye level and with the other hand made the motion of sprinkling salt upon it. That in Uzbek means "the best."

"Come to my office tomorrow morning. Bring your papers. Ask for me, and be of good cheer. I shall await you!"

My heart thumped joyfully as I returned to the crowded café. There, a few weeks ago, I had been a Jewish vagabond without identification, without job or money. Today I was fairly well dressed, a legalized Polish citizen with a name, address, and a promised position with the potent patrician of the community.

"With God's help, I may yet live through this experience!"

Thoughts flooded on top of plans, and plans enlarged and expanded until like the caliphs of legend I sailed off amid the clouds in imagination. Yes, on a rug as deep-piled and gorgeous as that of Comrade Chardiroff, my new benefactor, my new boss. . . . Quickly my mood changed: I thought of home.

Someday, of course, I must return to my parents. I must see the house in Mitau and put my arms again around Mother and Father, and look for a grown-up brother and sister. Was there perhaps someone else? A honey-haired girl I had occasionally glimpsed on the beach at Dubbell? I didn't even know her name. Could that university youth be now an adult? With manhood's aspirations? How my parents must worry about what happened to me. Would they still be hidden in the country?

I continued the reverie there on the crowded, smelly floor where men lay shoulder to shoulder. I had not had such thoughts for a long time, but it was not strange that they had come with a change of fortune, for I now had resolution again to carry on. Month after month had passed in Gusar, one much like another; as well write September as May. This was November, but my daily program had remained the same: at 7:00 A.M. to the teahouse, where a loud-speaker brought the news. But never good news.

The German armies still advanced. One was hammering the out-skirts of Leningrad. Dnepropetrovsk had fallen and with it the indus-trial Donets basin. The Russians were in broad retreat. It did not look encouraging anywhere.

After the broadcast I would tramp the streets trying to do a little business, perform a task, eke out a ruble for food, and each night return to the dismal café with nothing accomplished.

Now this would alter. I would be working for a man of wide inter-ests. What had he told me? A mill, a bakery, a tailoring shop, the cotton processing. . . .

"So I made a little mistake. Not mine, understand. But things work out." He had spat and flipped his cigarette aside.

Next morning I did not head for the *tschaichana*. Let the war news be as it might. In fact, to hell with the war. I had a new position.

Chardiroff's office was in a surprisingly large building for a man without political eminence. Glancing into a window as I approached, I saw young men and women pushing little balls on abaci. Others trotted among filing cabinets, and bookkeepers sat on high stools.

A guard stopped me at the main entrance. I was surprised.

Above him was a sign: *"Rajkomkombinat."* The United Work-shops of the USSR! The mills, the bakeries, the clothing factory, and everything of any account in Gusar—all centered here.

"Who do you wish to see, Comrade?" The guard blocked my path.

"Chardiroff," I said shortly.

"Chardiroff has no time," he retorted, rifle horizontal.

"I have an appointment."

"Who's the guard here, you or I? I tell you something, that's it."

84

This elderly fellow probably had been chiseling a few rubles by taking bribes from those who wanted to see Chardiroff. He made a mistake with me.

"Liar," I said, and pushed him aside.

Walking quickly down the corridor I read the signs. At the end door leading to the main suite I saw one that confirmed what I had already suspected:

"Comrade CHARDIROFF, Director."

My mysterious black-marketing friend was the top government boss of the region.

12

MY HEART beat faster as I knocked cautiously at the door. Is it not always so when a young man first stands before one of influence, seeking employment?

"Sachodi." At the word I turned the knob.

The mighty director reigned in a spacious, well-appointed office. Large busts of Lenin and Stalin on wooden pedestals flanked his desk, left and right. In one corner was a wide table, but nobody sat there. A large red flag draped the wall, above it written in gold letters: "To the best operation in the Community of Bukhara!"

"Come closer, come closer," said Chardiroff, his voice breaking a silence that only the ticking clock punctuated. It was a strong, forceful voice totally different from the halting, subdued undertones that negotiated for watches and gold. This man spoke with authority and power.

"Sit down, Jac. I just happen to have a little time. Let's talk. You want to go to work and I appreciate that, for every good citizen of the Soviet Union must work. You understand our regime and its principles?"

It surprised me how much his Russian had improved. Or had he used this speech so often he was familiar with the words?

"Yes, Chief, I wish to work, but at what? I have no idea what I can do."

"The important thing is what you know, what you've learned." Chardiroff interjected.

"I can carry bags and handle freight as I showed at the caravan court, but I've studied for law—very different from hustling baggage," I went on.

"What? You are an economist? Exactly what I need. The last one was arrested a week ago." And under his breath in confidential manner: "A Russian. And a drinker, a pig, and a crook besides. He's probably at the front by now."

"But I can't take over a job in which I've no experience. I can handle bags, but the economy——"

"Not everyone can sell watches, either," Chardiroff interposed, wagging a finger and laughing. "You won't have much to do. I shall appoint you Planovik—statistical director."

"What's that?" I inquired, hearing the title for the first time.

"The Planovik must prepare the work program and also be responsible for all work assigned. For example: If we get a thousand meters of yard goods from which three hundred and fifty soldiers' coats are to be made, you will see that the coats are delivered on time. You know, there's a war on!"

"But Comrade Chardiroff, I thought the director assumed that responsibility."

"On the contrary, Jac. All I have to do is make sure we get the material, that no saboteurs creep in, and a few other details. Ah well," he sighed, "what do you know of my responsibilities? One should have eight eyes—two in front, two in back, two to the right and left. Of course, I will support you as much as possible. Be assured we will get along very well. And now, no more questions. We start. Your salary is three hundred rubles and don't worry about your clothing. Where wood is chopped, there are always shavings." He winked jovially and laughed.

I hastily asked about written reports. "Comrade Director, I cannot write much in Russian." (I couldn't write it at all.)

88

"Durak" (Stupid), Chardiroff scoffed, "do you think your predecessor wrote any better? So, we agree? I'll call the secretary."

The offer was good and I had no alternative so I accepted. Had I suspected what lay ahead, I'd have been more careful.

A young Uzbek girl with a massive order book appeared and Chardiroff curtly dictated: "I, Chardiroff, Director of the Combine Gusar, order Comrade Feld beginning tomorrow, November 2, 1941, to be Planovik of our enterprises. Salary, three hundred rubles. Signed. . . ." He scrawled his name and that was it.

In the preceding months a number of Poles had taken jobs in the combine, as tailors, cobblers, and barbers, organizing the work efficiently on European lines. Production had improved by leaps and bounds, but all unknown to me as I labored at the caravan court. When I met my friends and happily reported I'd been appointed Planovik, they took the news with mixed feelings. Some congratulated me, others were envious of my good luck.

Old Elisier warned me, having formed his own opinion about responsible jobs in the Soviet Union.

"Be sure they don't affix a beard that you can scratch a long time before you're rid of it," he concluded gloomily. But I could scarcely wait for the next day, and half an hour early, appeared at my post.

"Good morning, Comrade Planovik," Storosch, the old guard greeted, the same man who the day before had tried to keep me out. "You may pass, brother, and please forgive yesterday's hold up. We all work for the State and want the best for our country."

"Never mind, Uncle," I said, concluding that office workers are the same whether in Moscow, Berlin, Paris, or New York. Here in Gusar they reported ten minutes before eight, sat at desks until noon, ate the lunch each brought with him, and then longingly watched the clock until quitting time.

Promptly at eight o'clock a bell rang and in walked Comrade Director. The day began, my first as a Soviet Government employee. I took a deep breath.

Chardiroff had given the second desk to me. He bent over a stack of papers, which he signed after careful study. I waited impatiently for my first assignment. Presently an Uzbek brought a sheaf of papers written in indelible pencil, along with a tabulation sheet covered with figures and red letters.

He introduced himself: "Comrade Akimov, head comptroller." Then he rushed immediately into an explanation.

"Comrade Planovik, I am at my wits' end. I don't know what to do.

"Workshop Two, which is the tailors', during the past quarter fulfilled only seventy per cent of its quota. The fourth quarter is nearing its end and, all in all, not half the yearly quota has been fulfilled, although we have engaged a considerable number of Poles. On the other hand, Workshop Four, the shoemakers, have already achieved one hundred and two per cent of their quota.

"My greatest worry, however, is Workshop Five, the bakers. God knows what they're doing. Do they sell the *lipjoschki* or do they just unload the flour on black market? Or do they eat everything themselves, the sons-of-bitches?

"Whatever they do, they have nowhere near reached quota, and because of it the damned town never has enough bread. You must know of such cases from Poland. What shall we do? I've suggested we keep a file and place the stinking bakers before the People's Tribunal!"

A nice job, this, I thought. What am I doing here, among this fellow's percentages, quotas, and files? I didn't understand any of it.

Chardiroff, buried among papers, didn't look up, and I didn't dare ask Akimov what the devil he was talking about. After all, I was the Planovik. Supposed to know everything. Suddenly a way out occurred:

"Look, Comrade. Leave your reports and quarterly statements and I'll check them. That will provide a picture of the whole situation; after that I'll call you."

When Akimov had left, I asked the director for an explanation.

"You see," Chardiroff began, "your job consists of nothing but quarters and quotas. A quarter: three months. Four quarters, one year. Twenty quarters, a Five Year Plan. Follow me, Comrade Planovik? You make sure the quotas are not too high and the percentages of production not too low, that is all!"

After that clarification, the scope of my position immediately became evident, but since the documents were mostly in Uzbek, I was no smarter than before.

Chardiroff continued to stare at his papers. After some deliberation, I presumed to disturb him again.

90

"Comrade Director, what should one do with a workshop which fulfills its quarter quota one hundred per cent?"

"Increase the quota by fifty per cent," he snapped.

"But suppose then they make even the hundred and fifty per cent?"

"What? A thing like that seldom happens, and only where the head comptroller is a crook or where he can depend upon his director."

"Let us assume," I continued, "that a good understanding prevails between the two."

"Then the director must have good friends in the Rajkom—the State Council," said Chardiroff promptly.

"And if this also were true?" I pursued.

"Then his confidantes in the Rajkom must have excellent connections with the Obkom, and not until the latter guarantees that the operation succeeds one hundred per cent and is airtight does it get the green light.

"You see, Jacchen, there must always be a certain understanding, and if it did not exist between us two, you would still be dragging freight in the caravan court. Now don't disturb me any more."

"One last question, Comrade Director: What shall I do with the bakers?"

"With what bakers?"

"Those who don't fulfill their quotas in Workshop Five."

"Write sabotage. People's Court!" He returned to his papers.

Comrade Akimov had obviously been behind the door all this time, for as soon as the term "People's Court" was uttered, he re-entered happily.

"Now I see that a strong hand has taken charge," he said to me. "Just don't feel sorry for the scoundrels. When the old Planovik was here everything got in a mess and that's why I didn't like him, the drunkard. Comrade Jac, I have the feeling we two will get on very well together."

He ordered the head of the bakers' workshop to be brought in at once.

An old Uzbek, thoroughly shaken and trembling, shortly appeared before the all-powerful Director.

"It isn't my fault," he defended, "we never get enough flour from Molonov, the supervisor of the camp. And he says the mills don't deliver enough to him."

"Silence!" Chardiroff cut him off. "This is not a question of a camp supervisor and his flour; it is a matter which concerns you and the fact that your quota is not fulfilled."

"But Comrade Director, how can I fill it when I don't get enough flour?"

"Save your excuses for the Tribunal. You can tell them."

"Comrade Director, why do you say Tribunal? We have plenty of bread in the city," the old man cried despairingly. "No one has yet starved in Gusar. Besides, there's a war on. The soldiers at the front have still less bread. I was a soldier myself, but I can't produce *lipjoschkis* by waving a paddle."

"What are you saying? Our soldiers lack bread?" Chardiroff bellowed. "Let me advise you: The Red Army has plenty of bread, but it would go without if it depended on bakers like you!"

He beckoned the secretary with the order book, and grated: "Write. Bakery Chief Bilbavev is perpetrating sabotage, and on top of it he spreads rumors that the Red Army goes hungry. We accuse him according to Paragraph Fifty-eight; Section A. Hand him over to the militia."

I would have choked before speaking to Chardiroff on the performance.

What I had witnessed demonstrated that one word too many and a citizen in this country went to prison. It was clear too that every mistake was translated into sabotage, that it was one step from freedom to the firing squad.

Swaying in shock, poor Bilbavev left the room. Storosch was waiting in the corridor, ever eager to turn someone over to the police.

"We are all good servants of the State," he had assured me.

Whenever Comrade Director received visitors, I had to leave the room, and because he had many of them I spent more time outside than in, or so it seemed to me. I also had to check the workshops, and from the dirty looks I received I could measure my "popularity." Nobody in the bakeries had been arrested by my predecessor, so they took an especially sour view of the new Planovik.

The first few days passed. I was not overexerting myself, but frequently suggested to Chardiroff where some supplies could be channeled to our uses, for discussions between high Party functionaries and the Director always ended with the same result: They received yard goods, shoes, leather coats, and accessories for which the ordinary citizen had to wait until he grew a long beard.

92

The first red-letter day arrived November 7, on which Communists mark the anniversary of the October Revolution. This puzzled the Latvians at first, but there were more serious enigmas in our new homeland, so we didn't worry about it. Preparations had been made for several days: red banners were put up, streamers and bunting placed over doors and windows. A temporary speaker's platform was built in the Combine court. It took a full day to decorate headquarters. I won't detail the slogans and inspirational texts this decoration included, but they were more than adequate. I enjoyed a quiet chuckle because most Uzbeks couldn't read them, so nobody would be arrested for misspelling.

Chardiroff stopped at my desk the evening before.

"Listen, Jac. Are you aware of what tomorrow is?"

"Sure I am," I said. "It's November seventh, a holiday."

"Right"—he slapped my back—"and a special one. For a Communist, more important than even the first of May. That can be celebrated without an October Revolution. But November seventh requires October's events. They made us the first labor-ruled power in history."

I chipped in with some of Lenin's philosophy and the names of a few early heroes, which took Chardiroff by surprise. He did not know of my concentrated Communist studies for examinations the Reds interrupted.

"Fine, Jac. One more thing: After the parade the Rajkom leader will make a speech. I also will speak, but in Uzbek. Your countrymen won't understand a word of it, therefore I want you to make an address in your native tongue."

"But Comrade Director!" I was horrified. "I have absolutely no platform talents. What could I tell them? You have older and abler men for the job. Let them speak in Russian."

"Old? Experienced? Do you think because the guard is sixty-five he can speak? No, whether you have talents or not, you speak. That's it."

"But I've never talked before any crowd."

"Then you'll do it the first time. Lenin once made his first public address."

"I believe you are joking, and anyway I would need a day to prepare," I implored.

"Nonsense," he laughed. "I don't prepare. You needn't prepare.

Just say the revolution was good, Lenin was good, Stalin is wonderful. We shall voluntarily carry out the Five Year Plan. Russia will defeat the Germans. We win the war. Hurrah. They'll all join in. You'll see."

He strode to the door, then added, "Go home and get a night's rest, my boy. Make ready for the holiday. Tell them to give you a bottle of vodka in the canteen."

The midday sun is still hot in Uzbek November. So the celebration waited till afternoon, when long columns arranged themselves at one end of town. Having no band, they brought up a drum. A few with harmonicas played. Others sang. Nobody was in tune and few could distinguish the words, for everyone sang in his own language and style. To make the procession more impressive, it retraced the route and ended at Combination Square.

The Rajkom representative spoke first. He was pathetic, but loud cheers acclaimed him. His frequent mentions of Stalin were greeted by more applause. Our director was next.

Chardiroff spoke slowly, uneasily, and gave the impression that he was searching for new but safe ideas. It was not a question of what to say, but what not to say. Then it was my turn. I nearly stumbled as I stepped to the podium, shaking in every muscle. I was scared weak, and my Polish compatriots made it no easier by their loud halloos. They grinned and poked each other, and I felt as if on a torture rack.

Following my boss's instructions, I delivered the speech Old Elisier had suggested. Every time I mentioned Stalin, there was an ovation. This provided time to think up the next line. It went much better than I expected. The Uzbeks and Tadzhiks, who didn't understand one Polish word, cheered loudest of all. Everyone was satisfied, and more dead than alive I sat down. The workers produced bottles and the main celebration began.

My Polish pals toasted me until their eyes became glassy, declaring the law had lost a great pillar when I turned to Soviet administration.

13

THE SOVIET road to personal achievement is pitted with deadfalls and tortures by detours. There was no mention of this in Marx or Lenin, when I memorized their principles during my university preparations. But now in remote Uzbek, I had a practical education in the mercurial changes of Soviet economic management.

I was about to be promoted with a raise in salary, when an unfortunate interruption occurred. A government commission arrived from Moscow. They were to pick up cotton in Gusar in exchange for a carload of leather from which to make soldiers' boots.

No more than arrived, they stormed into Chardiroff's office and made a great row. Then they turned upon me and created a second scene. They were enraged because of our poorly fulfilled quotas, and demanded to know what was holding up production. They bluntly asked Chardiroff what did he expect anyway from a Polish Planovik?

"If the quota is not met by our next inspection you will continue your term in jail," they promised me.

"*Djinde Orus,*" Chardiroff muttered, wiping the perspiration from his brow. Crazy Russians, indeed, but neither of us felt any too secure.

The situation offered little hope because the shortage of supplies and diversion of materials left no possible way to meet quotas. Of course we couldn't give that as an excuse—it would mean our necks. I would have surrendered my position gladly to return to baggage shifting in the camels' court.

But it is not so easy to give up a job in Soviet Russia. It might be hard to get one, but once hired, during war and under suspicion anyway, it was flirting with sabotage charges to suggest leaving. So what could I do? The People's Tribunal awaited, for I knew we couldn't carry out the commissioners' orders. Chardiroff continually put me off when I begged a change of scene.

"It won't be difficult for me to leave, because the Poles are still traveling back and forth," I persisted, until he finally relented.

"We've known each other for some time, Jac. It's not good that you simply run away. At the same time, I don't want you to endanger yourself in a job like this. So I've looked around for a better spot for you. Do you know the warehouse next door to the *tschaichana* at the bazaar?"

I nodded—a familiar building, the warehouse, where people got the necessities for daily living—but no more.

"Do you also know old Maulonov, the supervisor there?"

"Yes, I know Maulonov," I said.

"Well, the work in that warehouse is definitely better for you, because you won't need to write much—only to be good at figures, which you are. Besides, you can take over the bread supply at the same time."

"Why doesn't Maulonov want to stay there, if the position is so good?"

"He does, but I don't want him there," Chardiroff grunted, calling the ready secretary with the order book.

The Gusar warehouse was comparable to a department store in Moscow or Riga; it contained the city's main supply of bulk materials, manufactured items, yard goods, groceries, and leather supplies, including shoes. With my order from Chardiroff I sought out Maulonov.

96

The warehouse keeper was an elderly Uzbek with a long, drooping mustache and honest-looking eyes. He was upset that I had walked to the establishment, protesting I should not have done so when he could have come to headquarters for the order. He also stirred misgivings by his gratitude at being fired.

"It is high time the bakery and warehouse were turned over to younger, more energetic hands," he agreed. "I shall return to my tea in the cottage," Maulonov said, eying me in a fatherly, almost sympathetic manner. "Yes, the world to youth in these vigorous times. Honor to the old, with retirement."

I was genuinely touched when the kindly Oriental handed me the keys, and I stupidly took over. Then we returned to Chardiroff who had me sign the official documents of transfer—without waiting to check the warehouse contents. It was all new to me; I had no rulebook to go by. Maulonov, now completely in the clear, went along to give me some management suggestions.

The first thing I observed was a paucity of merchandise in the lockers. I carefully ascertained which coupons I should accept in distributing articles, and was computing the number of meters each cotton bolt contained when I heard something drop. The noise was repeated and turning, I saw Maulonov, thoroughly embarrassed, two pieces of laundry soap at his feet.

"Unfortunate, eh Maulonov?"

He looked imploringly at me, tears in his honest, brown eyes. "I'm a poor man, my friend. So poor that I have to steal a bit of soap from my own stores. Do you want to report me, Jac?"

"No," I said shortly, "take your soap and go."

He pressed my hand and mumbled, "You and I are kindred souls, and may Allah protect you." Then he was gone. I was soon going to need Allah and every other Omnipotent Power to get me out of this squeeze. While completing the inventory, my mind kept returning to Maulonov, for if the old rascal would steal on his way out, what all may he have taken while in charge? I also wondered at his exchange of glances with Chardiroff.

With my recent experience at the Rajkom, my new duties went along smoothly. I received merchandise, obtained the coupons, traded them in, drew my salary, and waxed content. My only worry was the bakery. Bread was also distributed from this storehouse, and people constantly besieged us for it. There was never enough on hand because there was not enough baked, and I needed no fortuneteller to point out to me that this was because there was never enough flour from which to make it. This troubled me, partly because of the scene at the Rajkom with the bakery boss and also because I knew conditions had not improved.

One day, after I had sent a detailed report of leather delivered to the shoeshops, Chardiroff sent for me and, kindly as always, asked how the work was going. As we talked, the situation in the bakery arose, especially the difficulty of supplying adequate bread.

"Something must be wrong in that flour depot," Chardiroff frowned. "I've noticed it for some time. How would it be if you took that over, too? Make the same kind of inventory you did at the bazaar storehouse. I'll increase your salary to five hundred rubles."

Five hundred rubles! My heart took a double hop, skip, and jump. With that kind of money I could afford ten loaves of bread on the black market every day, and since I ate at the government canteen, I could save plenty of money. I had visions of becoming a capitalist on my collective government salary.

That afternoon I closed the warehouse early and hurried to the floor elevator. The guard opened a squeaky door and I beheld sacks of flour piled high, ten to a stack, one stack against the next. I counted carefully, multiplied, checked each stack to be sure it contained ten, and found there were 250 tons of flour in the bin. The bakery used 30 tons per day, so we had a supply for about eight days. I put that fact down, also.

Every morning thereafter I hurried conscientiously to the flour storage and helped to load the sacks. This was from 7:00 to 9:00 A.M., for I had to open the store on time. A week had not passed, however, when I noticed that more than 25 tons were missing. How could that be? I was supposedly the only person with a key. The Uzbek guard swore on the Koran that I was the only human who had been there, but I began to wonder about the fine hand of Chardiroff.

I hustled to the warehouse and made out a report. In no time at all the chief of the Rajkom sent for me, calling me a foreign saboteur and thief. He blamed me for the bread shortage and every fault in the line of flour supply.

The measure was heaped when our leather stock in another warehouse was checked. Although my record showed I had used only half of it, there was none there. Maulonov had left me only about half of the leather shown by his figures.

Comrade Director Chardiroff muttered: "Soviet law does not know the guilty, but the one responsible. Therefore the one responsible is the guilty." He turned to me. "But, Jac, these misunderstandings occur quite often, and I'm fully convinced you are innocent. I'll help as much as I can."

"Sure, I'm guiltless, Comrade Chardiroff, but how will I prove it if they lock me up now?"

"You won't be jailed. Compose yourself. Go back to work and keep your eyes open," he soothed. "I'll see to it this whole matter peters out."

"It's too late for that," I objected. "The Rajkom knows about it. The NKVD has been hunting a scapegoat for a long time, and if I'm not a qualified stock supervisor I am a prime candidate for arrest. Besides, if I'm shot your position can only improve, and you could buy another gold watch."

"What does the gold watch have to do with it?" He whirled in his chair angrily.

"Quite a lot, Comrade Director. Because now I know where you get the money to buy such luxuries." I turned abruptly and walked to the door. Before I could open it he called my name, and turning I saw once more my smiling and kindly director.

"Don't take everything so tragically, Jac." He offered a cigarette. "I wanted to ask something else. Are the Polish trains still running, my boy?"

He lit a cigarette and slipped 300 rubles into my palm. We parted with broad, understanding smiles, and as I closed the door I knew I'd seen Comrade Chardiroff for the last time.

He would delay my arrest to give me time to disappear. I realized I had better make the getaway immediately. Never mind where I went. Just away from Gusar.

I gave my keys and papers to a friend who promised to drop them at the Rajkom office. Another pal took my suitcase to the station. Unfortunately, the traffic in Poles wasn't as casual as I had believed, and when I reached the railway station there was no train at all. So I waited until dark, hoping my luck would hold out.

A cotton freight pulled in, headed for Tashkent, and I scrambled up behind the locomotive. My suitcase was thrown after me, and pressing myself against the water tender I held my breath until we passed through the station. The train rolled on, and over my shoulder the lights of Gusar faded from sight. I would never again hear about an empty warehouse, the bread quotas, the Russian inspectors, or the official life of Comrade, the Director Chardiroff.

I rode the tender to Karchi, an assembly point where South Asian trains took on water. Some Polish transports were waiting; I spotted them by the chimneys poking through the car roofs. The *voyageurs* were preparing breakfast, and it seemed like a good time to trade my sooty accommodation for a better one. I picked a car at random and asked if I could go along.

"You can see we are overcrowded, with all seats taken," an irritable woman objected. I looked in, saw plenty of space, and said, "Yes?" This was obviously a private circle which had promoted a good thing.

I joined a group of young people and one married couple, had my name registered, and presently I was retracing the distance I had previously covered, but now as a legal traveler with free food, heat, and necessary facilities. Small wonder the Poles found these trains practical and that many rode out the war on them.

Every platform we passed was crowded. There were Poles and Jews everywhere. Among them were refugees by the thousand, many from as far west as Moscow, which by now was hearing Nazi tank guns. The occupied cities beyond the capital had spilled tens of thousands into the Urals and beyond the Volga.

These people were completely unorganized. They camped under the open skies, and most of them had nothing but what they wore. Others had plenty of baggage, especially when there were women and children in the family group. The government had made no provisions whatever for these homeless people; they rode the troop trains east until they halted to refill.

I could smell their misery from afar. Disease and hunger already had made heavy deductions in their ranks, and with winter's arrival deaths would increase. Food was the worst problem, and shelter nearly as urgent. It was rainy and cold most of the time.

From Djambul to Lugovaja, from there to Tchu, and on to Almaata —everywhere the same human destitution, the same field day for death. Refugees on all sides; invalids, the half-starved, and the ever-

100

roving thieves who lived on the misfortunes of others. We left the train at Tchu, hoping to find work in the factories there, for we believed that ultimately we would be put into some part of the war effort unless we were suddenly conscripted.

There were two miscalculations: first, the city as usual lay far from the railway station, and, second, there were no Poles in Tchu. Not one. I decided to return to Tashkent. I liked the place, and it seemed to offer the best chance to settle for the winter. Some of my companions took the next train to Novosibirsk, but I went with the Polish tide—toward Tashkent.

One meets a variety of characters on such a drifting career. There was a pale young chap named Felix, without baggage, without money, without even shoes on his feet. He advised everyone to continue to Djambul because many of our Jewish compatriots were there and working opportunities were better.

Foolishly, I allowed myself to be persuaded, although Felix was hardly an example of prosperity. As result I ran into a horrible predicament. Only those who have been stranded penniless and hungry in a community of strangers could appreciate it.

The Djambul station swarmed with refugees. They lay like insects after a storm, on benches, floors, the wet ground, and under dripping trees. Hunger and fatigue wracked everyone. Nearly all were ill, and our traveling group disintegrated as quickly as it had formed. Only Felix and I remained together. He said he knew his way about the town and a Russian who would give us lodgings.

The Russian agreed to put us up, but for 100 rubles a month, payable in advance. I took a few shirts from my bag and got enough at the bazaar to pay the rent and buy some food. But it was apparent we would need jobs to keep going, for my possessions were beginning to run low.

"Jobs are easy to get here," said the confident Felix. "I have some more connections in the town. How about my looking for both of us?"

A wintry rain was pouring on the clay roads, and some people actually lost their shoes in the sticky substance. What should we do? Together we had one pair of boots—mine. I also had an old military overcoat. I lent the shoes to Felix, because he could not walk into offices barefoot to apply for jobs. He would be home that night with better prospects for both of us.

I sat around the room all day, waiting. Night came, but no Felix.

Every sound took me to the door. When I finally went to bed my roommate had not returned. I didn't sleep, and next morning began some serious worrying, for now it was I who was barefoot, with nowhere near the price of new shoes. I had had nothing to eat for twenty-four hours, and this didn't help my morale either. "I'll wait until the rain stops, then go looking for him," I decided, but a chill collected around my heart.

Toward evening the storm abated, and in bad humor I trudged the flooded streets to the station. That was the rendezvous for Poles, and I looked eagerly for Felix. He was nowhere to be found.

"What happened to your shoes?" my friends asked.

"Don't want to ruin them in this mud," I said. That was understandable, for surface conditions quickly wore out shoes.

Wandering through the crowds, I kept inquiring for Felix. Finally someone said he had seen him on a train for Novosibirsk. It was a terrible blow. Deeply depressed, I slogged back to my room.

Not only had a trusted friend deserted, he had walked out in my shoes, the most important possession of a homeless vagabond. I was alone, friendless, hungry, shoeless, and without money in a city of cold-faced Asians. Felix had not only taken my shoes, he had shaken my confidence. I was afraid for the first time in months.

I curled up in the room, wondering if human beings when faced with basic survival, actually become like the hyena and other predatory animals. I couldn't get Felix's trickery out of my mind. Passages of Schiller's "Bürgschaft" came to haunt me. Bitterness surged through such reflections, and events of the deportation, the hard luck and losses by theft, which until that moment had not deeply affected me, took on more personal significance. I remembered Mr. Cohn and his lost suitcase. I thought of the frightened couple in Gorki and their robbery by the Blattnoy.

Well, I'd have to start all over. Perhaps I could run errands, stand in line for someone else's bread. I must get food. There was no ration here for the Poles. I could die as easily in this room as in a concentration camp. Trembling and apprehensive, I fell asleep.

14

THE NEXT day I walked barefoot through the mud, thinking of food, and the opening cadence of the Tenth Psalm came to mind:

Why standest thou afar off, O Lord? why hidest thou thyself in times of trouble?
The wicked in his pride doth persecute the poor: let them be taken in the devices that they have imagined. . . .

Hunger is a terrible thing at any age. When you are twenty-one and recently well fed, it comes as an unbearable shock. The nearness of thousands similarly afflicted, without prospect of sustenance, brought a desolation that was multiplied by their mass misery. I sloshed to the officers' mess, where with others I was prepared to beg.

But the spectacles of degradation repelled me. Sunken-cheeked

103

men were licking the plates at the kitchen door, and students from Soviet universities begged as insistently as Poles deported from Lodz and Warsaw.

As in most Russian towns, the bazaar was behind the railway station. There are many grades of bazaars in Asiatic Russia. The ones near the station are the lowest class, a free market in which "caveat emptor" must have had its beginnings, for buyer and seller made their own rules. One had to see such a spot during wartime in Soviet Russia to believe what took place.

Poverty and destitution established and maintained the trade. One went there only in extreme circumstances. Of course, there were also the human jackals, lurking in the crowds, feeding off the general distress.

The center of attraction was the Banacholka—the ragpickers' market. One could get anything there, including things the self-respecting European ragpicker would discard. There were torn and patched garments, one shoe but no mate, worn-out gloves, and grease-stained jackets.

There were dented petroleum lamps and fuel cylinders, filthy mats, torn oilcloth, and hunting cartridges with soggy powder. There were ladies' boots from the season of 1882, stylishly laced to the knees. There were stray patches of fabric, removed from other patches on patched pants. And many pieces of board, hose, pipe, and corrugated tin—anything to plug a hole or block a crack against winter winds. There were glasses filled with sunflower seeds—food for the birds, if the birds themselves had not already become food.

Amid this exposition of trash, ragged representatives of the human race circulated. I couldn't tell whether some were men or women, until they approached. One held above his head a dirty-looking portion of bread, shouting its sale price—"Two hundred rubles the kilo"—while keeping one hand over the place already gnawed.

At one spot salted herrings were going piecemeal. A Russian soldier purchased one, wiped it on the inside of his coat, pinched the tail between two dirty fingers and with the other hand expertly ripped off the skin. Next he brought out a flask of vodka from an inside pocket, took a long slug of it, and smelling the herring before gulping it, exhaled: "Ah-h-h!" His comrades waited impatiently for him to pass the bottle.

A fight took place at the kiosk where someone put his hand in an

104

officer's pocket. There being no policeman on the spot, the officer, after pummeling the thief, dragged him in person to a police station.

"Look at him, the well-nourished slacker! Instead of fighting at the front, this swine spends his time picking soldiers' pockets!" The officer's voice was loud and calculated to arouse the crowd's resentment, but most of the listeners were too weak to be patriotically stirred.

Two women of dubious talents smiled and raised wineglasses to the soldiers while this went on. I looked at them, wondering what service they contributed to the defense of good old Russia.

Drifting toward the peasants' quarter where kolchos workers brought wool and hay for private sale, I saw Kirghiz herdsmen lash out with whips when small boys sought to grab a handful of hay for their mother's goat. I was getting a lot of trampling from assorted boots, and my bare feet were soon scraped raw. If only I had a pair of shoes!

During the afternoon it began to rain again. Hungrier than ever, frozen, and with nothing achieved, I started back to my room. Then a voice—kind and friendly—came over my shoulder. I turned and looked into a pair of light gray eyes and a smiling face, the first I had met in Djambul. It was that of a young man in a long military coat and a pointed Soviet cap.

"I was listening while you were speaking to the Poles," he said. "You speak a Latvian Jewish, almost German. Where do you come from?"

"Bromberg," I replied, remembering my identification papers.

"I thought perhaps from Latvia. I am from Dvinsk, and would have been happy to meet a fellow countryman." He spoke sincerely and so disarmingly that I no longer denied my origin, but told him my home was in Mitau. His name was Sandler, and he worked at the military canteen.

"Why don't you come with me and have a decent meal?" he invited. "You're so down and out it will do you good to get warm."

I accepted gratefully. It was wonderful to thaw out, wash my feet, and drink a steaming cup of tea. I spent the whole afternoon with Sandler, who told me a Latvian division had been organized among the deportees and that almost 80 per cent were Jewish. He obviously hoped that I also would volunteer.

While he talked, my new-found friend brought out some rags and

105

suggested that I contrive temporary footgear from them. He also urged that I go to the military depot where there would be decent lodgings for the night. I began to suspect I was being prepared for a place in the new unit he had described, whether Latvian or something else. He spoke with such fluency and persuasion, I decided he must be a member of the Communist Party, which would explain his better living conditions.

Sandler was preparing a second pot of tea when temptation once more took hold of me. He had removed his muddy boots upon entering, and left them outside the door into the room. Since nobody else came that way, and it was still daylight, he probably considered them safe there. But he was entertaining a desperate man.

It was almost dark when I rose to leave. "You've been so decent; the only considerate soul I've met since leaving home," I told him. And that was God's truth. What I did next was not in keeping with my regard for this charitable chap, and I still feel ashamed of it.

After shaking hands and checking his directions to the depot, I said, "In the morning I will come to the canteen. You can tell me more about this division. Thank you more than I can say, for what you have done." We shook hands.

Then I closed the door, bent down swiftly, and picked up Sandler's shoes! I kept them close to my middle, and walked rapidly toward the depot, quivering with the fear that he would come running after me. Apparently he either did not see me do it or he was sure he would see me next day.

That was not what I intended, however. Once around a corner, I hurried to the Kolchos Nidvor, an assembly point for collective farm workers. It was a place to which only those who had failed everywhere else came for a job. The quotas were impossible to make, the work was sheer slavery, and conditions were the worst in all that region. It was my intention to "get lost" in this environment, for the time being at least. The first thing I did was wipe the mud from my feet and put on my newly acquired boots. They were a perfect fit—for my feet but not for my conscience.

After my experience with Felix, who I realized had been in the same predicament, I had indulged in harsh thoughts about my fellow sufferers. Had this choice been thrust upon me by an all-seeing Providence? Was this a form of retribution because I had been lacking in faith? I remembered my oath when the Red guards took me in

June, ". . . if God gives me the strength." My dishonesty with the towel suddenly smote me. Now again. . . . I sat for some time in self accusation and remorse.

But what was the alternative? Without shoes I would surely die. With those I might be issued at the depot I would also have excellent chances to get killed, fighting in a foreign legion for the Communists who despoiled our town and scattered my people. Stealing Sandler's boots was at least a compromise—if only my youthful conscience would be content. But it wasn't.

Keeping out of sight between the high-loaded, horse-drawn carts, I watched Kirghiz women throwing dice. I had no plans as yet; I wanted only to hide and at first opportunity slip away.

A few words in German came out of the kolchos murmur. Was I going a little off in the head? I listened intently, and heard them again. Someone was speaking real German, but with an unusual accent. German prisoners, here? How would that have happened? I followed the direction of the sound.

A cluster of men wrapped in sheepskins and wearing high boots, who otherwise looked no different from the Kirghiz, were talking.

"*Guten Tag*," I broke in. One or two replied, but otherwise paid no attention to me.

"Are you prisoners of war from Germany?" I inquired.

"We are Germans, but from Leninpol up in the mountains," one replied. "Do you know Leninpol? It's a village not far from Orlovka, in the Kolchos Rosa Luxemburg. Now do you understand where it is?" The others laughed good-naturedly, and one of them added: "Some of your Polish countrymen are joining us. They are definitely better off with us than here with the refugees. You, yourself, don't look in very good condition. Why don't you come along when we go back?"

"Could you really take me?" My voice broke with eagerness.

"Yes, but it's very cold up there and you'll need a fur."

"Never mind that, I'll get along without."

"As you wish," the taller German agreed. "We stay here tonight, but leave at dawn."

"Where shall I go until then?"

"Listen, lad. Go to Dunkanovka. Take it easy in the big *tschaichana*, and when we come by we'll pick you up."

I looked at him with grave doubts.

"Don't worry. We Leninpoles keep our promises."

Dunkanovka lay a few kilometers behind Djambul, taking its name from the Mongolized Dungab Turks from Turkestan who, like so many, were swept along in Mongolian invasions. I hurried through the darkness, thinking of the kolchos and my future with these strange people. Curling up in a corner on a straw mat I forgot my plight, forgot Sandler, his missing shoes, and even the NKVD which, if he had told them, must be looking for me. I slept until a nudge announced that the Germans had called for me.

"Get up, friend. It's cold, eh? What a hell of a climate." The tall peasant pressed a partially filled bottle into my hand. "Take a good pull; you'll need the heat."

I swallowed some vodka, one of the strongest drinks I had ever had at that hour of the day. A number of heavily wrapped passengers, including some Kirghiz, were in the carts. The horses started and the steel-tired wheels bumped creakily over the rutted road. A truck approached, filled with young Russians and Kirghiz bound for Red Army induction points.

"Down! Under the canvas," our driver yelled. "It's better for you." I stayed covered for an hour; then they told me to come out.

"See that stone?" the driver pointed to a marker at the roadside. "There ends Kazakhstan, and the Land of Kirghiz begins. Our settlement lies in the region of Frunze."

I looked over the flat Kirghiz steppe; there was nothing in sight except the familiar little clay houses with their meager strips of lawn, and broad fields. Beyond, a massive range of mountains provided a rim to this geographic griddle, and to the other side of the carts, the Talas, a swift but narrow stream, gurgled on its journey from the hills.

The cold was beginning to penetrate. My teeth chattered and I pulled the blanket closer, quietly praying that all my wandering eventually would come to a safe end. Another hour passed, and the temperature continued to drop. We were climbing into the mountains.

From one of the other carts I heard someone singing:

> *"Ach, du lieber Augustin,*
> *Alles ist weg!"*

Dear Augustin, was everything lost? I wondered as hour upon hour the animals toiled in their traces. It was bitterly cold now, and well past noon.

108

"Call me Klaus, friend," the tall German said. "Do you know the song about Klaus has gone to the woods?" He hummed the melody, but I had no desire for music. I was hungry again, and my conscience tortured me.

"Yes, I know the song," I said, "but I'm pretty cold for singing."

"Well, tell me your name then. You can give me a wrong one if you prefer, but we must call you something."

After I introduced myself, he made no further conversation and presently we came to an oasis where, without urging, the horses stopped. This was their feeding spot.

"Here we go, Jac, feed the animals. Instead of paying a fare you can help by getting some water for them."

I gave the hay on which I'd been sitting to the horses, then went to the pool for water. This done, Klaus produced cooked meat and white bread from a large white cloth.

"Here, you must be hungry, friend. Eat." He handed me a sandwich.

I looked at it and my amazement amused him. White bread, in this part of the world and under these conditions? With cooked, lean meat? This German settlement must be extraordinarily wealthy. I began to eat, hurriedly lest Klaus change his mind. But he laughed at my pleasure, took a long drink and passed the vodka to me.

So guilt-ridden had I become that I found myself eating furtively, glancing right and left as though someone might see me with white bread. But it was no crime. Everyone else had the same. While some of them built a fire to make tea, I asked Klaus how they came to have white bread, which I had not seen since before the attack on Poland. The Russians had none, the wealthiest Uzbeks had none, and yet these Germans in the middle of Soviet Kirghiz thought nothing of it.

"When we are on the road again, I'll explain," said Klaus. "Come, it's time to get going. Let's hitch the horses."

With system and a minimum of motion, the party packed lunch kit and themselves back into the carts and our little caravan resumed its climb into the mountains. With every mile the wind became sharper, until I cringed behind Klaus's bulk, curious as to how anyone could live, much less prosper, in such bitter cold.

15

"*ALL RIGHT*, Jac, I will now satisfy your curiosity. We are indeed Germans, and we've been here a long time. At least our ancestors came a good while ago. But it's a long story and you better tuck your chin into that blanket, because from here on our journey grows colder."

Klaus's breath made a small vapor cloud, and he grinned across the cart like a friendly bear lecturing a maverick cub.

"The tale goes back nearly two centuries and a half, to Czar Peter the Great and his famous trip, incognito, into Europe. During his shipbuilding apprenticeship at Zaandam in Holland, Peter met and was much impressed by several German Mennonites, one of whom he engaged as his private physician. He decided to invite more Germans to Russia, which he planned to westernize. This was in 1698.

"But even a Czar's plans are interrupted sometimes. Peter had a

111

lot of wars to fight, and by the time he beat the Swedes, Cossacks, the Poles, and Turks, he forgot the peace-loving Mennonites, who don't believe in strife.

"Another hundred years and there was a German-born Czarina, Catherine the Great, sitting on the throne in St. Petersburg. In 1786 this energetic and aggressive lady decided to improve Russia by colonizing some of the southern wastelands. She invited the Mennonites of Prussia and Friesland to immigrate to the crown lands of the Dnieper, providing free transportation, free land, religious tolerance, and freedom from military service. These Germans, persecuted at home by their own rising militaristic princes, were happy to accept. Many left the German homeland without passports, which meant they could not easily return, and soon a colony had grown up at Jekaterinoslav. It included about two hundred families, and they prospered.

"After Catherine the Second died ten years later, the settlers feared that under the mad Emperor Paul I, her son, they might lose their privileges, so they sent two men to the Court to get a charter—a document which for years was preserved in a fireproof building in Chortitz, but I cannot be sure it is there now.

"Paul, wishing to spread the movement his mother had begun, not only granted a charter, but added more privileges. For example there was freedom from taxation for any new immigrants for ten years. They received sixty-five *dessiatine* of free, arable land, the right to fish and to establish distilleries and maintain a monopoly of their product within the settlement. They could also substitute an affirmation for the military oath, which was against Mennonite scruples. Nor could the Russian government quarter soldiers among them. Oh, the German pacifists did all right with the Emperor Paul."

Other colonists went to the Crimea, Klaus explained, and some moved from the original Dnieper settlements to the Volga country, so that by 1870 there were thirty or forty thousand Mennonites in those regions. All kept up their German customs, were frugal and hard-working, and could, of course, be trusted because they did not bear arms and wouldn't go to war.

"These people lived in large brick homes with tile roofs, and always had a flower garden between the street and the house and well-kept vegetable gardens in the rear. They had splendid stables with horses of every breed and size, for besides the farm carts and plows

112

they also had a variety of sleighs and coaches," Klaus went on. Small icicles by now had formed in his beard, but he was accustomed to this, and brushed them off as he talked.

"But in the end, as often happens, the Russians became jealous of the prosperous Germans. There were pressures on the Czar's court to limit their privileges, to make them subject to Russian rule. During the Franco-Prussian War the Czar and Bismarck agreed that the newly created German nation would withdraw Prussian guardianship from the Mennonites and all Germans in far-off Russia.

"The decision was a great blow to the Mennonites in particular. It ended their freedom from military service and interfered with their quiet way of life. Their children, for example, would have to go to Russian schools. The Czars had praised our forefathers' industrious ways, and admired their diligence and skill at making things. As a result of their cleverness our people soon had wealth—not what you measure by white or black bread, but by rubles, many golden, glittering rubles, for which the best things of those days could be had. But the loss of freedom meant more to the Mennonites than rubles.

"They immediately considered places to move. Some wanted to try Africa, a few Australia, and America appealed to many because others of the same faith had preceded them there. A delegation was also sent to Siberia to see if there was opportunity beyond the Volga.

"The Czar soon realized he was losing some excellent citizens, and in 1873 sent von Todtleben, a special agent who spoke German, to persuade the Mennonites to remain. He promised that when called for military service, the young men could take noncombatant places or join the forestry service. A majority of the Mennonites accepted this arrangement, but some of the more scrupulous—and poorer—families went beyond the Volga, moved across the great steppes, and found a new place to live. My companions and I are the descendants of those wandering German Mennonites."

As the narrative ceased, Klaus tightened the reins. We were on a high ridge. The Talas, far below, glistened in its gorge and faintly, above the cartwheels' rumble, I could hear the cataract gurgling.

Then we entered a sharp gash in the high, rocky mountain. This gateway, carved by nature, opened upon a narrow, winding path with steep sandstone walls, its solemn silence disturbed only by the echoing voices of the drivers.

"Strange, isn't it? This protecting fortress that God Himself has

113

built us. It continues like this for fifteen kilometers, and at the other end is a new and more pleasant world. Yes, Jac, you will see. . . ."

Klaus had bent toward me, whispering in genuine awe at this natural wonder he must have traversed many times. When he spoke the last few words aloud, they were flung back from the rocks, echoing: "You will see . . . will see . . . see . . . see. . . ."

Although I was cramped with cold, I could not suppress my excitement and half stood in the cart to look about.

Klaus was delighted. "Like the place in the Books of Moses, no? Sela, down where the Edomites fled."

I was surprised at his knowledge of Hebrew Scriptures, for I, too, was dimly aware of a counterpart there. In the Holy Land region of Solomon's mines, was it not?—a place mentioned by the Prophet Obadiah, now known as Petra and an archaeological attraction, with sheer red rock pillars forming an entrance similar to this. I wished that among my possessions there was a Testament, so I could show Klaus the passage on the red-walled refuge of the Edomites, south of the Dead Sea.

Was I wandering in an area visited in antiquity by members of the Ten Lost Tribes of Israel? I remembered the anachronistic Hebrew signs and architecture in Gusar. There had been other instances, too, now that I thought about it. Klaus's voice broke into my reverie.

"When the German colonists moved across the Volga in the days of Bismarck and Alexander the Second," he was saying, "a rising Russia, besides fighting Turks and Poles, began to conquer the independent khans of this remote area. Thus Bukhara, Khiva, and much of the country you have crossed so recently, came under Moscow's control, although there was very little government or even civil connection with the people.

"Our troubles actually began with World War One." Klaus's narrative rolled on with the rhythm of the wheels as the horses plodded through the canyon in which two carts could barely pass. "The German armies invaded and, whatever our religious beliefs, we found ourselves struggling against our brethren.

"We did not fight only for an idea. It is never that way, is it, Jac? You may begin full of ideals and fervor, but soon you are fighting to stay alive, to hold on to the few essentials that keep one alive. So we battled German soldiers to protect house, family, and farm. I was a kid like you are, but I went through a great deal.

114

"At the end, what had we left? The nineteen-seventeen Revolution—the overthrow of the Czar and his regime—and a new kind of proletarian rule under the Bolsheviks. Worst of all, we had to ourselves only the right to starve. Our wheat-producing areas were in Germany's hands, the war still raged in western Europe, and instead of peace we heard that British, Americans, Czechs, Poles, and even Japanese troops were coming into Russia to prevent the Germans, who had helped the Bolshevik revolt, from using our people and resources against them.

"They did not know that famine was winning more battles than anyone. Millions of people died. Everything went wrong. We Mennonites began migrating to Siberia, exactly as the refugees today have fled. Some of our ancestors with horse and cart managed to cross the Kazakhstan steppe, in straggly caravans with little food and clothing.

"On that trek, Jac, I lost my mother. Nobody knows how many died along the route."

The gorge was widening. Suddenly Klaus pointed to a large bird swooping down to disappear behind the rocky crest: "The Kirghiz on a hunt. That hawk dives to kill hares for them. It is a sport as old as this trail."

Then he resumed his story. "A remnant of the Mennonite *voyageurs* reached Johannisdorf, a mountain village that hid behind the rocks, and which had been established by earlier German pilgrims. That was after Bismarck and Alexander had agreed to remove our privileges and to take the young men into government service, but some of them had already hidden away and built a prosperous community among the Kirghiz herdsmen.

"The name Johannisdorf, like the rulers, changed with the fortunes of politics. When the Czar's troops overcame the Khan's, it became Nicolaipol. When the Bolsheviks overthrew the Czar it was Leninpol. But, as you will see, nothing could change the natural gifts of our little paradise."

We were nearing the end of the canyon road and I was shivering so that Klaus also must have felt it.

"I told you a fur was needed," he said. "Here, wrap in this horse blanket. It will get still colder." He tossed me the one on which he had been sitting. I thanked him and after winding it around me, decided to keep up the conversation to take my mind off the cold.

115

"But how did those Germans gain a welcome among the herdsmen in the first place? They were Moslems, weren't they? And the Mennonites, however pacifist, were Christians."

"There is no written record, but the story is well supported that the Germans' knack at cultivation pleased the Kirghiz. The Emir, a broad-minded man, realized that his tribal economy would improve if more production was gained from the soil. He had heard of the success of Peter and Catherine with immigrants and thought the same plan would help feed his sheep- and goat-raising tribes. So the Germans were invited to settle wherever they wished.

"Searching for fertile ground, the pioneers came upon this mountainous gorge carpeted with clover. Where there is clover, grain will grow. So they staked out farms and started a village. They mingled freely and peaceably with the Mohammedans, trading produce for meat and wool, using skins for making shoes and harness. In this way both Moslems and Mennonites thrived, and presently they were so wealthy that cattle, sheep, horses, and goats were counted in the hundreds by each family.

"Yes, that was a happy era." Klaus sighed, and spat over the side of the cart. "Today? One considers himself well off with enough to eat and one costume against the weather. A bicycle, a phonograph, a small accordion, or a balalaika are absolute luxuries!

"But the old saying, 'Humans grow accustomed to everything, and man easily forgets,' holds true here. It makes little difference how we are governed or how we live—if we find some happiness. Besides, things with us are much better than in other kolchos. If only we were sure of staying put. . . . That damned Hitler. Why did he start this war?"

We turned a final curve and from the dim light of the canyon we came suddenly into a brightness that revealed, as Klaus predicted, a brilliant world apart from all others.

On every side, steep as though raised by military engineers, the mountains stood like massive sentinels in winter regimentals. Their white helmets were lost in fleecy clouds, through which the setting sun revealed snow-blanketed plains that sparkled as with billions of sequins. On the left, broadened by the intake from its tributaries, ran the Talas, a black ribbon through the whiteness. There was no wind in this tidy, high level plateau, for the sheltering peaks closed it out.

116

We might have been in the crater of a massive volcano, except that this was obviously the most fertile of farmlands.

I cried out in delight and Klaus, seeing my admiration, said, "We have still a ways to the town, so why don't you trot beside the cart to warm yourself up?"

As I jumped down, exhaling frostily, and tingling with the fresh mountain air, we heard a weird lamentation. Before us was a Kirghiz house where screaming women with brooms were dashing about in the snow. The column paused and I peeped inside where a woman was weeping bitterly and repeating a name over and over.

"Someone has died?" I whispered.

"Yes, her husband. Killed in the war. A neighbor brought the news, and these friends have come to chase away evil spirits."

Death is ever a messenger of despair to those left, I thought, and the rule is no different anywhere on this earth. Here I have scarcely arrived in the loveliest spot I have ever seen when in stalks tragedy. It is the same as when I left Mitau, only that was summer.

The first village was Dubrovka, its street lined with clean, well-constructed houses separated by the ever-present poplars. Was this real, or had I died and gone to some heavenly replica of home? It was not much different from Latvia's countryside. The nipping frost convinced me it was real. The carts were checked by an affable guard, I took a last long look in the twilight, and we resumed our uphill pull toward Leninpol some 40 more kilometers away.

I dozed as we bumped along, the untiring Klaus silent now and huddled in the other corner. Midnight stars provided the only light when we reached Leninpol. I was exhausted and stiff as the carts assembled on an open square, the horses were unhitched and stabled, and each traveler with his sheepskin cloak left quickly for a warm abode. Again I was alone—the only human, the only animal—without a roof or a place to lie down.

Klaus once more came to my rescue. "Sleep in the stable, or go to the schoolhouse with your compatriots," he suggested. "Take the blankets; it's nice and warm in the stable. The groom also sleeps there."

He didn't have to urge me. I bundled into a mound of hay with the warm odor of the horses about me, and soon was fast asleep, content as at home.

16

THE MORNING sunlight, shafting through a small, grated window above the door, awakened me. Usually, when I awoke after a rough passage during the deportation, I found squirming, frightened people about me. This time I was warm, refreshed, and alone. Except for the horses. For some reason the horses made me think I was in the stable on our tenant's farm outside Mitau. Horses, I may add, exude the same tangy perfume whether they be Latvian, Arabian, or Mongolian. These were sturdy Kirghiz steeds and their combined bodily heat had thawed and thoroughly relaxed one frozen, homeless, and grateful wayfarer. I actually had had a pleasant dream.

Blinking in the sun's rays, I recapitulated events in that dream.

It seemed I was back on a holiday with Sina and Ben, two constant companions of my schooldays. We called her Sinoshka, and she was the only daughter of my father's closest friend. Because our families saw each other nearly every day, the parents may have had plans for us although they never told us.

Sina was tall and at that awkward age, with a pug nose, fair hair, and gray, inquisitive eyes. She had a gay, rather frivolous outlook which produced no more than one serious thought in a week. Sina was interested mainly in fun, her objectives the program for the next weekend, holiday, or vacation.

Although I went out with her quite often, no romantic feelings developed within me. In many instances a third party, Ben, the best football player and sportsman in our group, would come along. Sina would dance most of the evening with him, until I felt like a male chaperon. It didn't occur to me that Sina, in her feminine fashion, might be trying to make me jealous.

One of Ben's handicaps was his father, Botshka, "the Barrel," as we called him, who to put it plainly was peculiar. Botshka had been a wrestler at one time, a husky fellow with good looks and immense strength. During a match he unfortunately fell out of the ring on his head, and after that he was never quite right.

On a Sunday when others strolled the avenues in their best, Botshka walked straight to the Duke's palace. There he would button his coat so it left a loop into which he thrust one hand, striking a Napoleonic pose. With head bowed profoundly, he would stride up and down in front of the drawbridge, muttering, "That's how it is, that's how it is." Sometimes he glared across the moat and shook a fist at the castle, adding, "And that won't help you, either!"

Naturally, the villagers felt that Botshka was living very much in the past, and poor Ben was bound to hear their crude comments. It had an unfortunate effect upon him, so Sina and I were both pleased when he threw off his reticence and went dancing with us.

Not that Sina was at all averse to building castles in Spain. We so often drove out to see her friends in the country that I knew every stone and fence on the route. While my horse, Orlik, trotted at his own pace, Sina would plead weariness, lean against me, to think up some new trick to play. She would take off "these silly shoes," or as happened once, toss them out of the carriage. Then, as I went to retrieve them, she whipped Orlik into a run with me dashing behind, shouting for her to stop. In some ways, Sina could be exasperating.

120

Now, in this God-sequestered mountain town of Leninpol, I had been back on a rustic romp with her! But only in a dream. We were riding in a carriage and she was putting questions to me, not as she did when teasing, but rather imperiously, like the NKVD fellows back in Gusar. Orlik, as if their agent, appeared to monitor our conversation.

In this mad dream the onlookers seemed to be Polish refugees, squatting around their kegs of beer, laughing and nudging each other exactly as during my speech in Gusar. I shuddered, wondering how badly these experiences were affecting me, that my childhood's Sina could appear so unreal. I was glad to be awake.

Dousing my face from a wooden bucket, I combed my hair and went outside, carefully returning the comb to my pocket. Where could I replace it, if lost? Where, for that matter, did one replace anything, however simple, in this land of no supplies?

The village was an artist's delight, sparkling in the sunshine, with steep mountains rising directly behind the houses. Stretching to the opposite parapet of crags, the plateau was a white canvas on which the winding Talas appeared as nature's signature.

A large sign, "Kolchos Profintern," surmounted the stable, in whose open-air court a number of youths were already working on the horses. With practiced strokes they brushed, curried, polished, and cleaned until the first animals led outside glistened for the inspector's approval.

"Klaus did not exaggerate," I thought, "this is surely a corner of paradise."

I walked down the street, craning up at the sheer cliff called Utschemechek—the Three Breasts—and so named because the massive bulged near the top in three suggestive mounds, all covered with a snowy brassière. Near the base a waterfall and a slowly turning mill wheel clearly explained why the town was located here.

A rotund German named Friesen had been the miller for years, and true to principles that antedated collectivism, he permitted the Leninpol women to go unattended to the scales. Several were already waiting with sacks of wheat on small carts. Others walked along the icy path, lined with leafless poplars whose upswept limbs were jeweled with ridges of ice. Each couple of hundred meters there was a pump, at which the women filled pails slung from yokes, and then hurried back to their houses. Some of the firstcomers were accompanied by a husband who poured scalding water into the pump's neck to thaw and prime it.

All this had a mystifying impact upon me. The town obviously lived as it had fifty years ago, barricaded from a turbulent world and its troubles. Did the people not know about the war? Of course, but it made no difference in Leninpol. Nothing had happened to change their lives—not yet, that is. Thank God there was such a spot left, but how long would it escape? Thinking thus, I asked passers-by where Klaus lived. It was well into the breakfast hour and I had not shared the feed with the horses.

Klaus's house was at the end of the road, and over its door was a greeting: *"Tritt ein! Grüss Gott!"* Enter! God bless you! . . . Yes, Jac, a long time since you read anything like that.

I knocked and a gray-haired woman opened the door, appraising me suspiciously.

"We have nothing ourselves," she began as if by ritual, attempting to close the door.

"But I want nothing, except to speak to the driver Klaus."

"Come later; he still sleeps," she replied, angrily slamming the door. I walked back up the street to the school where some Poles had more or less established light housekeeping. The men worked in the kolchos; the women remained at the school, cooking. But here again I was urgently asked to leave.

Women are a peculiar lot, I decided. When in trouble, they're happy to accept help no matter who offers it. Introductions are unnecessary. Nobody asks about your family pedigree. "Help me empty this tubful of dirty water; that's a good boy, Jac." It was that way on the Volga boat and again on the Polish rail transports.

But no sooner have they resettled themselves, with one well-dominated male to do the chores and bring home the groceries, than women become once more social-conscious, filled with rules, reproofs, and conventions. These wenches in the schoolhouse, for example. A few weeks ago they were glad to have someone hold a blanket to screen their roadside toilets, but now: "My dear fellow, have we met before? Who introduced us?" Yet I ask no more than a piece of bread and some warm tea.

After this spell of self-pity and increased appetite, I returned to Klaus's home and this time he opened the door.

"Ah, Jac. Come in. Seems you cannot forget your first and best friend? All right, find a seat. Let us have a glass of *pripse.*"

Pripse in that community was coffee from ground wheat. The gray-haired woman brewed and served it, with a sour glance. She was angrier when Klaus also asked her to bring bread and potatoes, but complied without a word.

Klaus took no notice, bidding me to feed up. "Have some more *pripse,* Jac. When you've finished we can discuss your future."

I finished the warm potatoes, and feeling much better asked Klaus how one proceeded to find a job.

"There is plenty of work in the kolchos, and it's important that you get started quickly," he advised. "With a little earned on the side, one can live pretty well. For example, the workmen here get a pound of gray bread and a liter of skimmed milk per day. I'd suggest you take work in the stable; it's warm there and that would offset your thin clothing, and sometimes if you do a hauling job for a farmer, such as fetching hay or straw for heating purposes, there will be some left over for you.

"Anyway, you will definitely do better than those who have to work outdoors. We just received a new Russian overseer. His predecessor, Neumann, was arrested a few weeks ago. Under alcoholic inspiration, Neumann spoke his mind and was immediately reported. The NKVD also picked up our stable foreman a few days ago, although he deserved it.

"Imagine this foreman standing every day before the schoolhouse map measuring the distances with a compass and figuring how long it might take Hitler's forces to reach Leninpol. Well, now he can compute the meters in the coal mines, provided, of course, he's still alive after the trip to Scheljabinsk.

"But whatever comes, my dear Jac, in this village as everywhere in the world, there are foolish people and smart people. The only curse is that for the sins of a few crazy ones the good must also suffer, so we have to endure more than you would guess. Some of us still piece out a living on our wheat allotment, but there are already quite a few who have used it up and are starving.

"Old Lady Franz has eaten her dog. I could tell you others who are down to the last loaf. If only they'll leave us here, but I'm afraid we, too, will be called away one day. 'Man proposes, God disposes,' as the old saying goes. Maybe the Devil will catch up with Hitler. Only it must happen quickly, or he may get here first. Come, it's time to go to the office. I'll go along, and we shall both talk to the economic supervisor."

The office was a short walk through the snow, and I noticed to one side a polishing machine at which two Poles turned the wheel. Others brought up wheat, then took the cleaned and sorted grain away. I wanted to speak to them and explain my presence, but Klaus hurried me along. "Your friends will be working until seven or eight o'clock this evening. The office closes at five," he said.

The economic supervisor, a young and self-important chap, invited me to sit, but I remained respectfully standing.

"Comrade, there is much work in our kolchos, but conditions are difficult. There's a war on, you know." The supervisor began as usual.

"Yes, I know about the war." I spoke seriously to make an impression. "Except for the war I wouldn't be here."

"Our problem is the food supply," the supervisor continued. "We have very little wheat left. You can believe me when I say not enough for planting. But the kolchos farmers don't choose to understand that point." He shrugged. "So we try to take care of all wishes. It's complicated."

Turning to Klaus he asked, "What is this young man's specialty?"

"I was working black." I spoke with embarrassment, the term meaning "plain labor."

"That's fine," the Russian said, "we have enough white hands. But your skill?"

"He used to be a stable worker," Klaus interrupted, "so perhaps he could find something in that line."

"*Choroscho*," the Russian approved, "take him to the stable where he will be instructed by the new foreman."

"Your pardon, Comrade Supervisor," I delayed, "but what about remuneration?"

"Remuneration? Wages in the capitalist sense do not exist here at all. You will receive daily a pound of bread and a liter of soup. Bear in mind, too, this is a preference over bread and skimmed milk. All the rest is credited to *trudoni*."

Leaving the place, I asked Klaus if *trudoni* meant credit of some kind.

"It means 'working days,'" he explained. "Every quota you fulfill is counted as a working day, which is then figured into wheat. When the

124

crop is harvested and the state's revenues have been paid, you get your share of the wheat. This year each of us got ten to fifteen hundredweight, except those who did not fulfill quotas. They received half or perhaps only a quarter of the share. So, as always, it returns to the old rule: As you work, so you eat."

"Do you mean that from this winter until next autumn I must wait for my payment in wheat?" A sudden horror of what I had walked into seized me.

"Of course. It's a question if we'll even get anything next fall. We are at war, the armies need a lot of supplies, and the men are mostly at the front."

"But what do I live on now?"

"You get the pound of bread and soup once a day, including Sunday. But use your head, that's important. Life is a game of wits, eh? With many new turns. Also, remember the daily bread ration is counted off your wheat allotment, later. You had better start working right away or you'll begin starving right away."

We had reached the stable and the foreman, a discharged soldier, received us suspiciously.

"Your new groom, Koljos," Klaus introduced me. Koljos grunted and when Klaus hoped he'd be satisfied, said, "I'm always satisfied. Come, let's look at the horses. They don't bite and don't kick, but they don't want to work either, a habit they got from the kolchos workers." Then, sharply, he asked, "Say, do the Russians live as undisturbed as this among the Germans?"

"I wouldn't know. Never was there," I answered. He cursed and limped away.

Five horses were assigned to me. I was to rub and brush, water and feed them, and to put on and remove their harnesses. One of the details was to clear away the manure each day, and scatter a bit of straw. Altogether, not a difficult task, except the odor of the animals and their stalls clung to me. I was a walking advertisement of the stables.

Meantime I fixed myself a place in the schoolhouse with the other Poles, all of whom were assigned more work than they could manage. Night after night we all lay down exhausted, and hungry.

The Soviet kolchos is well down the economic ladder insofar as skilled labor is concerned. There is hard work, with long hours and utterly miserable conditions. Sanitation isn't known in many of them, and both men and women soon shave their heads to avoid the pest of lice.

Among my few close acquaintances at the school was an elderly gentleman named Blumenkranz, formerly a chemistry professor in Rumania. In Leninpol he carried bricks, a wearying task. But I never heard him complain, and in his own quiet way, he became my hero. I sometimes felt he had passed the stage of recrimination or hatred.

One day he walked up to me and said, "Jac, isn't life wonderful? Today we learned my wife has an open case of tuberculosis and I have advanced heart disease. My children are all in the hospital, so as a family we are ready for the end. We can starve to death in unison and happiness. Be happy, old heart! What more do you ask?"

He smiled and walked away, lighter of step than I had ever seen, and I feared that his mind had snapped. In reality he was quite happy that they might all die about the same time.

The bearded Heinrich Kupfermann, however, was a different type. We called him "Heine" and avoided him when we could. A fellow of better class, he went to no job, but sat all day in a corner, cleaning his nails. When nobody could explain his actions, I wondered if he was a stool pigeon for the police and decided to give him wide detour. Later I learned that he was in reality a German Jew, a fact he had kept hidden until the Nazis one day segregated him with other Jews and he found it more convenient to flee to Poland. Then he moved into Russia, took refuge beyond the Volga with the others, and now moved in a circle of deportees and homeless who were disgusting to him.

"All right, each to his taste," I responded to this report, "but how does he beat this work-or-don't-eat regulation?"

"Wait till the snow melts and spring bread baking begins," I was told. "Old Kupfermann will then begin moving among the German householders, watching the women preparing their loaves and baking in the outdoor ovens. With his nice manners and clean clothing he gives them that 'God be with you' routine, and posing as an exiled anti-Nazi explains why he has to linger here, with us dirty Poles. It is unfortunate that he, a Lutheran and actually a German, must spend his time in such company. The result of this soft appeal is that the kindhearted Hausfrau gives him a loaf of fresh bread.

"He will make the rounds, even sing a little for the sewing circle,

126

and having no pride or ambition to work will come out of it with a nice store of begged bread. This he dries and keeps in storage, so he can spend his winters manicuring his nails."

The weeks passed and the young Poles worked long and hard at the polishing machines. They smuggled a few grains in their pockets, and I contributed a little straw for heating the room. Together we would cook a bit of *kasha*, an unpalatable gruel that at least stalled off starvation.

December and January passed. I was becoming accustomed to grooming horses and living in a common shelter at the school, when two visitations occurred. One was beamed directly at me; the other was to take in the idyllic settlement of Leninpol.

17

AS THE MONTHS passed and Nazi columns neared the Volga, the wounded were appearing in greater numbers in our mountain snuggery. The men, minus a leg, an arm, and sometimes both, climbed painfully from carts that returned from Djambul. Soldiers wounded in the body or head didn't have much chance to survive, we were told. One had to be able to walk or he didn't get back. I shuddered at the memory of that long, wintry ride and the thousands of other kilometers these wounded had come.

"Who wins the war? We don't know. Who does know? *Nichevo, nichevo.*"

Questions brought the same old shrug, the same disinterested negatives. The Germans had many tanks. The Russians had retreated. They had fought around the flanks and escaped into the forests. Then someone picked them up, a medic had sawed off the shattered limb,

129

and now they were here, to replace an able-bodied person. It was always the same.

The inference was plain. Those human wrecks, with the women, would be Soviet Russia's producers and suppliers. Healthy males were needed at the front. The spring campaigns would require millions of men. No community, however remote or forgotten, would escape.

By February the snow had melted to large extent and the frost had left the black soil. Huge tractors ground up and down the fields beyond the villages, although they were often laid up for lack of spare parts. It was to obtain these repair parts that the horses, rested and polished for the journey, periodically made the long trip to Djambul.

One night, when I went to meet friend Klaus and his *voyageurs,* I was startled to see a slender, familiar figure emerge from the first cart. Stepping into a shadow, I took a better look. It was Sandler! The one man whose coming I long had dreaded. He had traced and followed me nearly 200 miles to get his boots.

I had a crazy desire to flee up the snowy side of Utschemechek, to hide among the ample bosoms. Sandler undoubtedly had alerted the police, and there was the evidence he needed—still on my two feet. I watched in fascination while he helped care for the horses as I had done upon arrival weeks before.

I kept out of sight as a second column of vehicles appeared. They were trucks, and moreover, Leninpol's worst fears unloaded from them—NKVD troops. Tough, able-bodied police from Djambul, they had come to conscript the men of the idyllic Mennonite settlement.

The excitement caused by their appearance allowed me to postpone the encounter with Sandler. I was able to slip into the stable where I remained for the night, knowing Sandler would go straight to the Polish quarters. I lay in the straw, considering what to do.

Naturally, Sandler would take back the boots. But would he turn me over to these NKVD? If he did would I be included for military service, although not a Soviet citizen? What could I do to evade this possibility? By daylight, a plan began to take shape which, if I could manage the details, might get me out of this predicament.

Sandler was waiting when I went to the school for the morning *kasha.*

"Where are the boots?" he demanded, calling me a thief.

"I kept them, in event you called," I lied, handing him a package

130

containing his shoes. I had put on a crude pair of substitutes made from an inner tube, which I used in the stable.

Sandler grabbed the boots, examined them, and cursed me.

"I'm sorry, b-but there was no choice," I stammered.

"Oh, but there was. And it's here again."

He pointed to where two trucks with soldiers blocked the street. A large sign over one vehicle ordered: "Register here. All citizens eighteen years and over."

"I am not a citizen of the Soviet Union," I reminded him.

"Can you prove it?" Sandler sneered.

"Yes. Can you?"

Something in his expression told me Sandler was either a Russian citizen or afraid to admit he was not. My plan would work.

"Are you going to turn me in?" I demanded.

"I won't have to. They will turn you in, and you'll soon be on your way," he snapped, sitting down to change into his restored boots. The ones he was wearing looked like salvage from the Djambul bazaar.

Abruptly I left him. Going directly to the economic supervisor's office, I asked to be listed for more important work.

"But I thought you liked the stables?"

"I do, but what will be left in them? The Red Army is taking the best horses with all able-bodied men. You may have to reassign us Poles," I told him.

"I will look into this," Comrade Supervisor agreed as we started for the square to watch the registration. The NKVD officer was telling the crowd that every German resident must appear next morning with no more than 100 kilos of baggage. They would be transferred to the war labor front, because of the need for army supplies. Many of the Soviet workers had been moved to the front, and if any here preferred the fighting jobs that also could be arranged. He grinned each time he made this point, but there were no responsive smiles. The supervisor submitted his "combat availables," with one addition.

Once more I was witnessing mass-deportation preparations.

There was no selective draft with physical examinations, followed by a period in which to arrange personal affairs. The trucks had come after dark, and with this one day's registrations the area would be stripped of its best manhood. Depressed, the men returned to the neat little homes and the day they had so dreaded quickly passed.

Everywhere the women began packing travel kits of clothing, per-

131

sonal gear, and food. In many cases the last pig was slaughtered, the fresh pork baked or fried as though for a holiday. Some wives sewed frantically or darned socks until a late hour, so the husbands would be warm. All night the lights were on, with much dashing in and out to visit, to borrow, to arrange things. Dawn seemed earlier than usual, and many were unready for the assembly call. Husbands and fathers, some with children tugging at sleeves and coattails, appeared with sad and tear-stained wives. Many of these carried the lighter bundles, and all felt it was the last they would see of their men. I was harnessing the horses and greasing wagons for what would be their last journey from the town of Leninpol. The carts were made ready, the kolchos stables cleared of their strong, healthy horses.

"How many will become food for hungry city workers?" I murmured, but not so anyone could hear.

Quickly, NKVD officers read off the names in the order in which the men had registered. Occasionally an obviously unfit man was dismissed, to the joy of his family. There were not many of them. When a villager's name was called he tossed his duffel on the cart and stood beside it. At this, his children would let out howls of grief and the mother would put her face in her hands, weeping.

I walked back of the crowd, and there in a group beside a truck was Sandler. Somehow he had also been conscripted, although this was no surprise to me. I went near and he snarled recognition. The boots were muddy, for it was thawing.

"You will need them now, more than I," my voice was low.

"Maybe you'll get me some food, as rental?" he spat.

"Sure," I shrugged, and took half an apple from my pocket.

He threw it at me, with a string of curses.

There was a shouted order and the men jumped on carts and trucks, joined by the guards. An officer raised one arm; the column moved. Babbling women and children ran after the vehicles for a space, then slowed and stood, waving through their tears.

"Greetings to Hitler," shouted some of the left-behind cripples.

It was not a moment for jokes. I was further depressed over the bitter exchange with Sandler, now retracing that cold journey to Djambul, with his boots but without his liberty. He had tracked me down, but in the process the Red Army had caught up with him.

Life was all a gamble: win today, lose tomorrow. A pair of boots had brought me to this hideaway, and now it was empty of its able-

132

bodied men. The same pair of boots had diverted Sandler into the military service to which he had lured others. Life has its compensations, I concluded.

There was little remorse among the Russian wounded at the departure of Leninpol's males. The Russian veterans would take the vacated jobs, and in many cases the pleasant homes, including the future widows. Now they had the opportunity to jibe at the passive Mennonites, en route to factories, labor battalions, and combat units.

"Look at the Fritzes, the loads of baggage they take! They should leave that stuff behind. It will soon tire them and another will steal it. Either way, the devil is bound to get them." They laughed hugely at their knowledge of what these men would experience.

As the departing burghers rode from their town, they turned for a last look at the whitewashed houses, the stones of which most of them had placed in position. They had spent years in the hidden paradise, and but for the war might have lived there unmolested many more.

But time does not stand still. As the last cart disappeared down the slope a mystic volume closed. That was the end of Leninpol as it had been developed and improved by the descendants of Germans who abhorred war and had penetrated to this province to avoid it.

And now war had taken them away. I thought with sorrow of those who had befriended me.

Thereafter Leninpol became just another unloading station for the wounded, the deported, and fugitives from as far away as Moscow. Russians, Poles, and Jews, it soon was impossible to find jobs that would keep them reasonably busy and in rations. Many were soon going hungry.

The result was a familiar pattern: People sold what they had left in order to eat, and the local residents took their choice at a fraction of the article's worth. People stormed the bazaar, but for once there were more sellers than buyers. Kirghiz men had lived too long without double-breasted suits to need them now, and who wanted a modern, city dweller's hat and shoes? Meanwhile the price of bread and fat went up steeply. Soon it was possible to purchase a first-class costume for one slice of greased bread.

As the masses hungered, local authorities did their best to spread the food supplies thinner. Working peoples' rations were cut and cut again to provide a little for those without jobs or salable articles. At the hospital additional beds were put in the aisles until the place was packed. All available building space was filled with the overflow.

Then one day another convoy of NKVD arrived. This time all the younger German women and girls had to register, and the next day they were deported to munitions factories. There was nobody to weep except the old women and a few graybeards left behind from the first conscription.

That finished Leninpol and its Mennonite descendants. The Russians took over, the refugees were distributed among the empty houses, and the unhappiest spring since its colonizing came to the valley.

"Even the birds don't sing as they did other years," a grandmother whispered as she pumped water.

Since our school was now a hospital, we Poles were also redistributed among the village homes. I was luckily assigned to one of the better places, my landlady being elderly with a young grandchild. She was permitted to keep one room, but the other was given to me. It was next to the kitchen, and from the first I got along well with the woman because I brought heating materials from the stable. Besides, I was clean, behaved myself, and didn't come in drunk. I was able to sleep once more on a bed with white linen. It seemed like heaven.

Our supervisor had forgotten about my job request, so I was left with the remaining horses. When the other stable hands were drafted, I did the best I could alone. Brushing the animals, I computed my *trudoni* and made a notation on a scrap of paper. At night I would go to sleep, well satisfied that I had an excellent spot, all things considered. When autumn came I would have a plentiful supply of wheat.

"Then I'll eat *kasha* and milk, all I want," I told Grandmother Sarah. "I shall have plenty left over for you and the little one."

I wondered when I spoke thus why she didn't share my enthusiasm, and why she seemed indifferent when I spoke of next autumn, sure that I would still be there. Perhaps because she had seen so much more of life than I had. The last few weeks had been a terrible shock.

With such thoughts, I retired to the neat little room, making my usual brief prayer.

"Aushalten!" I had repeated this German word for "hold out" until it had become a personal watchword. In a way it was my whole philosophy, my objective, my single purpose in continuing the struggle. Endure. Stick it out. Stay alive.

It would have been quite easy to give up, to die. But that would not take me back to Mitau and my loved ones. I would never learn what had happened after we were deported, or whether the Nazis had overrun the town and seized what was left of the population.

Were my family alive or dead? Did my father and mother still hide in the country? Would I see them again?

During such daydreams I discovered I was remembering girls to whom I had paid little heed a year ago. Or was it now two years? Events had run together in my memory; the immediate past was a blur.

"Aushalten. Aushalten. Aushalten! Immer, Jakob, *immer aushalten!"*

Then something from the Books of Moses would come to mind and make me feel able to do it, as in the first chapter of Joshua:

Have not I commanded thee? Be strong and of a good courage; be not afraid, neither be thou dismayed: for the Lord thy God is with thee whithersoever thou goest.

The head of the Rajkom of Leninpol appeared with his staff to check upon the remaining horses. I displayed them proudly, hoping for some sort of reward, for I had become an expert horse valet by this time and they glistened in their spring coats.

"Fine, wonderful," the commissar said. His men took measurements, weights, ages, the sex of the animals. All was put down in notebooks. But after that they took nineteen of the twenty-two horses away, and left only three old nags for the kolchos. I was shattered.

Furthermore I was summoned to the labor office, where Comrade Supervisor said, "You see, Jac, only one stable boy is needed, and even he can be incapacitated. You must realize such a job is more deserved by one of our wounded, for a youngster like you can find something else. I suggest the polishing machine, with the others. You can get your wages in the fall."

"But what am I to live on until then?" I asked.

"That's your business."

"You mean I shouldn't eat?"

"You won't get your wages until months from now, so it's best to go to the polishing machine right away."

My friends were also out of jobs because of the many refugees, but when we went to the polishing machine it was broken down. It would be weeks before parts could arrive from Djambul, just as with the tractors. Everything was becoming broken, and little was repaired. More people were going without food, and the planting had not yet started. It was a terrible prospect, depressing in the extreme.

Back with Comrade Economic Supervisor, I was told to report to the machine-repair station, that they still had horses and the food situation was better. But the MTS (Machines, Tractor Station) sent me on to the combine, explaining that rations were easier there, and when I reached that station they passed me on to another. Eventually, I realized there was no job at all for a deported Latvian.

I'm an unlucky bird, I thought, but then a man who had lost a leg and an arm went by, and behind him a dozen fugitives climbed off a wagon. I decided things were not so bad and strolled toward the bazaar.

18

THE AIMLESS search for work was undermining my morale and I began once more to seek the crowds. If misery loves company it had plenty at the public market. Privation and destitution were in abundance there, ever willing to be shared. Perversely, one felt better seeing others who fared worse. If a cheerful word or helping hand were needed at least I had both to offer. Besides I was getting lonely as a refugee-at-large.

Near the men's latrine I noticed a group of young and old laughing heartily at some poor fellow's hard luck. Hecklers were shouting over the board fence and evoking a torrent of vile curses and uncomplimentary adjectives. At each tirade the Russians would hold their sides, laughing so hard they had to sit down.

"What goes on that's so funny?" I asked several boys who were jumping up and down in glee.

"Go, see for yourself," they invited, pointing to the doorless entry of the crude accommodation which passed for a public toilet. "A bourgeois is in trouble."

I went in, to discover an elderly gentleman from Moscow standing in one of the booths in his tunic and underwear. He had made the mistake of hanging his trousers on the fence, from which they had been promptly snatched. Now, in an exposed state, for his underwear had surely seen better days, he was being taunted by less sensitive persons who challenged him to come out and find his stolen pants.

Observing that I didn't laugh or harass him, the old man beckoned. Would I do him a great favor?

"Run up to the butcher's house and explain what has happened. Ask him for an old pair of overalls, and bring them quickly. I will give you something," he promised, whispering the address.

Partly for the tip, but more out of sympathy for an old fellow who, like many another, had been set upon by heartless youths, I agreed. Circling the crowd, I soon found the butcher's place, got the overalls, and returned.

As he climbed into the breeches the old fellow asked what I did and from where I came.

"I've had work until this week, but now I don't know. . . ."

"Deportee?"

"Yes. Polish."

"A long way from home," he said and then, returning to his own troubles, "What a filthy bunch. What a dirty trick to play—stealing an old man's pants!" He swore a few more choice phrases, called his tormentors a variety of evil things, and then in a magnificent non sequitur, asked, "Have you ever been in St. Petersburg?"

"Never," I replied.

"Well, you should see it; the white city by the sea with palaces and wonderful buildings. And the toilets there! My son, they are automatic with flushing devices that operate at the press of a button. But here"— he spat with disgust as we walked from the foul place—"here you must hold your pants with one hand and with the other fend off those who would steal them. What a long way we have come, thanks to the great October Revolution!"

We moved away amid jostling, laughter, and coarse comment, the old man blinking in anger and mortification. I wondered at his open criticism of the Bolshevik control, but said nothing.

As we left the bazaar, he seemed to sense my thoughts and spoke out: "You're a Jew, aren't you? With whom else could I speak? Perhaps with the Russians?" He leered and spat again. "What's your name?"

"Friends call me Jac."

"*Choroscho,* Jac it is. And I think I can do something for you. Come home with me."

Still believing him to be a refugee, I doubted this invitation would mean much, and anyway I was becoming cautious in my choice of companions. My critical look didn't trouble the old man, however.

Taking my arm, he confided, "You probably think I'm in this hell-hole because I want to hide from the Germans? Nothing is further from the fact. As a matter of truth, Jac, if I weren't so old I'd be at the front. I'd show them. But that's not important at the moment.

"It should interest you more, my friend, to know that I am here as representative of a large munitions plant. I happen to be Jefim Jurge-witz Nowitzki and a member of the Party for more than twenty years!" He thumped his chest a couple of times to emphasize his lofty estate, pulling the Communist Party membership card from an inside pocket. I admired it much as poor people gawk at the winning ticket in an international sweepstakes. I could hardly believe that my simple act of assistance had once more thrown me into the embrace of influence.

"Now, my boy, as I've said, I have to close a big deal and in that connection there will also be some work for you. If you are a smart one, perhaps more than just a job. So come along, we'll talk this over at home."

Comrade Nowitzki entered a large house where he lived alone with his large wife. This exclusiveness was enjoyed only by top members of the Party, for Leninpol was chock-full by this time and war's home-less tide was still running.

The tall, fleshy woman who opened the door towered above her spouse. "Back so soon, my Eagle?" she greeted. "Who is this you've brought along?"

Madame Nowitzki did not wait for his response but immediately disappeared into another room.

"Come in," my host encouraged, "it seems my wife's in good humor. She generally calls me old parrot. Today I'm an eagle, but of course she doesn't know about the recent embarrassment at the bazaar. We'll keep that dark." He chuckled, and in a few moments

Madame Nowitzki appeared with boiling tea. Over the cups, he explained his position.

"I'm here to organize a barter deal. I'll buy up the kolchos sheep and cattle, but not for money. We give a credit for merchandise. This consists of machinery, dry goods, nails, wire, pipe, kitchen utensils, tiles, shoe polish, and oil—lots of things, too many to mention." He glanced at me cunningly.

"First, we need a space in which to assemble the animals; then they must be slaughtered, salted, and packed in barrels for shipment to Scheljabinsk. Here, as everywhere, a plan has to be fulfilled. Quotas, you know. They must positively be observed, for as you know, Jac, there's a war on."

"Yes, Comrade Nowitzki, I know."

"Good. And you also know that if we get along well together we shall have more than merely bread and butter, my boy. What more does a man require these times but 'a load of butter and a little bread' —he's in business. A good living, yes?" He smiled again, and I was troubled lest it was all a mad joke.

"You aren't just making fun of me, are you?"

"Fun? Remember my young friend, Nowitzki never makes fun of anything."

He went into another room and returned with a pile of papers and a filing case from which he spread out documents. The usual book of orders was also there, and then he showed me the big, round rubber stamp which only very important officials possessed. My fears and suspicions melted at once, and I saw in this grumpy, profane old man another savior.

"I'll run to the kolchos and get my papers, then I can start work immediately," I cried.

"Good, Jac. But take your time with all that, for we have to wait anyway until Leonid gets back."

"And who is Leonid?" I asked, confused that a third party was involved.

"Our bookkeeper. He's still down in Djambul. God knows what he's doing there. He should have been here long ago."

I made arrangements quickly and with my transfer papers reported to Nowitzki bright and early next day.

"Leonid hasn't arrived yet, and I'm sure he's cheating me," said the old man.

140

"Perhaps, boss, he's unavoidably delayed?"

"Unavoidably delayed, indeed," Madame Nowitzki interjected. "He beats my husband all down the line. And Nowitzki's no boss, he's an old parrot."

The veteran Party member looked helplessly toward me, and I tried to quiet his excited wife by mentioning the difficulties of travel between Djambul and Leninpol. We had tea, and then I was allowed to go to my room at Grandma Sarah's.

Leonid wasn't back the second day, and Nowitzki's face revealed more than average concern.

"Wasn't I right?" Madame Nowitzki taunted. "He is no good."

"Sure, sure. He is cheating me all directions in Djambul," the husband morosely assented.

"Does he have merchandise?" I couldn't resist probing for details on this violation of trust.

"No, he has no merchandise. He has no money. Not one ruble. But he cheats me nonetheless. I know how, too."

"Without money or goods?" I spoke my doubts.

"You wouldn't understand. He does business at the free market, and naturally he won't tell me what he's making. My wife is right. It looks as if I'm getting old."

"You should punish Leonid," the tall woman snapped, putting down the tea tray. "It is sabotage. The whole works are held up because of your Leonid."

When I returned the third morning Nowitzki was beside himself. Leonid was still missing and my boss was so mad he couldn't speak without cursing. He hadn't slept all night, and his face bore a couple of fresh scratches.

"I was out cutting brush," he dismissed my inquiry abruptly, drumming the tabletop with nervous fingers.

The scratches looked like fingernail marks, but I didn't pursue this and presently Nowitzki reached a decision.

"Go to the kitchen, ask my wife for the book of orders."

Madame Nowitzki was stirring something in a pot and didn't look up when I asked for the book. "On the table." She pointed a thumb. "And if you ask me, it's about time." I understood what she meant.

Nowitzki opened to a fresh page, and producing the round stamp, gave me the book, a stubby pen, and some ink. "Write," he said, preparing to dictate.

141

"But, Comrade, it's a responsible task and this an important book. Don't you think you should personally put down this order?" Once more I was in a tight squeeze, being still devoid of Russian grammar and spelling, although I had gained a fair conversational flow.

"I don't have spectacles for writing, and you can do this just as well as I. So get going. Orders are orders," said Nowitzki, and began:

"I, Jefim Jurgewitz Nowitzki, as of today am dismissing the head bookkeeper, Leonid Leontovitsch Lifschitz, due to lack of ability. At the same time I engage Mischa Jac Feld as buyer for the metals factory Scheljabinsk, Leninpol branch. Signature. . . ."

With a curse he scrawled his name and plastered it over with the great stamp, which in Soviet Russia is the most impressive feature of any official document. Since most of the authoritarian underlings could not read they relied upon the stamps or seals, and the bigger and more numerous the more impressed they were.

During my travels, I had met a deportee who somewhere had obtained a Polish lodge stamp. It merely stated: "Good for two admissions and beer," but while his ink pad held out this fellow and his friends went a long way with its imprint on tickets and passes.

Returning the book to the kitchen, I calmed Madame Nowitzki, who conceded that at last her husband was showing some signs of being the boss. Once more I went back to my room and wondered when my new duties would begin. At least, I thought, I was due for better food, as Nowitzki's wife, say what one would about her feminine graces and temper, managed a good table.

We were having dinner the fourth evening when there was a knock at the door. It was Leonid, as if dropped from the skies. Madame Nowitzki immediately left the room.

The bookkeeper was certainly no candidate for Mr. Soviet Union. No, and scarcely for Mr. Kazakhstan, although he looked like a fugitive from the goat pen. Small and thin, he was also cross-eyed, and his pock-marked face, under a vizor cap from Kerensky days, added little charm to the general slovenly impression. He carried a heavy portfolio.

"Where in hell have you been all this time?" Nowitzki growled.

"In Djambul; where else?" said Leonid.

"Why didn't you get here sooner?"

"If you had been sitting on your end in Djambul, you'd know why

I stayed there so long," said Leonid furiously. "It's a miracle that I'm here now. People wait for weeks for a kolchos cart to bring them up here, but nothing leaves because the horses have all been requisitioned for the army. Luckily, I caught a ride with the Director of MTS in his automobile. But who is he?" Leonid pointed abruptly at me.

"That is Jac, our new co-worker," Nowitzki said.

"What for?"

"A funny question," said my boss. "Can't a poor boy also make something? He needs it."

"How much have you already made?" Leonid's raspy voice was loaded with accusation.

"By no means as much as you did in Djambul."

That was too much for Leonid. His voice cracked, he seemed to verge on tears through a mist of fury. "I went hungry and hardly slept; my wife and I were working every minute trying to get back here. And you sit there, talking the same as you did in Schaljabinsk!"

As I was to observe again and again, when Leonid cut loose Nowitzki became frightened and quickly changed his tone.

"All right, all right. Let's have some tea," he said. Since Madame Nowitzki had taken off, I had to brew and serve it, after which my boss indicated he had private affairs to discuss with Leonid. I was excused until ten the next morning, at which time I found him and the wayward bookkeeper the best of buddies, Nowitzki quickly explaining it had all been a mistake.

"So now, Jac, you see that when a Soviet official recognizes his errors he must correct them. Fetch the book of orders."

I did so and he told me to tear out the last page. "You remember, the one with that stupid order dismissing our friend Leonid. Go ahead —don't look at me like a cow surveying its calf!"

I was terribly upset, for not only was this the holy book of orders, but the page also contained my hiring as well as Leonid's dismissal. The good Comrade must have read my mind, for he shouted, "Tear it out. When I give orders I know what I'm doing. There are other orders on that page besides what concerns you. Leonid will rewrite them all. He can affix the same date and I'll put on the stamp. So nobody will know whether I signed them now or last week. You'll continue to work here, as we agreed."

My relief was tremendous, for it was the difference between eating and starving, but my awe for the "Book" from that moment took a tailspin.

Leonid was watching me crookedly all this time, but cross-eyed or not he seemed to be studying me carefully. After restoring the orders he introduced himself in the following fashion:

"As you already know, I am Leonid Leontovitsch Lifschitz, apparently a small and weak man." He fixed me with a gaze that seemed also to take in Nowitzki, for whose benefit I sensed he was also speaking. "But one thing, my boy, I want you to remember from the beginning: I have brought down more of the mighty than you would think. I, Leonid, am a man perhaps like all the others, but then again not. For not in vain have I worked on the same job twenty years, without ever having gone to jail.

"I have one principle, and that you will bear in mind. I want nobody else's money and will never touch it, but woe be to him who tries to get mine!" He rolled his off-track eyes and gnashed his teeth with a grimace that sent a chill down my spine. "I'll bite the throat of him who crosses me," he roared, hammering the table with a fist.

"Why are you getting enraged already?" Nowitzki interrupted. "You'll have plenty of chance for grinding your teeth. Remember, one must live, my dear Leonid. Worries come of themselves, and I think that Jac certainly has no intention of being dishonest. So why do you thresh empty straw? What could he steal from you, Leonid? You have nothing." The boss smiled.

"I don't say he wants to cheat me. I just want to straighten him out in a general way." The bookkeeper suddenly cooled down. "He should know with whom he deals."

Thereafter we met each day in Nowitzki's home, studying our orders, dividing the job into quarters, and checking for opportunities to make a little profit above our salaries. This would have gone on indefinitely except that Madame Nowitzki decided one day that her private domain had become a Soviet office and she would have no more of it. If the government placed important business in our hands it must also place an office at our disposal, she ruled, although the presence of many thousands of wounded and refugees had filled every possible building.

But the power of the State is all-pervading; what begging, complaining, threatening, and crying couldn't attain, Nowitzki's orders and

Party book soon obtained. A house was confiscated for war purposes and in it we were established.

Let the refugees manage for themselves. Tens of thousands were sleeping under God's stars; a few more wouldn't make much difference. Soon a huge billboard fronted our new offices, bearing the names of the participants in the newly founded organization: Jefim Jurgewitz Nowitzki, Leonid Leontovitsch Lifschitz, and M. Jakob Ivanovitch. I had been embellished with a new moniker for the sake of Soviet business. I hoped this time the enterprise would go better.

As in business the world over the first thing was to make a good appearance. We put on our best clothing, got haircuts and shaved. This also required some influence since the place was overrun with unshorn, bearded, and unbathed humans. But Nowitzki's order book and the big red stamp were good for priorities in what passed for barbershops, while home laundries took care of other needs. There were no end of fine women eager to get such work for a ruble or two.

Our office impressed everyone with its big sign, for who could guess that behind it were only empty rooms? Not even a safe or a file for papers and orders, which we kept in a drawer of the table. When word spread that I was in the firm, many whom I hardly knew came around with a kindly word.

"How is business, Jac? Everything going well?"

"Fine, fine. Business is very good, and I'm satisfied," I invariably replied. And what else would I say? I was eating; I had a dry, warm place to sleep; I was reasonably clean and clothed.

Six weeks went by, and then a great event occurred. A fully loaded truck consigned to our firm reached Leninpol. The driver had escorted the load from the Scheljabinsk factory by rail to Djambul, transferred to an army truck at that place, and proceeded up the road.

The arrival of consumer goods in Leninpol was as welcome as the spring weather and improved everyone's lot. The town had seen no such goods in months. The truck unloaded into our building and the adjoining shed. There were farm tools, household necessities, nails, hatchets, knives, repair parts for pumps and polishing machines, furnaces, tractors, and supplies for shoemakers and bakers. Most eagerly received were the pails, pans, tablewear, and other articles for the overcrowded homes of Leninpol. Overnight the assets of our distributing firm had skyrocketed from nothing to many thousands of rubles. I went out and proudly surveyed my new name in paint.

145

But every triumph has its problems, we soon found. The envious and jealous, the larcenous most of all, coveted this bonanza and there were many who hoped soon to see us behind bars so they could take over. It was obvious we could not leave the merchandise unguarded. I won the job without a vote.

I moved from my cozy little room, arranged a place to sleep in the office, and became overnight both government buyer and company guard. The first requirement was to learn how to sleep with one eye and one ear open.

19

JEFIM NOWITZKI was no professor of economics and I doubt if he could have written a page on the barter system, but sharing his activities was a revealing experience in the Soviet distribution of its collectively produced goods. I had studied it intensely during the Riga University preparations, but here I was actually a part of operations no textbook had suggested.

There was no Marx, Lenin, or even Stalin theory in practice; it was a pound for a pound, commodity for goods, a need-for-need exchange based on local rules of supply and demand. Meat, vegetables, and grain from the kolchos were turned in for drygoods, tools, salt, and other necessities from the supply house. We were agents by government permit, although I sensed as we proceeded in this fantastic trading that we actually were the middlemen whose counterparts in capitalist countries drew the harsh criticism of Communist agitators. Yet how else could this interchange be managed?

"We are at war and the young and able must fight or produce. It is the duty of the older, less physically equipped to further our cause by handling the details of civilian supply," Nowitzki said, and for once there was no cause for the prick of conscience.

The old Bolshevik hurriedly prepared for business, having large pens and sheds erected in the rear of our building into which kolchos cattle, hogs, and sheep were herded. There they were fed and fattened some more, for grain and hay were also brought in for barter. The spring sun had warmed Leninpol's plateau, so that the icy breastplates dripped from Utschemechek to moisten fields and gardens no longer worked by the attentive Mennonites. But we had more urgent affairs than observing scenery and seasons or mourning the dispossessed pacifists.

Everything progressed according to plan. The kolchos bosses drove in their stock, then lined up for equipment and machinery, staples and clothing according to their demonstrated needs.

Among the top priorities at this time, was salt. Plain, coarse, sometimes dirty salt. It was more precious than sugar to the Kirghiz, who used it as a medium of exchange when supplies ran low. Salt and tea, two rather common articles in the European household, were in this hidden place among things most prized.

So the peasants brought in livestock and if the cows and ewes dropped calves and lambs during the collection, we were that much ahead of the quota. We traded salt against the meat credit, and bartered merrily in all things the truck had carried.

Naturally, the Leninpolers did not get precisely what they wanted. In fact, they usually took what they least needed, or at best a shabby substitute for what they asked. But life is like that for the little people, and who could complain in such times?

"You don't like it, Comrade? Then perhaps you would prefer the Red Army satisfied your requirements?"

I heard it over and over and in my youthful naïveté grieved over the denials to these patient children of toil and trouble.

Nowitzki and Leonid didn't care. Noting that in order to obtain certain articles the peasants had to negotiate two or three more barters after the original exchange, I made bold to offer a suggestion.

"Why don't we take the supplies to the kolchos and then pick out the best and fattest animals in payment? Wouldn't it please them better, Comrade Jefim?"

"Hear how the young man talks!" cried Nowitzki, permitting himself a smile. "Why should we take the well to the bucket? The livestock comes here just the same. But if you like trips to the kolchos, you shall have them in future. But not to pick up cattle and sheep, my dear Jac. You will exchange salt which I shall supply. You will trade salt with the Kirghiz and follow my instructions to the letter. For one kilo of salt, you will bring back one kilogram of fat or two kilos of wheat. Those are the local prices; I have checked them."

That afternoon a pail of water was sprinkled over the salt to increase its weight, and next morning I left to trade my saline packets for wheat and fats. Only then did it dawn on me why I had been picked for employment by Nowitzki, Lifschitz, & Co. Jefim and Leonid did the bartering for the government; I bartered on the side for them.

Perhaps I should say "for our firm," for ours had blossomed into a four-way partnership with the arrival of another but not silent member from Scheljabinsk. We had been expecting him for weeks, but again that mysterious procrastination until presto! like a jack-in-the-box he stood before us—a man without hair and with a face like a porcupine. Squat, muscular, and beady-eyed, David Bronstein, a sweating butcher, waited admittance, still wearing in midsummer heat his felt-lined Siberian boots!

"Well, you bad-luck bird, you're finally here?"

"Are you waiting for the oxen to become lean before killing?"

Both my bosses used jovial jibes for salutations, but the harassed Bronstein was in no mood to share the laughter.

"Please, don't call me a bad-luck bird," he protested with a tired wave of the hand. "What happened to me in Scheljabinsk should overtake Hitler's armies. Besides, it wasn't my fault."

Nowitzki tossed me his "Leave us alone" glance, so I pretended an errand and left. I was becoming discreet in matters which required a certain diplomatic understanding. When I returned in the afternoon they were still talking. It was teatime and, with Bronstein and his wife and daughter billeted to the same building I occupied, we became by circumstance one happy family. At least we had a lull in the barter discussions, for which I was grateful. Bronstein's daughter was too young and not very attractive, which also helped. There would be no time in our operations for romance. The thought of it made me wince.

There is "a time to love, and a time to hate," according to Solomon, and a refugee in wartime soon accepted the fact. The unkempt females about us were dressed for work, not fondling, and both sexes at day's end were either too tired or indifferent for love-making. As to the village women, they kept to themselves and their code. My yearnings were therefore few, and the moratorium on sex was the least of my problems.

As a salt peddler I was an immediate success. Why not? He who takes hot cakes to the starving needs no salesmanship. I sold out each daily supply, but the profit unfortunately was split four ways. Nevertheless, it was a good living, and Nowitzki, although still on guard against being cheated, proved an ideal senior partner. He demanded and enforced equal shares.

Everything was orderly, carefully regulated, and there were no short weights. True, there was plenty of water over the salt, but doesn't it require washing? One wouldn't offer the gentle Kirghiz dirty salt. I flipped off these answers in my accumulating dialect, and business boomed. Our only problem was to keep the women from each other's hair as they heatedly debated which husband was doing the most for the beloved State.

Came the day when strict orders for slaughtering arrived. The quota figures were included. This was exciting news, especially for Nowitzki, who by now had definite qualms on whether he had reserved sufficient salt for the packing process. It should be noted that prewar Russia was little refrigerated except by its climate, and down Uzbek and Kirghiz way the cooling system was wind from Siberia only.

Now that summer had returned, the only way to dispose of the meat was to salt it generously, pack it in barrels, and quickly ship it to the consumer. Of course Leonid and I had signed as witnesses, so if we should run short of salt there was testimony that much had to be disposed of as unfit. Too dirty to wash economically, it was certainly not fit for packing fresh meat. That was our story and if need be, Soviet inspectors would be stuck with it.

"We get nowhere discussing the matter. I have the barrels so tomorrow we begin slaughtering," Nowitzki ordered. He scarcely needed to add that since my extracurricular bartering, the price of salt had gone down precipitately. The decline increased when various others fetched in salt from Djambul. We had salt to spare.

The excitement of a collective butchering is exceeded only by the

150

satisfaction of a collective packing. Barrel after barrel was filled, each containing 35 per cent salt instead of the prescribed 20 per cent, although this discrepancy we had to conceal at all costs.

"Each day grows warmer. It is a poor season to be preparing beef and pork. There must be no lack of salt to keep this meat edible," Bronstein piously repeated as we scooped in more.

The bosses and their wives worked tirelessly, the women providing advice when not transferring slabs of flesh. Comrade Bronstein unquestionably was an expert in his field; he knew how to cut beef so that well-salted bones went along in each barrel, and the pieces were so placed they took up maximum space. We admired his technique as we became happier in our work, the joy of seeing the quota approached nourishing mutual confidence and a communal spirit of friendship. We were calling each other by first names in no time at all, telling our family backgrounds, exchanging harmless experiences. At day's end we washed up and had our tea, after which in my youthful ardor, I would stroll once more in front of our office and read my new name in painted letters. M. Jakob Ivanovitch—even a pseudonym swells the chest in moments of triumph.

Of course it was too good to continue without unpleasant incident. I feared it was a snare like my friend Chardiroff's, set with different bait, but what happened was quite different and most distressing.

One night, a week after the slaughtering, dead tired with the day's packing, I awakened to hear light steps in the vestibule of our office-flat. I popped behind the curtain and looked out. Someone was entering the yard. The moon on his bald head identified David Bronstein. He was making his way to the locked meat house. I was seized by a horrible suspicion that our prowling partner was about to steal some of the stock.

Maybe Nowitzki is right: "In these days your property is stolen by the one who eats your bread." I preferred to go back to bed and forget the whole thing, but anger and curiosity kept me at the window.

When Bronstein reappeared from the meat storage, he was bowed under approximately a side of beef. It was so heavy I had an urge to rush out and help him carry the burden, except I felt he wouldn't appreciate my assistance.

Puffing and snorting, he entered our quarters so clumsily that even one numbed by vodka would have wakened. Avarice, I thought, makes a man forget that others also have senses. Fury rose within

151

me: So you are a thief, Bronstein, and one who does not steal from need or hunger, for we had plenty of food. No, you rascal, it is for greed and filthy profit that you cheat your boss and partners.

As he blundered into the kitchen and opened the trap door to the cellar, I tried to rationalize his actions: Was he saving us work by dragging the beef to the office? Did he intend to share it with us? Might he be a sleepwalker, dreaming that he was at work? All excuses vanished as I heard him slide the meat down the ladder, climb up, snap the padlock, and creep back to his waiting wife. Her only worry, I discovered later, was that I might catch on to what he was doing. I didn't sleep at all, hoping Bronstein would explain it all the next morning.

Breakfast passed and our partner said nothing. His wife, to allay suspicion, commented on her inability to sleep. "I walked in the garden, it was so balmy," she said.

"Yes, very balmy," I agreed. "It also kept me wide awake."

Both looked at me nervously, but Bronstein only said, "Let's roll a couple of cigarettes and get to work, Jac."

But I wasn't letting him off the hook so easily. Should I report what I'd seen to Nowitzki, or try to arouse the thief's conscience? I had never reported anyone, and decided against it. I wanted to hang around, however, so I said I wasn't feeling well. This allowed me to remain in the room, watch the kitchen, and prevent them from moving the meat back upstairs. By sheer chance I also got possession of the trap-door key when Madame Bronstein left it on the kitchen table. Not long after, she was beating her daughter for losing it, and a kind of panic invaded the household. Madame Bronstein frantically refused my offer to open the door, and finally called her husband. When he tried to send me on an errand I said I felt nauseated and could not leave the room. The game of cat and mouse continued next day, the Bronsteins becoming desperate as the warm weather threatened to spoil the beef. I thought by then they would have admitted the situation, but they remained silent. Bronstein's temper was ragged, and his wife seemed ready to cut my throat.

Next morning she insisted I go to the polyclinic for an examination, but I declined.

"It's a passing thing. Nausea," I lied, leaving the door open into the kitchen.

After the second day, knowing the meat was tainted by that time, I

152

slipped the key behind the water bucket and awaited developments. After all, there was no use making a personal enemy of Bronstein, but if he had no decency and honor at least he should have no illicit swag, I thought. Let him dispose of spoiled beef as best he could. But the episode took a turn I did not expect.

A cry of relief told me Madame Bronstein had found the key, and I heard her and her husband muttering about it during the night. Before sunrise Bronstein was in the cellar, his wife helping to retrieve the slab of meat. I turned over, deciding to let them finish as they pleased. Disgusted with it all, I fell asleep.

Bronstein after inspecting his booty decided all of it was not spoiled and lugged it to the *arik,* a water ditch that passed along the rear of the property. There he was washing it, bent over and unaware that anyone was about at that hour, when a familiar voice accosted him: "Good morning, Comrade Bronstein. So early up?"

It was the veterinary of the Rajkoms, always present during kolchos slaughterings to inspect animals and pass on the fitness of meat for food. He had a continuing feud with Butcher Bronstein and, at a recent Party meeting had been accused by our partner of issuing tuberculosis certificates for certain peasant's cattle which were perfectly healthy, in order to forestall their slaughter. Later he allegedly accepted fees to revoke such orders so they could be privately butchered.

"Ah, good morning yourself, Comrade Veterinary. Just cleaning up a little chunk of meat. Mostly bones, not much on them. I work so late, this is the only chance I have for such personal tasks." Bronstein was shaken at being discovered, splashing at the water trying to hide the slab of beef.

"Yes, yes, a truly industrious citizen. On duty before sunrise, at it all day, really a Stachanov. A veritable champion. And Bronstein, when you say only a little chunk, you are being rather modest, don't you think?"

The veterinary poked in the water with his stick, eying Bronstein as he calculated the amount of meat. "Almost half a steer, wouldn't you say?"

"Nothing but bones; ribs and gristle," Bronstein defended. "I bought it last night from a Kirghiz. Swindlers, every one. You pay for beef and get bones."

"A bad admission from you, David," the other smirked. "You, the best butcher in the Rajkom, on your own say-so. How come you let a stupid Kirghiz sell you nothing but bones?"

"Well, it sometimes happens," Bronstein said lamely, looking sadly at his prize and wishing it were in the bottom pit of Hades. Unlucky bird, indeed. He scratched at his ear.

The veterinary cut short the byplay. His voice was harsh as he surveyed Bronstein.

"Since when does one take a samovar to Tula?" he rasped. "And how long since you, who butcher three or four cattle each day, are obliged to buy your beef from a Kirghiz? Let me tell you this, Comrade Bronstein: It's a coincidence that I came by at this hour, but it was a coincidence by design. I've suspected something like this was going on. In fact, I felt sure it was happening.

"I'm not here as a trial judge from the NKVD, but as the veterinary. You are scrubbing tainted meat. Only a fool wouldn't suspect. It makes no difference where it came from, although a man with a bird brain could figure it out.

"At all events, if the meat you have in your hand smells bad, it is possible that all the meat you've so far salted and packed, also smells. And since we must assume that half a steer has been erroneously taken from your own supplies, my dear Comrade, you won't be offended if I confiscate it for examination?" The vet was warming up as Bronstein's pallor increased and he trembled in the cool of the morning.

"Furthermore, I must learn what kind of meat you are handling, Bronstein, whether from a Kirghiz—which while unbelievable is also punishable—and also whether you have been packing tainted beef in all your barrels. I put nothing beyond you! It is entirely possible that you will be placed before the Tribunal shortly, since every day of freedom will only increase your crimes!"

With which the veterinary dragged the side of beef to his cart, waiting under a tree where Bronstein should have seen it except for his concentration on stolen goods. The abject butcher trotted beside him, trying to help with the burden, but was pushed away as he strove to make a gift of the beef to his enemy.

"Have pity, Comrade Doctor, think of my wife and little girl. Take the beef, it's yours, and let's forget it. I swear it's not from our supplies."

The vet pushed him away and delivered a final ultimatum: "Why

154

didn't you think of wife and child some time ago? I don't need your gift of meat; I get mine from people whose cattle and sheep I declare ill. You know that better than anyone, for you alone reported me. Remember one more thing, in future: If one hand had washed the other, both hands would be clean, but now you shall have what you wished on me." He left the butcher standing in the road and drove away.

Bronstein, overwhelmed by what he faced, stared after the veterinary's cart and if he had possessed hair, most certainly would have pulled it out. He stood to lose a flourishing business, his job as government butcher, his family and his freedom as the NKVD took charge. But he did not take the blame, unlucky bird that he was.

He arrived home streaming curses at his wife, whose idea it all had been, he now decided. Terrified, Madame Bronstein couldn't console him, so both flung themselves on the bed and cried like children. The daughter also joined in the dolorous uproar. It was a pitiful end to an inglorious adventure.

I looked in, unable to decide whether Bronstein wept out of fear, remorse, or disappointment that his theft had backfired. But it was a sight to see a man who all his life had killed animals, behaving suddenly as if he were next to go to slaughter.

I went around to the office where I found Nowitzki and Leonid irritated at Bronstein's tardiness. It seemed discreet to keep quiet about his troubles, for while I had not yet heard the details, like Bronstein I hoped for a miracle that would cover his mistake. Maybe the veterinary was only frightening him? We waited half an hour, and Nowitzki had just suggested I look for the butcher, when in came the local head of the NKVD. Two members of the Rajkom accompanied him, and promptly ordered our boss to open all barrels thus far packed, because there was a report that spoiled meat had been used.

"Why does this suspicion arise?" Nowitzki asked, turning white. He had no cause to fear inspection of the meat itself, but we both knew there was 35 per cent salt in each barrel, not the specified 20 per cent.

We also knew the difference saved in weight had provided the meat we sold to reliable friends. Was there a traitor among them? While Nowitzki tried to think of a way out, the Comrade Veterinary was summoned and came in immediately, reciting his encounter with Bronstein at the *arik*. Nowitzki listened closely, his blood pressure

155

rising with each statement. When the vet explained how the stolen meat measured half a steer, Nowitzki's rage was as high as the hills. Leonid standing near me, stared at the floor and murmured, "A disgrace on us all."

Nowitzki couldn't wait for the end of the recital. He demanded that Bronstein be brought in so, as he expressed it, "I can tear the head from his shoulders!"

"Get him, Jac," he screamed, "get the miserable worm!"

I jumped through the door and rushed to Bronstein, who was still staring into space from his bed. His wife began wailing when she heard the summons.

"Why did you do it, Unlucky Bird?"

"Didn't you help him?" I asked the woman, and to my astonishment she said, "No."

I turned to David. "Better hurry. The NKVD is there, and Nowitzki is furious with you. What on earth have you done?" I pretended not to suspect.

"All right, Jac. I'm done," he got out. "It's time I take my medicine." He seemed reconciled to his fate, turned to his wife. "Hannah, prepare stockings and underwear for me, and don't forget a cushion. Cook me some meat as a farewell, please." He tried to smile, and kissed her on the forehead. Then he walked out of the room which, he felt sure, he would never enter again.

The inspectors had opened several barrels in the meantime, but it was our good luck that all were in good order. Only the lids were raised to permit a sniff for tainted meat, then closed. We were not apprehended for oversalting.

As Nowitzki realized he was in the clear, he turned ferociously upon Bronstein, the others watching closely. Grabbing the unhappy butcher by the arm, the boss jabbed a forefinger in Bronstein's face and yelled, "Behold our hero, Comrade Supervisor. This is how a man looks who, while others fight at the front to defend it, steals from his country!

"Gentlemen, as you know I've been a Party member twenty years. But this fellow believe me, is the meanest culprit I ever beheld. While others march to war, this one sneaks behind his comrades' backs, to steal the peoples' supplies!"

Nowitzki, an accomplished rabble rouser, was generating an emotional head of steam as he whirled the unresisting Bronstein around, seizing him by the shirt front and shaking him. The physical contact increased his rage. As he shouted epithets the blood vessels stood out in his neck and I feared he would have a stroke.

"I should kill you, traitor!" he screamed, and suddenly releasing him, seemed to be inspired. "By the beard of the great Lenin, I *will* kill you!"

He burst past the astonished NKVD into the packing room, snatched a cleaver off the block and rushed again toward the white-faced butcher, the weapon upraised.

"No, Nowitzki! No! You can't do that." The police chief seized his arm. "Have you gone completely crazy? We can't add murder to this difficulty."

"Let me at him," Nowitzki stormed, tearing loose and leaping toward Bronstein. "I won't have such vermin around me. There is no track in the slime unless a snake has passed. Is this why I lay behind the barricades twenty years ago . . . to open the way for thieving scoundrels?"

The officer stepped between, speaking sternly: "Comrade Nowitzki, we have made no direct charges. We find your meat well packed and fresh. Our suspicions have proved groundless."

"Never mind all that. My suspicions of this crook are proved. I'll take murder on myself to rid the country of such a dog!"

Nowitzki's third lunge almost succeeded. He raised the cleaver above the butcher, now on his knees in a corner, blubbering for mercy. I jumped to stop the cleaver's descent, just in time to hear my boss whisper, "Don't be afraid, stupid. Anything left for us?"

Bronstein sighed, nodded quickly, and collapsed all in one motion.

The officer snatched the meat axe and spun the boss around. "That will do, Nowitzki. It is not you, but I who gives orders here. We appreciate your excitement, but understand this: Nobody in the Soviet Union has the right of capital punishment, not even if a serious crime has been committed. How dare you threaten Comrade Bronstein's life on a simple suspicion? Are you missing any meat?"

Nowitzki grudgingly said no. The Rajkommissar turned to the veterinary, asking if he found spoiled beef on the premises.

"No, I cannot say I have," he stammered.

It seemed all at once that they were trying to avoid police intervention in a small, human misunderstanding. None except Bronstein and I knew the actual circumstances, and we weren't talking. The

157

veterinary, too, seemed satisfied now that his enemy had had a good scare.

Bronstein was dismissed with a shove, Nowitzki's glare completing the exit tableau. What an actor! I thought, but kept my face blank.

Everyone shook Nowitzki's hand, the Rajkommissar with a firmness that bespoke absolute approval. The NKVD grinned admiringly as he stood, disheveled but every inch a hero and defender of the State's property. Leonid was in a corner, gnashing his teeth. And I, in utter confusion at the uproar I had helped to bring about, began to feel a definite guiltiness for having tried to discomfit a thief.

We stood in silence a moment after the officials had left. Then Nowitzki began to smile. The smile spread over his gnarled face. It evolved into laughter, the rare but loud and unrestrained laughter of Nowitzki. Leonid joined in. So did I, for without exchanging a word we all realized what had been put over.

Tears of mirth in his eyes, the boss held his belly, spread his feet, and delivered himself thus: "Comrades, this is your boss, Nowitzki. What do you think of him? Did he get us all out of that jam? Just compare him to that meat worm, Bronstein, who has been trembling and praying in the corner. Now we'll go after him.

"I don't know whether he has cheated the government, but it is clear that he has stolen from his best friends and partners. If not before the People's Tribunal, he must at least face one other court—and we shall be his judges. Come!"

20

WE HAD scarcely entered Bronstein's door when he, in a flood of remorse and confession, flung himself about the boss's neck.

"I am so glad you have come, Jefim," he gurgled, a genuine flush suffusing the peaked face. "I have sinned against you all. But especially against you, my good boss. I am ashamed to face you; I am such a miserable thief!"

Bronstein obviously had prepared the speech, and as I listened something like a faint bell tinkled in memory.

Was this a face-to-face demonstration of the Russian passion for confession? We in Latvia, no less than the people of all Europe and across the seas in America, had always wondered at the manner in which accused Russian Reds helped their prosecutors by extravagant admissions of guilt. Much of it was attributed to torture and terror, in conditioning of their minds before the trials, but none of it explained the joy some prisoners took in destroying themselves.

Now I watched David Bronstein, Soviet government employee who had just escaped serious involvement with the state police, demonstrating that inward happiness at clearing his soul.

Was it part of an Oriental philosophy in which one must purge oneself of failure? Dissidence, deviation, indifference, and treason to the Communist cause are serious matters at any time; in war they were unforgivable. In Bronstein's mind the dreadful thing was not primarily the theft of a side of beef, but that he was caught in the act. The impact upon his conscience was the same as if he been seized while giving information to the enemy.

"I have been stealing all the time," he rattled on, the words tumbling like the rapids in the Talas. "I have taken meat from the government and from you, my best friends. I have stolen and salted and said nothing to anyone, so do with me whatever you wish."

Nowitzki attempted to speak, but the butcher switched from self-immolation to a pledge of materialistic penance.

"At the same time, I want to prove I'm a true Soviet citizen. It is not only important to recognize and admit one's faults, but to make amends for them. Did you not quote the great Lenin to that effect, my boss? Comrades, I have kept that thought in mind."

A cunning expression crossed Bronstein's haggard face and he glanced from side to side, furtive trade-mark of the longtime government operative.

"My partners, up to this day I have salted and hidden away in the cellar of our neighbor, who doesn't know about it, two full barrels of excellent beef. I shall get them. They are yours!"

"There must be more," Leonid interrupted. "Who can trust a thief?"

Nowitzki, seizing the initiative, decided not to dally. "I don't want to test him again. All I know is that in this place even a pig's bristle is valuable. Let's go, comrades. David, we accept your statement and we shall meet here this afternoon to sit in judgment upon you. Understand?"

Bronstein understood perfectly. After the scene for the NKVD's benefit and this sudden offer to square himself with the firm, I had a hunch both Bronstein and Nowitzki had been through such experiences before.

"Bring the two barrels with you," Leonid warned.

"Agreed."

160

"Good," Nowitzki finished. "Now we have to talk over our case."

"*Choroscho.*" David accepted without reservation.

Madame Bronstein had brought out her best when we reconvened: the good tablecloth, best dishes, some choice home-baked cakes. She actually had flowers in a vase. It looked like a party, and we were the honored guests. Filling the tea glasses, she signaled her husband who brought forth, instead of coarse brown sugar, the highly prized saccharin tablets—an absolute luxury in the USSR.

"For such an occasion, the best," Bronstein explained, putting two in Nowitzki's tea.

He went to the foot of the table, sitting opposite the boss to whom he looked expectantly. The wife and daughter had already vanished to the kitchen, but we knew they were listening behind the curtains.

Clearing his throat, Nowitzki opened "court" with a brief but tolerant preamble:

"David, I believe you learned something from this day. At least I hope so, for a few hours ago it would have been quite simple for me to have seen you off to prison. However," he hastily went on, "up to now no man has been placed behind bars because of me." He spat on the floor and thundered the next sentence. "No, and may God forever defend me from such a necessity. But remember this: If one partner steals from the others, jail is really too good for him!

"Bronstein, I happen to know this is not the first time you've been in serious difficulties. Your name, 'Bird of Bad Luck' preceded you to Scheljabinsk, and now up here to Leninpol. But you also know in this world nothing goes to waste entirely, neither the good nor the bad. . . ."

The butcher thereupon let go such a sigh it almost wafted the flowers from the table. He nodded profoundly.

". . . As to what really is responsible for this situation," Nowitzki continued, "I wouldn't know. Possibly your weak character, that bird brain, or"—he dropped into a whisper with an eye toward the kitchen —"maybe your wife."

Bronstein supplied two more emphatic nods.

"Anyway, you can all write this in your caps: None of us here operates in order to get rich. We are only trying to make a living. It could be that what we do is slightly larcenous, but in my view it's

161

more an act of self-preservation. Call it self-defense, Comrades. But we do want to live more like human beings, for after all's said and done we are human beings, aren't we?"

He suddenly banged the table with a fist.

"Hear me, David? *We* are human beings. But *you* are a swine!"

"Yes, Comrade Boss."

Nowitzki was working himself into another rage, face red and eyes darting sparks. Bronstein half rose from his place and looked at the door, measuring his chance to escape.

"Sit down, swine. So you wanted to get rich, and you gambled the livelihood of us all? Do you realize what you've done, Bird of Evil?"

"Yes, boss." Bronstein sat.

"Everything is clear?"

"Clear as daylight, Comrade Jefim."

"Fine, then we can proceed to the judgment. Stand up!"

Bronstein rose, a bit unsteadily, and pale.

"First," said Nowitzki, "everything you've stolen from the warehouse becomes ours. On top of that, you will, during the next few months, deliver two more barrels of salted meat without our detecting that it's missing. I don't care how you do it, legally or otherwise. Buy it on the open market if you wish. But get it.

"Third, as restitution and appreciation of our friendly understanding, your salary of three hundred rubles this month will be spent on vodka, which we drink tonight. Do you understand?"

"Understood and agreed, Comrade Boss." David Bronstein extended a hand toward Nowitzki.

But the latter wasn't easily melted. "Not so fast, David. Sign this first."

Nowitzki pushed the salary envelope under his nose. Bronstein signed without protest.

"Choroscho," said Nowitzki, "now it's forgiven. But not forgotten, David. Not forgotten." He tapped Bronstein's bald pate with a bony forefinger, after which we solemnly shook hands. I hustled to the commissary for several bottles of vodka.

That night at the party there was no further mention of Bronstein's side of Soviet beef. We were comrades and partners once more, each with a realization that while the State's interests must be protected, there was surely no crime in trying to live like a human being.

"But one mustn't be a pig about it," I warned myself.

Our project continued without grievance or undo suspicion in the following days, and Bronstein conscientiously kept to the conditions laid down. Leonid, of course, retained a definite mistrust, but a man who looked both ways at the same time must be allowed some latitude. I inclined toward Nowitzki's broader view, that it would profit none of us to stir the controversy anew. We did not pursue Leonid's urge for rechecking Bronstein. Instead, we worked the harder to make up for momentary loss of confidence, and to our astonishment as barrel after barrel was labeled, lidded, and rolled into storage sheds, we filled the quota ahead of schedule.

This in Soviet Russia is one of the rare rainbows in the economic firmament. The quota is a continuing treadmill on which striving workers never seem to catch up. But here we had suddenly reached the goal—a jack pot that few would ever attain.

Nowitzki had to call the Chief of Rajkom in person before he would accept the fact.

"Only because my own eyes tell me, do I believe," said that worthy official.

Nowitzki telegraphed headquarters in Scheljabinsk, somewhat jubilantly: "Plan fulfilled in advance. Quota met. Await new directives. With comradely greetings, Nowitzki."

Ten days later came the reply: "Congratulations. By all means continue along same lines. Greetings. Petrov." Next day there was something more useful; the second truckload of barter products, topped with Comrade Nikolai Iljitch, the Russian boss of our boss.

After the usual introductions and effusive greetings, Nowitzki casually mentioned tea and a few nips of vodka and Comrade Iljitch required no persuasion. After a few rounds, during which I was established as the "confidential assistant," tongues loosened and Comrade Nikolai without preliminary asked the local price of salt. He added that for personal requirements he had put a barrelful on the truck, and nobody batted an eye at such a supply for a weekend's journey.

"You're six months too late, my dear Iljitch," said Nowitzki. "You can save your salt. It's practically worthless because everyone has plenty."

"What do you mean, worthless?" the big boss roared. "Are you trying to say your salt is better, or that the Kirghiz don't use as much as formerly? Or do you merely try to knock down the price, you sly fox?" He squinted meaningly at Nowitzki until Leonid came to the rescue.

"None of those reasons, Comrade Iljitch; it's only that salt has no value except in barter, and since we've done that so well, nobody's short. Jac, here, did a great job. . . . Well, you explain it?" He turned to me and I confirmed his statement.

Iljitch's face fell and he didn't finish his drink.

"Look, Nowitzki. After all this trouble, you simply can't let me return empty-handed. You know the hideaways here; Jac can show me the routes."

Nowitzki winked and agreed that if I wished to go he could spare me.

The barter goods had been transferred from the truck, so at dawn with only the salt aboard, we rattled down the rocky mountain road. I knew the way from previous trips, but seasonal rains had made it worse. In the half-light of morning Iljitch hit hole after hole, bouncing against the cab's roof and emitting a repertoire of Russian oaths. I had suggested it was better to go by horse and cart, that the Zis would not navigate such a trail, but he cursed us all and vowed nobody deserved to travel such a highway.

As we jostled along the truck seemed to resent the maledictions, and Iljitch had to get out repeatedly to check springs, tires, the radiator which was leaking, and to make sure we hadn't lost a vital part at one of the mudholes. Small wooden bridges, too narrow or light to cross, forced detours of several kilometers. The day was about spent when we reached our destination, the remote Kolchos Kisil Su. It means "red water," and to pass it one rode by the old Kumbas, a memorial to the dead, along the course of the wayward Talas. It was an isolated settlement of lonely nomadic people, usually bypassed when the trading goods ran out or the peoples' representatives got tired.

Unfortunately Comrade Iljitch rejected the advice to leave our vehicle at a distance when nearing this community. Previous experience had shown that enthusiasm on the part of the customer sometimes leads to unpleasant events. Now we saw a flock of ill-clad Kirghiz racing across the fields, screaming and waving their arms.

What did it mean? I hurriedly told my superior that the peasants probably remembered the last load of supplies to come their way, more than a year ago. What wonderful things it had fetched! Red shirts for father, pots for the stove!

"They don't worry about food; they raise that themselves. But clothing and household articles seldom reach here," I explained.

Presently we were faced by a character screaming *"Dambal, dambal!"* (A shirt, a shirt). He wore a potato sack and black felt hat, and behind him came a crowd in similar rags, laughing and pushing each other in the scramble for consumer goods. In no time our truck was surrounded so we couldn't move.

"Damned sons-of-bitches," Iljitch shouted. "If lightning were to strike here, it would restore my faith in God."

As a matter of fact, we weren't too well placed. Should a kolchos supervisor show up in that mob, he might well inquire why we had only a barrel of salt and nothing more for the natives.

"Jac, we'd better get out of here. The devil take you and your Kirghiz friends, but if they recognize me I'll get Paragraph One-o-seven."

"What is that?"

"Paragraph One-o-seven: Speculation. Penalty: Prison, five to ten years at hard work. Can't your Polish noodle absorb that? Come on, turn around and let's go!"

When the engine started, the Kirghiz, having spotted the salt barrel, screamed broken Russian revilement. Some even managed understandable epithets. But Iljitch was most enraged when three youngsters scrambled aboard the Zis and began filling their caps with loose salt, passing it to those running behind.

"Stop it, stop you thieving bastards! The devil have such no-good bums!" he shouted through the broken rear window. Whereupon one threw a handful of salt in his eyes, and all jumped off and ran with the peasants toward the kolchos.

The cursing of Comrade Iljitch defies repetition. He climbed down wiping salt from his eyes, but did not, as I had confidently expected, order a retreat. As he said, he wasn't an old Bolshevik to no purpose; he would damn well get rid of his salt at a profit or tour the whole province.

We stayed aloof at the next kolchos and Iljitch walked in to make his trade. The salt was bartered with a fair return in farm products and we made the bumpy return. Next morning, Iljitch and chauffeur returned to Djambul, and life for us returned to normal.

Asian summer now turned its hot breath upon us and only the extra altitude made Leninpol bearable. Fruit trees sagged under lush burdens, grainfields ripened to golden waves, and the neat white homes lay sunning as in previous summers, only now they were under new management. The recently assigned tenants tried to keep up the German gardens, but with varying degrees of success.

As the confidential agent of Nowitzki, Lifschitz, Bronstein, and Ivanovitch, I traveled everywhere along the kolchos circuit. It was my job to line up the livestock and boost our bartering products and, as I early discovered, a generous larding of Latvian blarney greased the deals. In short, I was subverting Marx and Lenin by injecting old-fashioned capitalist salesmanship.

Naturally we didn't so label it, nor did I foolishly flaunt its effects before my bosses. It wouldn't do to let them feel I was clever. Much better to remain a convenient scapegoat, although my Planovik experience in Gusar had taught me to beware of traps. But as Nowitzki would unquestionably agree, one had to think and act as a human being, did he not? I proceeded on my rounds with due caution.

Everyone was working at the harvest; even the refugees found things to do. My colleagues of the Polish trains were digging irrigation ditches and installing equipment; they worked long, hard hours, but that was better than starving in idleness.

"We are helping the war against Hitler, too," they explained, for the word was passed that our valley was a prime Red Army food source. The propagandists had merely to point toward the plains of shimmering wheat or the foothills stippled with grazing herds.

One urgent task was maintaining the huge harvesting combines, those cumbersome machines that rumble across collective acres, mowing, threshing, cleaning, and sacking the grain. Soviet Russia had always prided itself on these monsters, but the fact was they had a dismal habit of collapsing at the critical hour. The peasants hated them.

For one thing, many were underpowered, or at least the tractors that propelled them were inadequate. This caused stalling, clogging, and jerking of the moving parts so that the castings broke. A mechanical failure meant sending to Djambul for parts, or way off to Scheljabinsk, with weeks of demoralizing delay.

Since God's weather waits on no man, and the Soviet system couldn't change it, the peasants were left to finish the job with hand sickles and the few farm horses that remained. If they didn't complete the harvest the penalty was starvation. It didn't require threats to spur them.

Thus evolved the resentment of the combine, which broke down because it was overworked and underrepaired. Whenever I appeared with a needed replacement I was hailed as a hero of the Soviet Union. Had I been able to dismiss combines forever and restore their horses and simple reapers, the Kirghiz tribesmen might have made me permanent chief. But I kept such mad dreams to myself.

New orders continued to flood our firm, and with amazing luck we were able to fulfill them. We established a business routine that, incredible as it seemed in those circumstances, was not uprooted or disturbed. It actually functioned. Scheljabinsk was satisfied, Djambul was happy with us, and we—contriving to take care of ourselves as we went along—were contented as the fattest cats in the sun. As Comrade Nowitzki so succinctly put it: "We are, after all, human beings. Call it self-preservation, but we should live like human beings."

There were two things to avoid in this way of life, however:

One must not become a swine, and "contrive" too much. And more important, in preserving one's human status and maintaining a certain living standard, the prudent Soviet citizen must not get caught.

167

21

THE PEOPLE'S Café on Leninskaya Street was the only public eating place in Leninpol. One section of it was not geared to the
custom or the tastes of the discerning gourmet. It had four walls and
a dangling kerosene light under which long wooden, unwashed tables,
without cloths and flanked by benches, accommodated the ravenous
clientele. Here workers with a spare ruble in their pockets came for
one purpose only—to fill with a bowl of grits or *kasha* a corner of
their empty stomachs. Few, it seemed, received enough under their
state-controlled rations.

A curtain divided the People's Café, and although it was made
neither of iron nor of ideologies, it separated those with influence
from those without as sharply as if they lived in opposite worlds. This
always intrigued me, for were we not in classless Russia, the country
of no distinctions?

At the Rajkom's political indoctrination club we were frequently lectured on the politics, education, and superiority of the Soviet economic system, and no opening was lost to laud its pure equalities. Party spokesmen of various degrees orated heatedly and with ten times the necessary wordage on how we were progressively freeing the world from its capitalist chains. They liked to use Leninpol as a compact example of how surely this could be brought about, how effective the collective state control.

But sometimes I had my doubts, even while leaving these inspiring lectures. I would recall that just a year ago this place had been a prosperous semi-independent community in which the individual energies and private thrift of the German-descended settlers had developed self-supporting farms and villages. Now the settlers were gone, and hungry muzhiks clamored to the *offiziantin* for an extra spoonful of *kasha*. And their highnesses, the *offiziantin* or waitresses, ignored all flattery and supplications to dish out more than the regular allowance. These women, knowing the demand far exceeded the supply, adopted a public servant's indifference toward those who worked with their hands and actually laughed when the customers lapped the plates clean.

But on the other side of the People's Café curtain, ah, that was something else. There the Party functionaries, at individual tables with cotton covers, requested a menu and with lordly deliberation debated whether to order fried chicken, a schnitzel, or *shaslik*. These customers were better dressed than the others and were smilingly served with the deferential attention befitting men of position in this undistinguished province of the classless Soviet Union.

Did this sort of thing spur ambitious to attain membership in the Party? Plenty of eager citizens were always trying. Was this also one reason for reiterating the philosophy of share-and-share-alike, the fairy story we constantly heard at the political club?

I went often to the People's Café, for in my comparative prosperity I could afford a little snack, and besides I was a growing boy now twenty-two. Did I say boy? I felt considerably grown-up, and by now the Riga University education, so rudely interrupted by the NKVD, had been supplemented by experience.

Why should I read books about politics, sociology, economics, religion, and philosophy, when all were on practical display at the club or the People's Café? Here was truth in action. Look on one side

170

of the curtain, then look on the other. It told more than thousands of emphatic statements by our commissars. I saw the man of toil, weary and unwashed from his day in the irrigation ditch, refused another portion of cabbage soup. But on the other side, the one who had sat in the shade directing his work, was gladly served a second helping of meat stew. It did not fit with the lectures. Only if one had the proper connections could he expect to enjoy "equality" at mealtime. In the People's Café it was painfully clear the service was much more "equal" on one side of the curtain than on the other.

Nevertheless, we dutifully reported for club lectures and the large hall usually was filled to capacity. This was readily explained: The only promotion these forums required was a tapping at the window and one word: *"Sobrania!"* "Meeting!" and everyone put aside other plans.

Older persons went so as not to be suspected as counterrevolutionaries; the younger reported because they wanted to get ahead in the economic system. But about a third of the populace actually believed what they heard. They were convinced Moscow was freeing the world from a hated, capitalist slavery. Besides, "there's a war on," we were reminded, which probably accounted for whatever enthusiasm was real.

"But where do we finally fit into the picture?" I asked my friends from the schoolhouse dormitory. They were now in the fields, helping with the harvest. So they drifted into the café and we would talk. Having come from moderate capitalist backgrounds we were skeptical. At the club the speakers invariably had an answer.

"Hunger is always a problem, but if you, the workers, cannot understand that we must hunger in times of peace, I shall explain," the man would begin. "We hunger in peacetime to become hardened for war. It is a conditioning of the body and mind for the great struggle ahead!"

So we were at war, and now we hungered for that reason—how easily and logically it was explained! But the stomach did not respond to this sophistry. Back in the café men cursed the waitress who did not bring a second order of *kasha,* while a homeward bound couple tried to reconcile the lecturer's words with empty larders and wan children asking for milk.

Nobody became insistent at the meetings, however, or asked more than was considered discreet. Serious disagreement in thought or action brought a Politruk next morning, to haul the inquisitive one to a hearing by the NKVD. There he might receive proper clarification. As we agreed over the simulated coffee and *kasha* on the wrong side of the People's Café curtain, it comes down to this: "If it is true that those who suffer great injustice on earth, are destined to sit at God's feet in paradise, then we are lucky. Surely, after our millions are accommodated, there will be no room for those living in luxurious, capitalist areas!"

Now the barley and wheat were ripe all at once, and the mighty combines with their drivers cursing merrily, as if to keep them going on profanity, moved like Oriental dragons through seas of golden grain. Accepting a sort of voluntary service, office workers and all in the villages went to help the reapers for several days, for despite the throngs of deportees and refugees there was a temporary labor shortage.

That was another trouble with the system, I observed. Somehow, the work came in bunches, with dull periods in between. It made a startling zigzag on the productivity graph, to which the brisk Rajkom director devoted much attention. Not that he could do anything about it. Wheat and barley grow and ripen at their own pace; the harvest, as people the world over understand, must be gathered when ripe.

Since the Soviet harvest comes in at the same period over vast and scattered regions, every kolchos wanted reapers at the same time. If a mechanical breakdown occurred it was tragic. All hands were immediately ordered to the sickles and hoes, in the fashion of their tribal forebears. I saw whole sections of the valley enlivened by rhythmic moving arms and bodies, as if attuned to the wind and sheaves.

A change seemed to come over the whole province during the harvest, a sense of achievement and triumph transforming the most indifferent. We had produced an important store of grain for the fighting forces. This had been done while our skilled men were away. Although we were strangers in a strange place, the contagion of having planted, tilled, and reaped vital food provisions made everyone glad.

What a contradiction the task presented. While thousands of terrorized people elsewhere fled the roar of airplane motors, we sang to the hum of the combine engines. The bomber was an instrument

172

of death and destruction; the combustion motor here was a means of gathering the true object of human effort—our daily bread.

The warehouses soon filled as everyone worked long hours without complaint. Kolchos farmers were out there from sunrise to dusk, hoping desperately for their meager share of the crop when it was delivered. Everything was paid for in measures of wheat and barley. I remembered my overdue wages for working in the stables, although now that I was a businessman in the collective state, this account did not prey upon me so much. With the others, I spent about two weeks in the harvest fields, and in honest appraisal, must confess they were healthy, enjoyable days.

Returning one evening weary but content, I passed the little house where Kaljos, my early companion in the stables, now lived. I was attracted by screams and sounds of children wailing, followed by the worst imaginable cursing. Remembering the past winter, I knew that Kaljos was capable of such words.

"Drunk as usual," said a farmer friend. "Should we call the police?"

"Don't be silly," another replied. "We're his friends. Let's go in."

Two of us entered, the other waiting outside as reinforcement. The interior was a shambles and Kaljos in alcoholic aberration was addressing an empty chair at the table. He didn't notice the intrusion.

"Excuse us, Comrade. We thought someone was being killed," I began.

"Killed? Who kills them? But they should be exterminated, the brats!" He glared across the room at one child, hurled a half-eaten apple at Genka, his stepson, who peeked from under the table.

Then Kaljos turned blearily to us. "As you know, Comrades, I married the German woman Klara, to prevent her being sent to the labor front. But when no food was left in the accursed house, I went to the old Frieslander—that lazy speculator with the pointed beard, who cleans his nails—and exchanged the cow for five hundredweight of wheat. But now that it's also gone, Klara accuses me of having drunk up the cow! What a thing to say of her loving husband."

Kaljos slumped in his chair and the kids resumed their howling.

"Shut up, you brats! . . . It's enough to hear this from my new wife, but these hellions each day I return from work, sit in that chest where the wheat was stored, making noises like a cow. Today, when I fetched a guest, one of the boys was under the table whimpering and immediately cried, 'Where is the cow?' Before I could explain, from inside the *sunduk* comes the other's voice, 'Moo—moo!'

"So you see, brother Jac, what a thankless pair they are. These kids love the cow more than a father."

At this point the mother appeared, ushered the children outside and said quietly, with a note of resignation, "It's all right. He treats me the same, now that there's nothing more to eat." And she brushed the tears from her cheeks.

So the harvest came in, autumn imperceptibly took over summer's time, and I looked toward my second winter in the valley amid the mountains. How it had changed in that year! But the routine went as always, each one to his task. The familiar polishing machines were once more running in the kolchos court, the dwellings were prepared for winter, and to the joy of one and all, everyone who had worked so long and hard received a part of the promised wheat wages.

New excitement had come with the autumn, however. All Soviet Russia held its breath, listening to the war news. A titanic struggle was taking place on the lower Volga—the Battle of Stalingrad. As reports filtered back of the lines and it became evident the Red Army was holding, and then turning the tide, it was impossible to crowd into the Party hall where the news came in. People cheered wildly as each word of victory was spread.

"We can stop them. The Germans are human beings and can be beaten!"

This in many dialects and mixed tongues was the thrilling message of that autumn of '42. Not that the battle was quickly over. It was a dreadful siege, wearing far into the winter, but the Nazi panzers did not cross the Volga. The snow was falling steadily, and the roads were deep in drifts. The Germans would not be coming our way. It was the Russians' turn to attack.

One night the speaker could hardly restrain himself in announcing defeat for the Nazis, for it was coupled with another blow to their conquests in North Africa. His voice was drowned out by cheers as he told how the Germans reeled in the snows at Stalingrad, and that the Americans had landed in Algiers.

I was on my feet waving my cap and shouting with the crowd, for this was the moment we had awaited so many months. As the fate of von Paulus's armies was sealed, a definite ray of hope warmed my heart. I might again see my family.

During the heat and work of summer I had been immersed in our business, helping food production, so that the thought of peace and a return home scarcely suggested itself. But with winter, and with such good news after nothing but defeat and retreats, memory rekindled the burning within.

And then there came a sudden letdown to my good fortune.

As we all realized, our unique firm would have evaporated long ago, had it not been managed by an old Bolshevik like Nowitzki. He had the necessary connections. But one day as we sat down in the office, he said quietly, "Finished."

When we asked for details he said we were completing our last order.

"As you comrades must know, we have lived well and without molestation for a long time. Each should have some rubles saved. But you also realize that the trees don't grow all the way to the sky, and if we don't wish to lose everything, including our liberty, the sensible thing is to stop this business before it's too late.

"It's true that man is seldom content with what he has, and that he rarely gives up a business because of risks involved. But I am content and I am giving up, and I advise you to do likewise if you wish to be safe. I might say that if any of you intend further operations in the Soviet Union, remember the parting words of old Nowitzki: 'Risk one ruble and you get two in exchange. Risk two, and you may get three. But if you risk three, the devil will catch up with you!' "

Each of us took the news in his fashion. Leonid didn't care, knowing he would continue as bookkeeper with Nowitzki. Bronstein was unhappy because he could never be satisfied anyway, and he was still upset about the two extra barrels of salted meat he had to provide. I was the only one without immediate reactions, for I knew I could live awhile on my savings. Nowitzki invited me to walk home with him. He wanted to talk.

"Jac, do you remember our first encounter when they stole my pants?" he began. "Such are the coincidences by which people meet. A good turn for a good turn, eh? I'm worried about you. Once I'm gone, you can be picked up for the army next day!"

"The army?" I said nonchalantly. "I don't have any talent for military service, boss."

"They'll teach you talents," he replied. "You're young and physically fit. But it would be a shame, for I imagine by now you have nobody left for whom you would be fighting."

He mumbled the last as if thinking aloud, quickening his step as if to keep me from hearing the soliloquy. Was it something he had recently learned?

Nowitzki turned suddenly and spoke emotionally. "Jac, it's not only war against Hitler, or for the Soviet Union. I'm talking of any war, any time or anywhere. Have you ever been to the front? Have you seen combat?

"I remember when we were in the trenches in 1916. We'd leap over the breastworks yelling hurrahs and *'Nashtikach!'* as we made bayonet charges against German positions. We took prisoners, too. And among them, a fact that still bothers my conscience, were Jewish sergeants, Jewish officers, and Jewish privates, wearing insignia of rank and fighting as hard as we were. Now did that make sense? What had either side to offer us Jews, if we prevailed?"

"Yes, Comrade Boss," I replied, "there really isn't much for us to fight and die about. The Nazis chased our people from Germany. We had barely accommodated the refugees when the Soviet tankers came and the Reds took our Latvian properties. Then the NKVD deported us. So that is why we wander up and down, working for the Red Armies now, perhaps one day fighting with them. But why? And for what?"

He pulled out a letter, handwritten.

"Take this and go to the Rajkom center in Talas. Report to the director of motor transport. You know how to drive. *Choroscho,* that's for you. The director's an old friend of mine, and if you get on with him they'll not take you into military service. But you must get out of Leninpol.

"We also will be leaving tomorrow. But tonight, let's spend a last evening as friends and partners together. We'll be waiting for you. My wife has everything prepared, special!"

22

THE OLD Kirghiz sang happily as he drove the two-pony cart. I felt like singing, too, being his only passenger on the way to new adventure. I had money in my pocket, warm clothes on my back, and the promise of an industrial job which would keep the Soviet Union from drafting me into the Red Army. Moreover, in the lunch box at our feet, there were meat sandwiches specially prepared by Madame Nowitzki. Best of all, I didn't have to walk the 30 freezing kilometers to Talas.

It had been a wonderful party, that farewell to the firm of Nowitzki, Lifschitz, Bronstein, and Ivanovitch. Plenty of vodka and lots of laughs. My boss had started several times to make a speech, but each time something interrupted good Jefim, so there were no formal remarks at all. There was no need for them. We understood each other perfectly. It was a pity the Kremlin didn't know of our co-ordinated talents, for we could have demonstrated some efficient tricks to expedite the war production of the USSR. Did I say that, or did Jefim? No matter. It was true.

Life on the steppes was much like an elevator. Up and down, but never much standing still in the traffic. A year ago, going up this route I had been a fugitive without a coat. Now I traveled like a well-equipped commissar.

We turned right at Orlovka, a town which, like Leninpol, was once a Mennonite settlement, now pre-empted by Russians and the name changed from Johannisdorf. The road improved and we met trucks, the passengers muffled in furs. It was a pleasure to ride at leisure, protected from the biting winds. We passed a cluster of cone-shaped kilns.

The Kirghiz spat. "Here we baked the damned tile, Comrade."

"And why are you on such bad terms with government tile, Grandpa?"

The old gent shrugged and said, "Because we don't need tile for our kibitkas. They are made of clay and straw. You saw them in Leninpol. But here they need tile for the new jail."

"They need bigger jails?" I asked.

"Not since the war. Years ago I hauled the tile here, and when one of my horses died from overwork they put me in this jail for a year." He cursed and spat toward the jail, urging the ponies to a trot.

"The NKVD headquarters," he muttered, looking straight ahead.

The bazaar was typical, and the town of Talas was not much different. One Kirghiz community is like the rest: a motion-picture theater near the market, an unpainted hotel called Inn-Tourist. There was a milling crowd of badly dressed, unemployed refugees and one character in large cap and bells, who seemed to be the last representative of private enterprise. He carried a big drum on his back, the sticks connected to his heels which he waggled to establish rhythm. He played a *garmoshka* as accordion players the world over, except that he also waggled his head to beat time. For a fee of one ruble, a tortoise in a box passed up cards on which the customer's future was printed. A few doors away a photographer had his samples in a small glass case. One of the exhibits portrayed a policeman in high boots, holding a pistol to his head, Asian application of Russian roulette.

178

"I can make one like it for you," the photographer offered, but I hurried away.

The garage was in a large, fenced yard at the opposite side of the city. Several vehicles, resembling the Ford of 1929, were coming out of the gates. Drivers taking them to Djambul were doing a side business with hitchhikers, for pay. Since the repaired trucks were the only transport to Djambul, the drivers could pick their customers. Peasant women received first attention because they had just disposed of spare products at three times the State's pegged prices. Black marketeers and other gentlemen of profit were also preferred, and as usual, wounded soldiers had last call. They couldn't pay much, and those on crutches—*kastilniki*—were usually left forlornly beside the highway.

No wonder they're having trouble getting heroes for the front, I thought. What a sorry reward.

The manager's office was reached through the usual screen of guards, flunkies, and secretaries. His name was Nikolai Ptschilinzew, which sounded suspiciously like that of a Polish guy. He was tall, with broad shoulders and calloused hands which suggested years at heavy work. His red nose also hinted at more than an amateur's interest in hard liquor. He took my letter, and sized me up, head to foot.

"So that's you?" He waited and the voice was deep and confiding as he moved closer. "And how is Comrade Nowitzki, the old rogue? Homesick for Scheljabinsk, is he? What's your name?"

"Jac. And my former boss has been recalled to assume Party duties at Scheljabinsk," I said.

"Recalled, hey? Don't kid me, Comrade. Old Jefim calls himself back when he wants to. I know him. Does his wife still beat him as she once did?" He began to laugh and swatted me heavily on the shoulder.

"I was his driver for a good many years, and if he sends you to me, it's okay. You are hired. Report tomorrow, my boy, to the head driver, Anushka."

"Anushka? But that's a woman's name, Comrade Boss."

"Sure she's a woman, or a girl—the devil knows what." Ptschilinzew grinned. "All I know is I wouldn't swap her for three men. She will show you more about this work than anyone can, and also how important it is. Just now we're picking up wheat from the outlying kolchoses for the elevators at Djambul. And by the way, you insure with your superior the truck you're assigned, loaded with such merchandise. Missing work is considered sabotage, and for sabotage there's but one punishment. The war, you know.

"In the old days with Nowitzki, Jac, we took it easier. Had enough to eat, got drunk, and smoked to our heart's content. But now—the war. All for the front. We, the bosses, make the same poor wage as the drivers."

He referred again to Nowitzki's letter, his pensive expression transmitting the unspoken question: "Do you get what I'm trying to say, young man?"

"Comrade Nowitzki was a generous, honest boss," I volunteered, having already detected the depth and ardor of the garage manager's patriotism. He looked at me steadily and I as earnestly returned his gaze. Thus the implications were not lost upon either, and in a few moments details of employment were completed. I was enrolled as chauffeur in the Soviet Socialist Republic's government garage.

Next was to find a place to stay. Since the day was spent when I left the repair center, I remembered the Inn-Tourist which proclaimed "five white-covered beds to rent." I proceeded directly toward it, warmed by the self-confidence of a man with money to spend. Several other travelers, having failed to catch a ride to Djambul, joined me. One, a clean-cut young veteran, limped on an ill-fitting wooden leg.

"You don't mind our coming along, Comrade? You look as if you knew a place to sleep."

I told him we could all try, but the rooms would cost plenty.

"White-covered, it says."

The clerk in the small pension was totally indifferent. "All filled. You must be here for the first time, young fellow."

"Yes. I got work only today," I said.

"No rooms left," he snapped.

"I thought it would be like that," the soldier said. "We were here several times. This hotel is for Party members and high officials with government orders. The better class, if you know what I mean."

I said nothing, and the soldier talked on bitterly.

"I might insist, with this"—he tapped the wooden peg—"but they've probably got their orders. And why should I let their bedbugs chew me? An unimportant man like me can sleep in the open. Will you join us?"

I agreed to go with the group, but on condition that later I'd try again for a room. If I found none, I would come back and help

180

mount guard. This, the soldier indicated was prudent if they didn't wish to be robbed.

Camping with strangers had lost its appeal since my travels began. It was a considerable hike to the chosen spot, and the "shelter" was a tree by the river. By now the trees had no leaves and the ground was frozen. A little soft from my lush Leninpol life, I decided against it.

Back in the town, knocking at one door after another, I quietly inquired about renting a place to sleep. The answers were short and somewhat lacking in hospitality: "We're full up. This is no welfare organization! Get the hell out of here."

They added up to the same thing, if the words did differ. I was dejected and indignant and about to return to the riverside tree when I tried a neat-looking house.

"Can a chauffeur from the auto-repair center rent a room, half a room, or just a place to lie down and sleep? I can pay."

After a moment or so the householder himself appeared, asking whether I was a go-between for someone else. He studied me as he spoke, a bearded man who showed the mark of primitive living through the years.

"It's for myself, and if you take me in, Father, you won't regret it." I showed my papers and after conferring with his wife, the man said, "Come in. God be with you."

He assigned me a corner in a large room where the bed was a wooden bench covered with sheepskin. While I washed up, the man changed into a coarse linen shirt and loose trousers, then sat on the bench and began a discourse on world affairs, the state of the war, and the sinfulness of mankind.

"The anti-Christ is at large in our world, young man. He will destroy us and then be condemned to the pains of eternal damnation!" he ended his declaration.

Katarina, the wife, hurried to the cellar and with small, quick steps laid the table. There was an earthen pot of sour milk and a loaf from which my landlord cut three good slices, remarking, "Comrade, whoever you may be, while there is bread in my home, no guest shall be hungry."

The old couple knelt for grace before the ikon in the corner, I bowing with them before we shared the frugal meal. Another hour of solemn conversation and I turned in as befitted an employee of the State.

Bright and early the next day I reported at the garage. The trucks under repair stood outdoors in long rows, and the men working on them were equally cold and silent. This was natural in a country where everybody was more or less a newcomer, but the reason here lay in the fact that two men were assigned to each vehicle and nobody knew who would be his partner. That was the brigadier's decision. I asked where I might find Anushka, and someone jerked a head toward a Ford on which she was working.

Brigadier Anushka was scrambling out from under, covered with oil and cursing vehemently and as well as any man. She was a sight. Cropped hair topped a wrinkled face, and her eyes were cold and squinty from peering into the bowels of machinery. She wore a quilted tunic, black wool breeches, and calf-length boots. She continued an uninterrupted flow of profanity that ranged from classical to quaint, some of it new to my ears. Until she had expressed her full opinion of that particular job I waited quietly, rolling two cigarettes. When she paused for breath, I offered her one.

"Can I be of help, Comrade Brigadier?" I did not so much as smile at her oaths or ask their reason. A flicker of gratitude and a flash of femininity softened the weathered face as, with the back of a greasy hand, she brushed at her mouth.

"You are a gentleman, not like these others. A Pole, yes? I do need some help with this crankcase; run get an overall. When this machine is fixed we'll have a drink and talk."

Under the truck I discovered we had to remove the pan and dismount an extra oil container, a simple process I could manage.

"Comrade, you go ahead and wash, I'll handle this," I said. "It's not for a girl to get smeared like a cat in a tar barrel."

Anushka half turned as she lay on the cardboard pad, staring in undisguised surprise.

"A girl you say, Comrade? I am the mother of two children who depend on me for food and clothing. I haven't been away from these trucks in three years. The job makes it possible to live, but on the other hand"—she shrugged with that philosophy of the Russian peasant woman—"one day it will cause me to die."

"But if you have two youngsters you draw support, if your husband is at the front."

"Husband!" she snarled, fury suffusing her as maledictions poured out in a new torrent. "To blackest hell with husbands, those God-damned parasites who can do nothing but breed babies. My children,

182

no more than many others, know who their father is. But this I can tell you, Comrade: I'll raise them as well as any fine-feathered female who nibbles white *piroges* at home while her husband sits in jail for stealing!"

She spit into her palm, grabbed the wrench and loosened a bolt while I looked on in admiration. There wasn't a speck of feminine loveliness or charm in Anushka, but many a high-ranking lady could have learned maternal loyalty from her.

There were other women mechanics in the motor pool, but none evoked the slightest chivalry among the males. If occasionally one of the women asked help in starting a motor—Russian trucks seldom had self-starters in those days—she got a sneering, "Do it yourself, Comrade. The Soviet Union grants men and women equal rights."

Although I was hoping for a truck, I wasn't immediately assigned. It was better to expand my mechanical knowledge, Anushka decided, and put me to work with a man called "the Nut."

Timofei Alexandrovitch, called Timka, was a peculiar fellow. Anywhere else he would be a "character." He always carried a book, *Questions of Leninism,* containing the basic principles of communism and their application. He spent the lunch hour memorizing entire passages, and at the slightest excuse would quote them and make a speech. He was, at the same time, a qualified automobile mechanic and philosopher, anxious to pass his knowledge along to others. In a word, Timka was an idealist.

Early in our association he saw me hit my fingers with the greasy hammer, a painful accident.

"Here, let me have it," Timka said, straightening the sheet metal with a couple of expert raps. "That's how you do it, Comrade Jac. Fingers are for holding, not for hitting," and he went back to his bench.

At lunch I offered Timka a Machorka. "If it's for helping you," he said, "I can't take pay for instruction. If it's a sign of friendship, I accept. Believe me, Jac, I'm a friend to man or beast, good and bad, young and old. But I've never had a real friend and I'd like to have one."

He exhaled and unburdened himself. "I know they call me the Nut."

"Who calls you that?"

"The real nuts. Those who begin in the garage and end at the penitentiary in their chase after money. What a bunch of fools we struggling humans are. Most of us never realize until near death that we've mislived our whole lives. Do you believe in God?"

"Why do you ask?"

"Because I'd like to know why. Do you believe He created the heavens, the earth, and also man, Brother Jac?"

Nobody had ever put it so directly, so I pondered.

"You believe; you're a believer," Timka chuckled. "But then"— his tone changed swiftly to anger—"can you also tell me who put greed into men's hearts?"

"The devil? Maybe the devil." I answered like a poor pupil.

"No, my friend. We do it ourselves. One man cuts off another's head for his own advantage. The devil lives within humans. We become devils in person." He slammed shut his book. "But I, Jac, believe neither in God nor the Devil. I've been looking into Darwin's theory. A lot in it. The correct theory." He made an ugly face.

"Take that fellow over there, Akakiwe, the electrician. Nobody, except his African uncle, could look more like a chimpanzee. Yet he claims I'm a nut. Tell me, Jac, why do men see only their neighbor's faults? . . . Do you know about Diogenes?" He thumbed the book quickly, and I assured him Diogenes was familiar.

"A smart Greek," said Timka. "Never obligated himself. The King asks what favor he can grant, and Diogenes says, 'Please, step out of the sun. You're casting a shadow on me.' Perfectly unselfish. No hint of avarice. A bona fide Communist."

Timka took several pulls at his cigarette.

"If the world comes to an end one day, it'll be through human greed. You may look for the cause of wars in many directions. One says economic pressures, another says overproduction, scarcity of markets, bad distribution, unbalance between supply and demand— good, wise-sounding arguments. But poof! The answer is greed.

"That's the sole reason the accursed Hitler attacked Mother Russia. Like other warlords, he promises more loot and territory, but the people get nothing except misery. Greed at the top, greed at the bottom."

The bell sent us back to the job, but Timka having found an audience, whispered an invitation: "The Kolchos Club next Saturday. I'm the speaker. Be sure and come."

184

Saturday brought a new Timka to my rooming house: he was the local *bon vivant* in yellow shirt, red scarf, nicely polished dress shoes with well-pressed trousers falling below the ankles—a real dude. I must have betrayed my amazement.

"What, this? Why shouldn't we live? We work hard." He dismissed the fancy attire. Then he was expounding again.

"Jac, I've figured out why Hitler must lose the war. It's his transport. No good. I was talking about it with one of the combat casuals just today. The capitalist automobiles have failed miserably. At Stalingrad, for example, Hitler had thousands and thousands of trucks at his disposal. But each was of a different manufacture. Each needed its own replacement parts. That's a capitalist device to make money. More of the greed I mentioned. I know all about it.

"But in a world war, capitalist pursuit of profit is a mass hindrance. When replacements never appear at the front, transport sags, the rear is endangered, the campaign goes to hell. Follow me?

"Now in all Soviet Russia we have only three types of trucks: Gaz, Zis, and Jag. One and a half, three, and four tons respectively. If any gets stuck at the front, the Red soldiers need but grab a needed part from a wrecked vehicle. They're interchangeable. From this you can see how smart and farsighted our leadership is."

I was beginning to suspect Timka of propaganda. He had the answer for everything from his book. When he needed a current illustration, he could find a handy witness among the walking wounded. Nevertheless, I reminded myself, there are lots of broken-down Soviet trucks in our motor park.

The Kolchos Club was smaller than Leninpol's, but the decorations were the same as everywhere: pictures of Lenin and Stalin, red draperies, the speaker's podium. When the hall was full the program began. An elderly peasant, strong but inarticulate, acted as chairman. He began haltingly with a tirade against the German invaders, but quickly turned the gavel over to a Comrade Sidarov, Rajkom Director.

It was Sidarov's mission to pry more war funds from the kolchos and garage workers. He built up to it quickly, saying that so far all had contributed 20 per cent of their incomes to the country's war chest.

"But now, Comrades, we have a new opportunity to show our

patriotism. Let us make a new resolve, that instead of twenty per cent we will from now on sacrifice twenty-five per cent of our net income to the State!"

The speaker waited for this to sink in, then swept the hall with a glance. "Who is against this proposal? Who, Comrades? Let anyone who is against, raise his hand!"

There was complete silence, and obviously nobody was dumb enough to raise a hand.

"I didn't expect any other response, Comrades. So let's write that it's accepted unanimously."

Timka was the first to applaud. Others followed. What could they do? Sidarov bowed like an actor, and it looked as if the meeting would adjourn. But the peasant chairman suddenly stood before Sidarov. He asked to speak.

"Comrades, I wish to add some words. You know, our bull is getting old and tired. Yes, old Mars our breeding bull at the kolchos. I have to tell you we must levy a small tax to buy a new bull."

"What for?" screamed a small peasant, leaping onto a bench. "Why can't we borrow one?"

"Rent one," yelled someone else.

"Why borrow or rent? We have old Mars," others shouted. Having just lost 5 per cent more of their earnings they resented an additional cut for a new bull.

"What for?" bellowed the chairman, sounding like a bull himself. "The other kolchos don't lend their breeding bulls. Who is to produce our calves? Maybe I?"

"You have my permission," the little peasant retorted. "I give not one kopek."

The hall was in uproar, farmers shouting opinions while orderly procedure went to pot. They feared to protest the extra war tax, but a new bull they could do without. Sidarov calmed them by promising to raise the price of the needed bull at the Rajkom. Only then did the hubbub subside.

But the kolchos peasants were in no mood for Timka's concluding *pièce-de-résistance,* "Napoleon and Borodino, Hitler and Stalingrad." By the time he had finished, the dance had started, and the rural patriots had consumed half their ration of vodka.

186

23

THE NEXT few weeks, working with Timka, were in the nature of another buildup to a bitter letdown. It wasn't Timka's fault. His Marx and Lenin lore spewed forth to grease our working hours with Socialist slogans and rosy theory, no matter how grimly they were contradicted by surrounding practices. Perhaps that's why the end result was so unpalatable.

The trouble, as always, was in my own optimistic make-up. I still had abundant faith in people. I liked my fellow men. That included a good many I knew were no good. But by that time I realized how fortunate I had been to survive, and a mounting gratitude overbalanced the cynical realism that our Soviet comrades exhibited.

But that "Honest Jac" outlook, I would presently discover, was not only a personal disadvantage; it interfered with other people's programs. Patriotism or no, that was bad.

It all began one day when Brigadier Anushka, convinced I had absorbed enough about motor vehicles, assigned me as auxiliary driver on a truck. I was delighted.

"Now we'll get to Djambul," I told Timka.

"You're going to Aktach, the opposite direction," the dispatcher said.

Aktach means "white stone," and there was a wolfram mine there, high in a craggy mountain range. We loaded flour, salt, clothing, shoes, and hand tools, and started along the rutted dirt road which was passable only a few months of the year. After traversing several muddy streams and foaming rapids, the trail climbed steeply and we were soon in second gear, the motor whining as we threaded along precipices at dizzy heights. With each mile the road became more dangerous, not a warning sign, not a guardrail. It had been hewn from a cliff, and the chasm fell away some 2,000 feet. It gave me "butterflies" to look down. The temperature was dropping, too, although the radiator boiled over as fast as we refilled it.

We took turns at the wheel, and when the regular driver noticed my uneasiness he interrupted his bawdy, unmelodious singing to cheer me up with: "Yes, Jac, many a man has fallen off this road with his truck and gone straight to hell. But don't worry. It won't happen to us because they don't want our kind down there." He resumed his singing.

The mine was a few hundred meters beyond the village, and run by a Tartar, who was delighted to see us. He promptly unloaded our truck, then sat us before his living-room fire with a glass of high voltage "mountain dew."

"This makes up for the thin air," he quipped, and my head swam as I gulped it.

The driver talked late into the night, but I was all in and soon slept. We had a mountaineer's breakfast, then with me in the driver's seat and full of fear, we began the perilous descent. My comrade was soon in full voice, but had he known I was driving a mountain road for the first time in my life, he might not have been so carefree.

During a stop to change positions, he couldn't keep his secret longer.

"Do you know what this is?" He waved a beautifully engraved paper under my nose.

It was a ten-ruble gold note, but even so its significance was lost on

188

me. Probably a different type currency for this remote region, I thought.

"Money?" I supposed.

"Money. You're damned right, and better than money," he replied. "These are gold coupons. Redeemable in pure gold. For this ten rubles you can buy more than for ten thousand ordinary rubles. Gold! Understand?"

"No, I don't understand," I said, for I didn't.

"Well, listen. These miners are paid in gold, because the work is considered so important. The pay is worth much more than you and I make. The only problem is that they can be redeemed only in the So-Loto-Port-Snab in Djambul and none of these fellows ever get down there. So they sit on their coupons for years, enjoying nothing better than *kasha* like the rest of us."

He smiled maliciously, and continued: "Yes, things are very neatly arranged in our country. You do special work, like digging out the wolfram, and get paid special gold coupons. But you can't get into the city to redeem them, so the old Tartar buys them up for flour, shirts, pants, shoes, and plenty of other junk the miner doesn't need or want. But at least it's something for his uncashed ruble notes. See? All you need in a place like this is brains.

"I shall now redeem these for him in Djambul, and when we get back to Aktach, we take a lot more merchandise. And our friend makes it worth while, as he trades again for twice as many gold coupons, and so it goes. We both do all right."

"What about the wolfram miner? The guy who works all day in the earth?"

"Him? He never sees the light. He sleeps when above ground. He doesn't need more than what the Tartar trades him." The driver dismissed my point. "Besides, this is a dangerous trip up here, and involves plenty of risks."

"I see." I was glad to end the conversation, for I recalled clearly another situation. . . . "As the quota, so the wages." And again. . . . "He who does not work does not eat." Remembering my introduction to the Soviet labor system at Jangi Bazaar, my mind was filled with odious comparisons.

One day while I was working on a repair job in the yard, I was summoned to appear before the director.

"Well, how goes everything? I hear you've been driving to Aktach a few times? We try out our chauffeurs on that tricky route before we give them the truck jobs for Djambul." The director was smiling and enthusiastic. He said I had qualified nicely, that he and the brigadier were satisfied I could handle the Djambul route.

"First, however, you must become acquainted with the routine," he added, giving me a searching look. "I shall assign you to a veteran and trusted chauffeur. His name is Stozenko, and I'd suggest you introduce yourself. He's over there, fixing a truck."

Comrade Stozenko wasn't much pleased when I found him, and didn't look up from his work. In his bent-over position, he presented a rear-end prospect that I resented.

"I hope we will get along well together," he muttered, still keeping his buttocks foremost. "Funny, how these four-wheeled contraptions always strike when you need them most. It's not the first time it's happened to me, although I know this motor inside out. I suppose now it will perk up, with you a novice, taking a hand."

Seething with anger, I came back at him.

"Why do you speak so ill of your vehicle, Comrade? I've always heard a good driver loves his truck. You're the first I've heard complain. Maybe too many *lewaki?*"

The word means "stowaways," or "hitchhikers," and it stung Stozenko as if a poisonous spider had reached that derrière. He straightened and spun around.

"Don't get mad," I said easily. "I just wanted a front view. Go see the director; he has something to tell you."

"Director?" He regarded me slowly, head to foot, then hurried to the office. When he returned, his attitude had changed to one of co-operation.

"You will drive to Djambul with me, to learn the way. After a few trips you'll have your own truck. I hope you have better luck with it than I'm having. Look at those tires." He instructed me about loading time, preparations, and hour of the departure. It was an overnight trip.

We went to the Sagod-Serno warehouse, where wheat came in from the kolchos. There was a line of trucks ahead of us, men and women loading as the sweat ran down their faces.

Some of them seemed about to fall exhausted among the sacks of grain, for it was hot in the elevator and the air was filled with dust.

190

Many of these workers had done prison time because they were caught checking out with a few grains of wheat in their pockets. A little hidden to make *kasha,* but damning evidence in the People's Courts.

Stozenko seemed to know the supervisor well, and when our truck was loaded we were permitted to pass the guards without any checkup. We turned quickly into the main road, leading straight to Djambul. Not a word had been spoken as I absorbed this important step in my first official trip.

As usual, plenty of people were waiting along the roadside, waving and holding up money to try and promote a ride. Stozenko gave no recognition and the truck did not pause.

"Don't you want to pick up a few rubles?" I couldn't restrain my curiosity, having known about the hitchhike racket for some time.

"Sure I like extra rubles, but not that way," he answered. "Don't you think the NKVD sees which trucks take stowaways? They can count. But Stozenko makes money, just the same. Moreover, the wolf is not starving and the sheep are safe." He dropped into a confidential tone. "This has to be handled in an entirely different fashion, Jac."

"How am I to understand that?"

"Why do you think you're riding with me? So I can explain. Or do you think Ptschilinzew puts any old idiot alongside me? Now look: how many tons does our truck carry?"

"Two tons," I said. "You have the papers. They say two tons."

"Papers, hell!" he snarled angrily. "It's because of papers we can do business. They state two tons, but we carry two and a half. Obviously, we have to pay the guard and the brigadier something for that extra five hundred kilos, but even so we make more on a trip than if we were to pick up fifty passengers. What am I saying? Fifty? I mean the equivalent of five hundred riders!"

It was plain the veteran Stozenko had been given a full go-ahead regarding my "reliability," for he explained the whole crooked process.

"This is a game only for the most trustworthy drivers, and you will soon be one of them, the boss says. You certainly don't want to be like Stephan—he was drafted last week, thank God—who also had this run. But the soil got too hot for him; he made more on one trip than we do on ten! That's how it is if you have connections. And Stephan had them through his good friend Besugli."

"Who's Besugli?"

"The weighing master at the elevator in Djambul. I want you to meet him. Stephan had a real hookup with him. You can imagine what they pulled off. Stephan didn't need to depend on brigadiers or guards; he just sold the entire load when and where he wished. Then Besugli gave him a receipt and weighing papers; they worked it fifty-fifty.

"Ptschilinzew didn't go empty-handed, either. He often had to haul Stephan out of trouble when he got drunk and into some tight squeezes."

"Didn't this Besugli's tricks attract attention? Didn't anyone get wise?" It seemed a reckless policy to me.

"How could anyone prove it? Wait till you see. Go in and try weighing twenty thousand tons of wheat to see if any is missing. You can sooner grow hair on a marble."

I shook my head. Wherever I turned there was graft and dishonesty. It hung like a cloud over the Soviet Union's war production. Stozenko kept talking.

"Besugli has the government's full confidence. He knows everybody. Wonderful connections. We call them *blat*. Yes, Jac, that's a business. Who are we compared to such?"

Blat? Another tinkling bell amid my crowded recollections. The Blattnoy! They were a little more direct in their robberies. They took travelers' suitcases. These conspirators took the people's bread. By the truckload.

As the truck rolled toward the city I recalled scenes from the many collectives I had visited. At Stalinabad. At Leninpol. Along the railroad tracks across the Asian plains. The tired, emaciated figures of the kolchos workers, dressed in rags, plowing, tilling, planting, and irrigating the whole year, while longingly waiting for their meager share after the harvest—a share far short of that stolen by these slickers on one trip.

Was this the end result of Communist upbringing and the Socialist theories hammered into my head by Riga professors? And repeated by lesser pundits like Timka? Was this the share-and-share alike stuff I had been hearing about? My face grew hot, but I realized that I must not let Stozenko detect the fury rising in me. He had no reason to know that I had worked beside such peasant prisoners and deported slaves or that I was fed up to the ears with the whole ghastly system.

My head ached, listening to the plans he outlined for my partici-
pation.

Presently we were in a deep mountain cleft, and I recognized the
gorge through which I had traveled with Klaus. A truck was standing
beside the rock wall, the driver huddled with his passengers.

"Are they waiting for us, Stozenko?"

"For us to pass. They're waiting to make the pay-off," he replied.

"In this gorge, Comrade? Couldn't he do it just as well in Talas, or
Djambul?"

"Durak," he grunted. "If he waited to collect at the end of the ride
they'd run off and he wouldn't get one kopek. If he tried at the beginning, in Talas, they'd haggle until the inspector appeared and collected the fares for himself. But here, in this mountain gorge, neither
can happen, and they pay exactly what the driver demands. If not,
they can always get out and walk. But nobody does.

"As a matter of fact," Stozenko said with a tolerant wave of the
hand, "it's a complicated and dumb thing to pick up passengers. I
suppose most of our drivers do it, but only because they can't think
of anything smarter to do to keep their heads above water."

He blew the horn and we drove past the group, leaving the canyon
behind as the road unfolded straight to Djambul, an hour away.

The first stop was in the outskirts, where in the doorway of an
Uzbek house the peaked cap of its owner appeared momentarily.
Stozenko drove to a large gate at the rear and a little later, having
been relieved of ten sacks and with 5,000 rubles in our pockets, we
proceeded to the elevator. On the way I made a rapid calculation: At
300 rubles per month, the average wage of a worker in those parts,
it would take nearly a year and a half to earn that much money. It
had taken us fifteen minutes to finish our transaction.

The elevator in Djambul was the most impressive structure in the
town. It had the aspect of the Paris Bastille, and was probably guarded
as closely. But mere guards didn't forestall my smart compatriots. The
elevator was the clearinghouse for the collectively raised grains of that
region. From all directions and over distances as great or greater than
we had traveled, drivers fetched the precious harvests.

We passed a double guard and moved up to the scales with our
truck. There stood the fabulous Besugli, in the flesh. He was thin and

193

old, and to my amazement he was dressed more poorly than most of the workmen. The clever old rogue, I thought. He gives no hint of his ill-gotten wealth.

His eye flicked from the scale to us and then back to the weighing bar. Besugli gave no sign. The bar balanced, everything was in order down to the last gram.

"Choroscho. Unload, Bin Twelve." The voice was thin, but crisp.

We drove diagonally past rows of bins at which other trucks were unloading. Then we reached an enormous heap of wheat lying under the open sky, unprotected from the elements—Bin 12. We added our load to the pile. There was a plan to erect a storage building, but none of the preliminary work had begun, so the grain was already commencing to mold and rot. I felt wretched, knowing what an effort every shovelful had cost someone.

The formalities completed, we hit the road for Talas. This time we also picked up a few passengers, "for vodka funds," as Stozenko explained. The boss would be waiting for it.

Whatever could be said of the whole conspiratorial business, there was one inescapable point. The director had to go partners with his employees. He couldn't work these deals without help. Was this the real dividend of the Workers' Paradise? I turned this proposition over and over in my mind, looking up at the stars and wondering vaguely if perchance there were characters on them who also perpetrated such evil. And did they dress it up with so much political hypocrisy?

After a few more turns with Stozenko, during which I was introduced to one and all as a "reliable man," the long-anticipated day arrived and I received my own truck. It was a beaten-up Ford, no better but no worse than the others had. The boss nodded with a smile when he saw me at the wheel.

"Careful, Comrade, you have a new motor," he said with a wink. "Drive carefully, particularly in the Djambul suburbs."

That afternoon I began my first independent trip. I had been going over the truck and doing necessary repairs, but because I wasn't sure of its performance and also because I had certain reservations about the operation, I decided against any crooked business the first time out.

The guard let me pass at the warehouse gate without questions. The brigadier greeted me with a grin, but as soon as I explained that under no circumstances did I want more than orders provided, his expression darkened.

"Jac, have you gone crazy?" he whispered. "Stozenko has announced you for today. I've already discussed it with the guard. Besides, the old man is suspicious. He will never believe you didn't take more, but will insist upon the amount we agreed upon with him. Think it over; every second is money."

I shook my head. "Impossible, Comrade Brigadier. I've thought it over, carefully. I won't do it, but not because of moral scruples. I'm just afraid of this old rattletrap truck. Suppose I'm stuck along the way and someone else has to take over my load?"

"*Trus!*" he hissed, "coward." Then he strode to the scale where the extra sacks lay ready. The guard saw me at a distance and opened the gate. "Good trip," he shouted as I drove through.

When would-be riders thronged around, I kept going, but later took a peasant woman with a couple of baskets. Conscience clear, I proceeded toward Djambul. With a normal load and no crowd of riders I made it in good time. Besugli greeted me with surprise. "So, Comrade Pole, you have become an independent?"

I nodded.

"Well, I hope you don't sell the whole load, then leave the truck at the railroad station and disappear," he wisecracked.

I hadn't liked Comrade Besugli from the outset, and now I liked him less.

"Why do you say that?" I came back, looking hard at him.

"Such things happen," he shrugged. "Last year, I recall, the fellow who did it was also a Pole. First he went on a spree, then took off with the cash."

"Do you have something against Poles, Besugli?"

"Nothing, except what I just mentioned," he said.

I was blazing with anger. "Do you want me to tell you something?" I whispered, stepping close. "I know cases where only the wheat disappeared, but driver and truck went home with no questions asked. What do you think of that, Comrade?" I laughed in his face.

Besugli was shaken. He glanced around to see how many heard my remark. "What do I think? Why, the devil take scoundrels who steal from the country in time of war. That's what I say, Comrade!" He puffed up, red in the face, as if he meant it.

"That's exactly how I feel," I threw at him, starting the motor. Then, pulling slowly off the weighing platform, I shouted, "And I'll be mighty happy, Comrade Weigher, if the devil catches you!"

He was watching from the platform as I drove behind the warehouse.

Next day at the motor pool, when I went to the office with my receipts, the director called me in.

"How goes the truck, Jac?"

"Very well, Comrade Director."

"And how was the trip?" He bored me through with unfriendly eyes.

"Also good, Comrade Director."

There was an embarrassing pause. Coldly and with suspicion, he surveyed me. "Is everything in good order—with the truck, of course?"

"Yes, everything with the exception of the profit," I said evenly.

"Then get to hell back in the garage and work," he roared in a rage.

Stozenko gave me similar interrogation.

"A good profit, Jac?"

"Not much, Comrade. From one passenger, that's all."

"Do you mean that?" He looked at me with enough doubt to fill all our trucks. What I had truthfully reported was too improbable for him.

"You don't believe? And if you did, you couldn't understand." I said slowly.

Stozenko shook his head, studying me.

"Well, believe me or not, I didn't take any risks because it was my first trip. It didn't seem very smart to do it," I said.

"If I believed that," said Stozenko, "even if it was the truth, I just couldn't figure what kind of man you are."

It was as clear-cut as that. A driver with a reputation for reliability was suspect because he had done an honest job. They were convinced I was lying, that I had stolen and kept it all. It was the philosophy of corruption.

When I prepared to load wheat next day, I received a frosty reception. The guard demanded my *propusk*. I produced the pass, but after looking at it he said curtly, "No good. Expired. It needs a new stamp

196

every day, otherwise you can't go through. Go to the office for a new stamp."

After some delay I returned with the properly stamped pass and was held up by several trucks. I realized I was "getting the works." The brigadier also was unco-operative, and I took care to stay near my truck so he couldn't tamper with it. They regarded me as an informer or spy—all for refusing to play it crooked that first trip. From now on I would never see one kernel more than specified on my load, and if I didn't pay attention a few sacks might be missing.

The climax came with payday at month's end. With the rest I went to the office for my 300 rubles.

"Comrade Jac," said the bookkeeper, checking my file, "after careful calculation, we find you owe the operation four hundred rubles."

I looked at her, dumbfounded. "Four hundred rubles, I owe? But how? Why? What about my wages?"

The senior bookkeeper joined the discussion. "It's quite clear," he said. "Is this your first experience in an auto repair center? The law is the same everywhere.

"As agreed, you get three hundred rubles wages. But you have used seventy liters of gas more than allocated to your truck. Naturally we cannot determine here if your vehicle burns that much or whether you've sold it on the black market."

He pushed a form toward me. "Read for yourself. For every excess liter of gasoline, the driver must pay the operation ten rubles. Seventy liters amounts to seven hundred rubles. We deduct from that your three hundred rubles in wages, leaving a balance owed of four hundred rubles."

"And what am I supposed to live on?"

"That's your affair."

I turned away.

Outside I found Stozenko working on his truck, and told him what had happened. It was not a surprise to him. Others he knew had been given the "freeze out" treatment.

"You brought it on yourself, boy. If you don't know how to eat white bread, try eating stones," he said. "And remember: from now you'll learn to live like those who depend only on their wages. When your debt amounts to a thousand rubles, they'll have you before the court for sabotage."

Things were no better by the end of the next month, so I promptly went to Anushka and asked to be put back with Timka.

"Do you really prefer grubbing in the garage to sitting at the wheel of a truck?" she asked. "I can't object, but really, Jac, you don't seem much brighter than Timka!"

She gave me a woman's sympathetic smile, the nearest to understanding I had had from anyone to whom I had appealed.

Conscience, and a queer sense of patriotic fitness, had put me deep in the Soviet doghouse.

24

THIS WAS the fourth winter of my deportation, the cold and bloody winter of 1944. It was getting bloodier for the Nazis, too. Our broadcasts at the Kolchos Club grew more encouraging, just as the walking wounded became more numerous around the hall.

They were everywhere, poor fellows. Living in the cattle barns, sleeping in the tearoom, huddling in the village streets, trying to be of use, despite missing arms and legs. I seemed to notice especially the recently returned. Their bandages were newer, and the bloodstains red, not brown and dry from lack of changing.

According to the radio, the battles were now "fluid," that is to say nobody exactly knew what was happening. The Germans called the front "elastic," but Soviet announcers, rigidly censored, made no claims that weren't verified, because to exaggerate would only hurt morale. But the fighting was now around Dnepropetrovsk in the

Donets basin, and up toward Kharkov, Kursk, and Orel. When the Red Army claimed these places, the Germans did not retake them. Each day the need for men was reiterated.

After resuming work with Timka, I accepted the future stoically.

Old Ptschilinzew, the calloused graduate of hard labor and the friend of Nowitzki, as an experienced conniver and boss of the motor pool in Talas was certainly not going to take chances with me. I had failed to go along with his racket, but worse, I knew too much about it. Thus, although I was "reliable" I was also dangerous, for I had been shown the inner workings.

"You'll probably hear from the office soon enough," Timka prophesied. He was right.

The office girl handed me a letter one day in February, suggesting I see the bookkeeper. Thinking it concerned my unpaid gasoline levies, and nerving myself for a trip to the Tribunal, I presented myself at his wicket.

"Comrade Ivanovitch," he began, using my formal and assumed business name, "I have the honor to present your draft summons. Your old debts will be canceled, and you will get an extra three hundred rubles."

He carefully counted the money which I pocketed.

"Now see to it the war is quickly won," he said, with what passed for a friendly smile.

"I'll do my best, Comrade," I replied, shocked by the unexpected turn of events. The Tribunal was pretty ruthless if they wanted to get rid of you. The Red Army offered practically a death sentence.

But I was by no means an isolated case. Next day at the assembly point, men from seventeen to fifty-five were present in considerable number, and they had brought along their families. This was a sad ritual at all Soviet draft points, but at Talas with its peasant populace, they even fetched the cats and dogs to say a last farewell.

The men had no patriotism whatever. Many hoped some miraculous disability might show up to excuse them. Occasionally a keen-eyed individual would be wearing thick spectacles or a sound-limbed candidate came limping on a crutch. Some hopefully presented a list of ailments, real or fancied. No such excuse would have helped me.

Only Ptschilinzew could have rescued me, but he was definitely glad I would have a chance to be a combat hero. I bucked myself up with the thought that not everyone stopped a bullet, so why should

I? Still, many a citizen had been hit by something, otherwise why didn't they come back?

The medical examiners were all women, who promptly ordered us to strip. Naked, and somewhat unkempt, for toilet facilities at our garage were obsolete, we submitted to a slave-market survey that brought blushes even to the Kirghiz.

We were weighed, measured, and then, in the fashion used to requisition horses the previous winter in Leninpol, the examiners poked us in the bellies, felt under our jaws, peered down our throats, and had a look into our ears. One businesslike lady went down the line checking for hernia and v.d., a somewhat personal reconnaissance. But who else was there to do it? Every able-bodied male physician had long ago gone to the front.

By the time this was finished and each had a slip saying "valid" (which meant fit and ready), we had regained some sense of humor. I squatted under a tree with other potential heroes, and opened a bottle of vodka.

"Vsjo Ravno?" said an elderly Russian. "What's the use? You don't die twice, my boy, and the first time you can't avoid it. Let's have a slug in the meantime."

It was evening before all had been processed for the trip to Djambul. Our motor pool supplied the trucks. Once more the women and children, as I had witnessed along the Volga and at Leninpol, set up their wails and lamentations. Mine was the only unmourned departure. I belonged to nobody, so was first on the truck. Then I heard my name being called.

"Jac, take this. You'll have use for it."

It was good old Timka, and he handed up his precious book on Leninism. More acceptable, he gave me a pack of Machorka.

"I know the reasons you're leaving," he muttered. "But never mind. Come back to Talas when it's over and I, the crazy Timka—Timka, the Nut—will be director of the motor pool and Ptschilinzew will be fixing the trucks!"

Touched and also surprised, I fumbled for words.

"My dear boy, in you I had finally found a friend, only to lose him so quickly. Don't forget what I've told you, and read the book diligently. You can learn plenty from it, I'm telling you." He waved a hasty salute and the officer sharply ordered all into the vehicles.

The baggage was loaded, several Comsomol girls in red kerchiefs sang battle songs, and then up drove Comrade Sidarov, Rajkom Director. His bon voyage was much briefer than kolchos speeches. It amounted to six words: "Good-bye boys, I am staying here!"

"Forward." The command from a staff officer set the trucks in motion. His sole assignment was hauling recruits to Djambul, much as I had been assigned to haul wheat. Except he made no hidden profits transporting extras. There was no black market in human beings. They were cheap and all over the place.

Under a bright full moon the snow-topped mountains serrated the sky as we rattled along. Beyond Orlovka we cut by the Leninpol road. I thought of Nowitzki, his advice and his partnership. It made me warmer inside, for it was only the intercession of this clever old fellow, with his compassion for a kid who had done a small favor, that had postponed this war-bound ride so long for me.

At top speed, singing a few military songs, some dozing, others cursing because they couldn't, we reached Djambul and were put in tents for the rest of the night. A red-haired second lieutenant with blaring trumpet awakened us, yelling for us to line up. Our first reveille. Yet we were expected to respond as if fully trained. There was no breakfast, either. All they wanted was to count us.

This is a specialty of the Soviet Army. The officers are always counting their men. They keep checking like a boy with his marbles. It goes mighty hard with them if the count is short. As in any man's army, it is difficult to substitute for live, human bodies. The count must be reasonably correct. Since it is a habit in the Soviet Union to "bug off" when possible, the officers make a strict rule of this counting. I soon became accustomed to such extemporaneous census.

At noon the supply officer arrived with rations. They were supposed to last three days. But we had wolves' appetites by that hour, and most of the men promptly ate everything. At five o'clock another trumpet and loud commands sent us to the railway platform. Scores of weeping relatives said farewell to the Djambul contingent. We marched past a civilian train whose passengers tossed cigarettes through the windows for us. Several empty cars had been attached for us. Next to the locomotive, and fenced with barbed wire, two heavily guarded conveyances carried special passengers.

"Now I know where we're going," a middle-aged Russian whispered, turning suddenly pale.

On the platform was a grim tableau. A large group was kneeling on the planks. They must not turn heads left or right. Neither were they allowed to lift their eyes. NKVD with Tommy guns ringed them, fingers on the triggers. The kneeling passengers were male and female, and by their clothing one could see that some had held important positions in life. There were also some evil-looking Mongolians whose hard features suggested uncertain pasts.

"*Katorshniki,*" my neighbor whispered. "Criminals. I know, for I once spent some years in the penitentiary with such. I swear by the Holy Mother Mary, we're going to Siberia."

He stood like a man in a trance, lips moving to frame the word over and over: "Siberia . . . Siberia. . . ."

"But this train is for Moscow," I encouraged.

"By way of Siberia," he said.

"There's no war there. Why send soldiers that way?" But the thought of Siberia made me also shudder.

"Look, Comrade. You'll see. Surely they're not taking the *Katorshniki* to a sanitarium. This train goes by way of Scheljabinsk; I've been on it before, as a prisoner." He began cursing, steadily.

Another recruit joined the discourse. "Siberia is part of Mother Russia," he said blithely, "and you can cure your delirium in its quiet. Neither will you catch malaria. . . ."

"Shut up, you simple son-of-a-bitch!"

The ex-prisoner stepped toward the fresh guy, aiming a punch. But just then a shout, "On the trains," interrupted what would have been a first-rate fight. Everyone leaped for a seat, the only method of avoiding a stand-up ride all the way—unless one swapped tobacco for a spell in someone's place. When I crowded aboard, everything was taken so I flipped my bag onto the rack and nimbly climbed up beside it. I was expert at riding the baggage shelf, and it provided opportunity to keep a close watch so nobody carried away the wrong parcels.

Through the window I surveyed the platform where, two years before, I had wandered barefoot in the mud with thousands of other refugees. Fugitives were still there, but different ones had replaced those I knew. Where had they gone? Were many still alive? The familiar whistle—one short and a long—interrupted my musing, and we pulled out. Some recruits were already playing twenty-one in one corner; others sat staring straight ahead, as if consigned to the undertaker.

Train rides through Asiatic Russia run to a pattern. Generally, they're not pleasant. In wartime the trains were a rolling community of complaint, confusion, and cursing. Nobody knew where he was going, and nobody could tell him. It was a continuous moving into the unknown, with all the fears and inner suspicions that a Russian journey entailed. The fact that we had two carloads of "solitaries" up front was no psychological soothing syrup.

At first it was familiar stuff to me. Crowded, uncomfortable, shocking to some to have to adjust to crude behavior and primitive conditions for private functions, the trip took us past Tashkent and Tchirtshikstory, onto the main line toward Ehrenburg and Scheljabinsk. The beautiful but dread plain of Samarkand faded behind, we entered the massive mountain portals, then emerged onto the steppes. The day blended into another night, night gave way to a new day, and we traversed the Kazakh prairies.

Army recruits are different from deportees, I noted. Some sat smiling in their sleep, doubtless dreaming of home and families; others lay back, hands folded beneath their heads, eyes open, silent.

It began to rain, and as we rolled north from Tashkent the rain changed to sleet, then to hail. A noisy row began over a card game. The car was choked with tobacco smoke. Nobody could open a window and the icy gale prohibited such folly anyway. Youngsters at the far end of the car sang, "Cornfield, you are my little cornfield." In 1940 over the BBC there was a similar tune, the British soldiers singing, "You Are My Sunshine."

For men who ride to war, it matters little whether it's toward the Western or the Eastern front. It's away from home.

Kazakhs appeared whenever we stopped. What did they want?

"Tschai?" The same old quest for tea. I remembered the deportation train with Mr. Cohn, old Rummel, and the testy ladies of Riga and Mitau. Were they still alive?

A Kirghiz draftee spoke in dialect: "Genghis Khan made this trip with thousands of men on horses. He wandered over these steppes. A long way. But we will go farther, Comrade. Much farther."

The feeding of the recruits was reduced to a minimum. Fifty grams of sausage and 500 grams of bread were rationed each man, a day's supply. Instead of tea, we obtained hot water from huge samovars found in every station. But to get the water, one stood in long lines. Civilians with pails and cans also clogged the queue. It was the community's central water supply, and arriving trains only aggravated its inadequacy.

204

While still waiting my turn at the first stop after Tashkent, there was a toot and the train moved. I scrambled aboard with other angry men, some of whom hadn't eaten since Djambul, three days back.

One said to me, "Comrade, when you are starving, lie still. Never move. Believe me, I'm a specialist in that."

When I unwrapped an onion and a piece of bread he drooled, begging a portion. "It will hold me until Kazalinsk," he pleaded. I shared what I had; Kazalinsk was eight hours away.

The town lay near the Aral Sea, which is full of fish. Kazakh women crowded the platform, selling smoked, boiled, fried, and uncooked fish. Warm, wonderful fish from which the odor of stale fat smote us like the perfumes of Sheba.

The soldiers took advantage of the eager women, however. They thrust hands out of doors and windows pretending to sample the goods, then without paying, snatched fish, plate and all. Without understanding the local tongue, the Kirghiz merely laughed as we pulled away from the jabbering, cursing females.

Driving snow replaced the rain and icicles sheathed the windows when we neared Scheljabinsk where we detrained. It was still the middle of Russian winter. Shivering in our light clothing which had been adequate for Djambul's warmer climate, we were permitted to warm ourselves in the station, although civilians were strictly barred. And the Katorshniki again knelt in the platform snow; there was a look of death about them.

Two hospital trains pulled in while we waited, and the wounded held out canteens for water. I hastily got some and entered the car. They were from the Kiev, Kharkov, and Tula fronts, and several asked if any of us were from villages they named. Word-of-mouth communication was the quickest way for Soviet war casualties to get news. Everyone shouted at passing trains, hoping to find a friend or neighbor.

The interior of the hospital cars was ghastly. They smelled of infection and antiseptics. There lay once strong, healthy men, now cripples for life. Hands or feet were off, the bandaged stumps of arms and legs hanging over benches and cots. Women doctors and nurses were in charge, doing what they could. Medical supplies were scarce and not modern; the better stuff was kept nearer the front, or had been lost in the retreats.

All questions about the fighting lines withered within me. This was madness. Fine men, many my own age, had been maimed and converted into liabilities on society. For what? For the insanities brought about by people they never saw, didn't know, and couldn't understand.

"I'll never shoot anyone, and I'm not going to be somebody's target, either," I said to myself.

The Moscow-Novosibirsk train, snorting white smoke and steam, rolled into the station amid a flurry of orders that compounded the noise. We lined up for rations, and at running pace boarded the cars. Almost immediately we pulled out for Siberia.

Now the birch forests began, guarded by the fir grenadiers. Frost made a blackout of the windows and we scratched peepholes to scan the peaked-roof huts, the villages of unpainted wooden houses. All were covered with snow, the sagging roofs giving the impression that winter had forced all man's structures to bow down. Spirits sank as the temperature dropped toward zero; we had no felt boots or winter underwear and everyone shook with the cold.

At the well-kept stations people were getting water from the one ice-crusted pump, but the other buildings were weather-beaten and sad. When I asked why the station was always the best, a Russian smiled.

"Advertising for the tourists, Comrade. Foreigners don't get off anyway, so our government puts the best where they can see it."

Wearied, bored, and ready to settle anyplace in order to get off the train, we arrived finally at a muddy town on the Ishim River. It was Petropavlovsk. A young lieutenant counted us once more, marching the men, each with his bundle of baggage, along a dirty street toward the military camp. A band waited at the gate under a huge picture of Stalin, and cold and starved as we were we had the "pleasure" of a short concert. Next we passed in review for another high-ranking group, the lieutenant shouting "Higher the leg, one-two, one-two!" Thus we came to the camp's open square where another officer counted, and escorted us to barracks.

A sign said *Banja,* (bath), and ordinarily this would have been welcome, but it was freezing cold, our feet were wet, and we had eaten nothing in two days. The men shouted about food before washing, but an officer ended that proposal.

"Bathe first and get your hair cut, you filthy bums. The longer you take, the longer you wait for food."

What Comrade Lieutenant says is the law. That much we knew,

although not yet in uniform. So we stripped. First, to our surprise, came the haircut. It took but four or five minutes per man, the clippers taking it down to our skulls. Like an assembly line, we marched in, naked. There was still some spirit left, however. A Kirghiz comrade near me asked the barber: "Did you handle your customers bare-assed in peacetime?"

This fetched him a kick in the rear, but of course the barber expected no tip, either.

In an hour the group was shorn, bathed, and ready to be reclothed, at the expense of the Socialist state, each one spilling a bucket of water over his successor's head before drying and lining up for another count.

We were now in a storeroom where quartermasters produced our future costumes. The distribution was unique, the product hardly patterned on New York or Paris. All uniforms—blouses, breeches, drawers, belts and caps, except the rubber-soled boots—were tossed in a heap on the floor. Everything was clean, although previously worn.

"Get going, boys. Pick out whatever fits," the corporal shouted.

The next few minutes were total chaos. There were about thirty in our squad, and all dived into the pile. It was like a wild bargain day in a department store basement. Like pigs at feeding, the biggest and burliest were first. Lesser fellows were trampled.

A recruit would emerge holding a tunic to his chest, pants slung over a shoulder. He might have a belt to fit Malenkov, pants for a pygmy. This naturally entailed another sortie, which for men so long unfed was a true test of courage. However, who wants to go naked at 20 below zero? We waded in, and sometimes a good pair of breeches went in two directions, but of no further use to either tugging candidate.

I had long dreamed of the day I might come into a pair of socks again, and this seemed my chance. (I did not know the Red Army used foot bandages.) After finding none in the pile, I naïvely asked the corporal if I might have some socks.

"Maybe you'd like patent leather pumps, too?" he screamed. "Get going, others are freezing out there."

I dressed hurriedly, noting a suspicious brown splotch on my blouse. As we prepared to reassemble, the inevitable absurdity in such a grabbag occurred.

The littlest Pole in our company stood two full heads shorter than the average. Moreover, his personality was retiring, and he lacked energy for the melee. During the free-for-all, he had been pushed aside so often that he waited patiently until all were supplied, then took what was left.

He did all right for pants and the shirt fitted him here and there. But the tunic must have been modeled for Peter the Great, a legendary seven-footer. There was a roar of laughter as the little Pole donned it, for about a yard trailed behind, and the pockets swept the floor.

Desolate and miserable, the little man ran from one to another, beseeching someone to trade coats. But all were satisfied, and the corporal was urging us to hurry. A practical minded recruit finally said, "Just cut off the bottom; it will do."

Elated at this solution, the dwarf soldier borrowed the corporal's knife and quickly amputated part of his garment. In a moment he joined our ranks, a bit ragged at the edges but much relieved in spirit.

Mustering the squad outside, the corporal's eye fell upon the Pole whose pockets were gone and his coattail missing.

"Front and center you!" he bawled, not knowing the little fellow's name. "What imbecile gave you a knife?"

When he realized the tailoring had been done with his own blade, the corporal blew his Siberian thatch. Pouring a cataract of curses on the crestfallen Pole, he ordered him before the lieutenant.

"I'll show you. What incredible nerve to destroy the Red Army's uniform! God-damned Lilliputian!" In indignant rage he ordered the trembling recruit to the guardhouse.

"Step closer, men. Eyes left," yelled the corporal. "Has anyone else been cutting up?" There was only silence.

"About face, march!"

Some turned right, others left. A few kept straight ahead.

"Halt, fools! All turn left." He repeated this order until it was understood. As we again entered the square, there remained only the tail and pockets of the little Pole's tunic.

Presently a bugle announced mess. But again we were disappointed. Although it was nearly night, our orders were for breakfast. And that's what we got. We were in the Soviet Red Army.

25

WE GOT UP from the table hungry. Every man could have eaten three times what he had. I remembered my mother lecturing us on diet, but mother did not let us go three days without meals. It was no use protesting, or calling for seconds. Having distributed a few slices of our daily 500 grams of bread, the mess corporal solved his problems by disappearing. Military regulations forbade foraging about the town, even had there been some prospect of buying food.

"Tomorrow is another day," the officer in charge had quipped, as he doled out a fraction of each man's ration. From each about 100 grams had been withheld by the kitchen crew, amounting to a sizable sum if "sold on the left."

"Selling on the left" was a Russian expression among those who lived dangerously with the black marketeers. Where there was no inside arrangement like Nowitzki's and Ptschilinzew's, an operator tossed his "take" on the left side of the highway. Maybe it was only a few potatoes. Or a couple of shirts from the consignment. But it was the driver's "cut," and he would return after dark (when he was sure of no witnesses) to retrieve his bit of merchandise. I had no doubt some chiseling went on in the camp kitchen, for I could estimate 500 grams of bread rather accurately. The portions were about 100 grams short. Of course, the commissary might not have had enough to meet the regulation. Times were tough in Siberia.

Our next revelation was the *semlyanka*. This was the army trainee's shelter. Some armies use tents, others build barracks. In Siberia they performed like the resourceful beaver. They used what was at hand.

A long waist-deep ditch was excavated, the clay heaped against a plank roof built over it. When the clay dried, it made a snug and practical hut, not much different from what the beaver produces by gnawing down trees, floating driftwood, leaves, and mud against them to make a dam and under it a warm and dry series of apartments. Although our *semlyankas* each had a window and door, no light got through and they were dark as the grave.

"They want us to get accustomed to our permanent hole in the ground," a sour Kirghiz remarked. Being handy with clay and tile, the South Asians took an unsympathetic view of our quarters, even when fresh "linen" was provided in the form of straw.

Dead tired and ravenous, we flopped into our rustic nests and soon the coops vibrated with provincial snores. The bugler next morning had trouble getting us awake. But a heartless corporal kicked those who lagged, ordering, "To the ice hole, soldiers!"

"Ice hole? Why?" someone mumbled.

"To wash off the dirt," he roared.

A tub-sized hole had been hacked in the frozen stream, from which recruits were dipping icy water and splashing their faces. Some rubbed necks with snow. It was barely daylight, but if there is a faster way to wake up and make one's toilet than in that Siberian camp, I did not find it. The breakfast porridge was like heaven's gruel.

Company after company lined up in the square, and under a lieutenant and corporal marched into open fields for the first day's training. The rifle and its uses was the first subject.

Any fool knows this weapon is for shooting, but we also learned how to use it for sticking, clubbing, grenade firing, and for parading and saluting. The lieutenant did not emphasize that it was also good for freezing fingers, especially when left long on the shoulder. It took

210

a time to discover how to keep the fingers intact while handling this cold steel instrument. One does not manipulate a rifle wearing mittens.

Almost a month of concentrated rifle training convinced the officers we were ready for inspection. All would have gone well, if the Kirghiz had not embarrassed our corporal.

These odd fellows had remained aloof, as usual. During field work, they indicated full understanding of the drill. When the superior explained, they nodded in unison, going through their paces without error.

Now, however, as the lieutenant concluded by asking did everyone understand the rifle, one by one they said, *"Nyet. Ne ponimayu."* The officers were indignant. They thought the tribesmen were pulling a bad joke. But the Kirghiz insisted they didn't know, prolonged the training, and drove the noncoms to despair.

"What's the idea with you fellows?" I asked one of them one night, for I had picked up a smattering of their dialect. "You aren't so stupid you don't know what the corporal means."

He grinned while picking his teeth with a twig.

"No, not stupid," he agreed. "But if you want the truth, we Kirghiz don't understand why two must eat from such a small kettle of *kasha,* why the little fellow who trimmed his coat must carry a heavy rifle, while a big, fat Russian deals out soup in the warm kitchen. We especially don't know what they expect from the Kirghiz people. For many generations we have avoided war. If the Russian lieutenant knows so much about shooting, let him go to the front and kill the Germans."

Not long after, we were reported ready for combat training and sent to Tokushi, a village beyond Petropavlovsk. We were quartered in homes where the husbands were at the front, and I had the impression this was the first government order that the peasant women had approved since the war began.

April had come to Siberia. Big, wet snowflakes fluttered in our faces as we drilled, melting as they fell. The dreary fields became softer as the frost relented, and our grouchy lieutenant, who tried to foster company spirit by getting us to sing, began antitank tactics. He put gas masks on the men, although he wore none himself, then forced us to charge across uncleared spaces with bayonets. Since we could barely breathe in the mask, the exercise was exhausting. We gasped as if the enemy had been after us with flame throwers.

But one must obey. We had found that out the first few days. Wet and weary, we reached our objective only to meet a simulated tank. Four of our unlucky comrades had been drafted to push this, for it was a wooden imitation. All others were required to defend Moscow.

"Dig in, dig in!" The corporals ran around and we began making the mud fly. I was nicely imbedded in a puddle when I saw our Kirghiz friend paying no attention whatever to the oncoming "tank." He took a belly flop only when the lieutenant yelled, "You're dead, you idiot! You didn't take cover. Now lie there pig, till we're finished."

The mock attack was lost completely on Yul, the Kirghiz. Leaning on one elbow, he calmly rolled a cigarette and lit up. He was enjoying a puff when the lieutenant again spied him.

"How dare you smoke during tactics? Lie down, you son of a dog!"

"You said I am dead, Comrade Lieutenant. Where's the harm in a dead soldier smoking?"

Furious, the officer put the Kirghiz under three days' arrest.

Combat maneuvers got us no more to eat, however. If anything, the bread portions were smaller. We lined up for roll calls every hour, it seemed. Driven by hunger, the men were sneaking off, foraging. Several were disciplined for stealing a potato from the kitchen. Our uniforms were caked with mud and in rags from diving into the rocky ground. The hard-pressed Soviet Union couldn't afford field clothing for trainees, so we looked as though we had been dragged through the brush from Omsk to Tomsk. Many felt it would be better at the front, where nobody would object if one stole a snack now and then.

The day arrived for swearing us in. Under dripping skies, the companies lined up for roll call before a commission of high rankers. We were a sorry-looking lot. Many had worn out their boots and now walked in foot bandages and torn breeches. Everyone was wet, muddy, cold, and hungry. There wasn't a smile, unless among the Kirghiz.

A well-polished major, inspecting, showed high displeasure.

"Ragged bunch of tramps. What a mess," he thundered at the camp commandant. "No soles on their shoes, a raggedy-assed crew if ever I saw one. Who's to blame for this?"

"Not I, sir. We reported the need for uniforms, sir." The commandant looked scared.

"Well report it again. I'll see they get new breeches." The major thrust his fingers into holes, ripping them wider. To the tunes of a specially ordered band we marched to the Workmen's Club while dirty-faced urchins ran alongside chirping, *"Ras, dva! ras, dva!"* to our cadence. In the flag-hung hall the major made a speech, explaining how the original Red Army had been even worse uniformed, marching barefoot in rags to defeat the foe.

"It's not the uniform or medals, it's the spirit and ideology that claim victories," he shouted.

All of us would have settled for a warm meal and dry pants.

Thirty in a group, we moved up for the oath. A bunch of Poles came up and the staff officer inquired, "Any foreigners in this unit?"

"Are Poles considered foreigners?" someone with foresight inquired.

"Yes, if they previously have sworn allegiance to the Polish Government," the colonel replied.

Several, including me, stepped forward in the hope we might be dispatched to the Polish sector.

"Stand over to the right," the corporal ordered. "We don't use soldiers who change loyalty like their footwear."

My heart thumped. What did he mean? Was this good or bad?

Other units were sworn. Most of them couldn't read, so the Politruk's man recited the oath and they repeated it after him. By the time all were inducted, our group had increased to a dozen. The colonel turned to us.

"Does any one wish to volunteer for the front?" His voice sounded expectant, but nobody raised a hand.

He repeated the question, still getting no acceptance, then turned with heavy sarcasm to the major.

"They're obviously not anxious to join the fight. Let Ivan pull his own chestnuts from the fire. These Polish heroes should be issued curved rifles so they can shoot around corners!" The officers joined in the laughter.

The major spoke sotto-voce to the corporal, who gave another order.

"You'll serve the Motherland in a different fashion," he grated. "Starting now, you're assigned to the labor front. Pack your rags. You leave tomorrow for Omsk."

"Labor front isn't fighting front," one of the Poles whispered. "Let them laugh and revile us. It only exposes their anger. I think things go better than we could have hoped."

213

I could scarcely believe such good luck. As I packed my meager belongings, there came again that sense of gratitude, with a growing confidence that maybe, some way, someday I'd get through this thing alive. At least I was not ticketed for the raging battles in front of Moscow and Kiev or back in my ruined homeland, Latvia. There was no time or opportunity for farewells to the unluckier Kirghiz.

While the regiment entrained for Petropavlovsk next day, our Polish group was put on a "first-class" cattle train for Omsk. But again luck smiled. In winter, an open-air ride through Siberia is a sure pass to the cemetery; but spring was in the air and we enjoyed the ten-hour journey through budding aspens and birches, across streams bursting through winter's ice.

Omsk looked exciting as we approached at night. After so much forest and swamp, any town looks good. The lights were on and the station warm, so the corporal—still in charge, to make sure we didn't escape—allowed us to sleep on the floor. It was as comfortable as the *semlyankas*.

A truck arrived early to take us to our new war project. It went through the center of the city, crowded with beautiful buildings.

"This is a much better place than one would expect in Siberia," we agreed. But again disillusion followed.

As we crossed the Irtysh River, the theaters and office buildings were left behind and memories of Warsaw, Riga, and other European cities of which we had heard, again faded. The town frayed into the usual expanse of unpainted, one-story houses and unpaved, rutted roads. Distances between the villages became greater and finally we came to long stretches of open fields. The truck kept going, however, and after several more miles we approached the entrance to a sprawling factory.

There was a high concrete wall around the place, on which armed guards stood at intervals beside watch towers. We recognized mounted machine guns, being now familiar with such lethal hardware. Sounds of machinery came from within, and presently we were admitted. The truck dropped us at Community Dormitory No. 6.

"Your new hotel," the corporal jibed. "You can sleep until called." He laughed maliciously, and departed.

A forced-labor installation has some good points, we decided, for the first thing we saw were double-decker beds with straw mattresses and blankets. Not even the training camp had given us such luxuries.

214

There was only one drawback: those guards with the guns, and the watch towers. We also were advised that nobody—meaning absolutely no one—ever left the premises without official permission. Then it dawned: a wartime concentration center!

"There is nothing here but discipline and rules. Blind obedience, nothing less," an inmate warned. He then added a few more facts. There were no wages whatever and we worked three eight-hour shifts on a round-the-clock basis. All equipment was new and modern, and on all sides red posters proclaimed: "Everything for the front!"

When we reported for work our bedraggled uniforms were not badlooking compared to the tatters in which other workers toiled. I was assigned to Nikita, a Russian working in the garage. The factory made armament replacements and repaired tanks and war vehicles, mostly trucks. Nikita said the garage was the best spot in it, because no definite quotas were assigned.

"Once in a while we work on a director's car or one for an army general. Then maybe they slip us a few cigarettes, extra," he said.

A canopy of security obscured this place for reasons not apparent to us rejectees of the Red Army. Workers took an oath of silence on what was being done; nobody changed jobs or departments; nobody went anywhere except from job to sleeping quarters. Compared to this factory, a monastery was like a Paris night club.

Although there were no quotas or wages there were plenty of penalties. Failure on the job was punished by a reduced food ration, tardiness by a diet of bread and water for a week. If a machine broke down, or a worker collapsed from fatigue, hunger, or nerves, he was imprisoned for sabotage. It was, in short, a well-regulated hell on earth—all dressed up with guards, machine guns, and patriotic slogans.

"Well, Jac, what do you think of this operation?" Nikita whispered across the straw pallet about two weeks after we arrived. "The Soviet state should be the richest in the world, because everything belongs to it. Even our bodies are its property, and without much cost of upkeep certainly on the feed they give us."

"True, Nikita. But I'd settle for a starvation diet if only we had a toilet nearby."

"In the big Russian cities they have them," Nikita chuckled, "but here in Siberia toilets are unnecessary. Know why?" He continued to laugh in the darkness. "I'll tell you.

"You saw that big building in the market place of Omsk? It has four floors but no toilets. On the first floor, students live. They are too poor to eat, so naturally they have no need for the commode. On the second floor are the Stachanovs, the pressure producers who work twenty-five hours a day, and have no time to use the w.c. Up on the third floor are dispossessed merchants, bankers, landowners, and speculators. When someone knocks at the door it so loosens their bowels they never get to the toilets, so why install them? On the top floor is the all-powerful NKVD who do what they wish. They treat all Soviet Russia as a public outhouse, so. . . . Do you get the picture, my friend?"

"A good story, but dangerous to repeat," I answered. "Good night, Nikita."

I thought things over before sleeping. Yes, this factory was the jumping-off place in human degradation. Hard work, hard bed, hard bread. What a life. Yet, what must it be like for those *Katorshniki,* the real criminals? They might be somewhere nearby; under what conditions? I shivered and began to dream. It was a nightmare of corporals and crooks.

As the months passed a rainy, windy season began that blew up heavy storms to add to the misery. About the middle of August it felt like October, and we stood in utter rags, the Polish group looking more like scarecrows than trim soldiers from Petropavlovsk. I spoke to Joseph, one of them, about trying to make a break out of the factory.

"Are you insane?" he said. "How far would you get in that army blouse and dirty pants? Without papers?"

"I don't expect to walk the boulevards, greeting policemen," I retorted.

"Ah, yes, but you take a terrible chance. The war will soon be over."

"No, Joschi," I replied, "we will be over, long before the war is. Another winter in a place like this. . . . Besides, I've traveled without papers before."

I confided that I still had some money on me, something most inmates lacked. As to papers, they could be managed.

"Don't talk more of this thing," he cut me off. "I only hope we've not been overheard or we may as well get lost in the Taiga."

I realized an escape would have to be a one-man effort, and began to think along that line.

216

It was obvious that a direct break would get me a burst of bullets and quick burial. So I worked out a plan to leave in normal fashion, if possible with a stated mission and pass. Already I had worked up friendly contacts with certain drivers and assistants, when they brought in cars for repair. I gave them money for cigarettes and then split with them. I also promised to buy a few bottles of vodka, which I knew could not be smuggled in but which we could obtain if they'd take me on a ride into town. As proof, I laid 100 rubles on the fender.

"I'll speak to the supervisor about letting you take the place of my co-driver, who is sick," a fellow promised.

I began to have hopes. But weeks went by, and I dared not breathe a thing to a soul.

It was the end of October when the supervisor called me over casually. "You are to accompany Stemka to the tire factory to help load a truck with tires. Get washed and pick up your *laissez-passer* at the office."

As I climbed into the truck with Stemka, Joschi appeared, looking at me longingly but with gravest forebodings. We did not exchange a word, and a moment later the guard waved us through the gate. I looked back as we got a mile or so from the high walls and the guarded towers of this wartime production plant of the USSR, the place where there were no union rates and hours and no pay checks for supplying the fighting forces. It was a lasting insight upon the lonely workingman's life on the Siberian front.

Stemka took me through a couple of small hamlets where lowing cows and sheep's bells moved him to his first comment.

"*Kulaki*," he said as I glanced at him, for that meant farmers in a language close to that of my home.

"Whom do you call *kulaki*, Comrade?"

"Certainly not you and I, for we have only bugs and insects for livestock," he quipped. "Before the Revolution the farmers where I came from had more stock than we have bedbugs in the barracks."

I paused, for many a man has joined a conversation that led back to a concentration camp.

"It's before my time, Comrade. I wasn't around in those days," I said lightly.

"Yes, but you come from a country where property—houses, farms, factories—are still private. Although I can't believe it, it must be wonderful," Stemka went on. He talked of 1925 when his father had a transport business of horses and wagons, but was later imprisoned as a bourgeois when the NKVD found on him a few gold rubles, left by his grandfather.

My thoughts were far from history, however, for immediate events demanded my getting away from this chatterbox. Traffic increased as we entered the Leninskaya, and near the bridge tall buildings rose around a park. This was the provincial government complex, around which were parked the horse-drawn carriages of the Party members and directors of the economy. There were no automobiles, however, these having been requisitioned for the war.

Beyond this was the workers' district, where laundry hung frozen on the lines and starving dogs prowled. The windows were part glass, patched with cardboard, although some of the important specialists and technical experts lived there. The adjacent factory was our destination, and from the number of new planes taking off we knew it was making them. In fact, this was Siberia's biggest aircraft center. We loaded our sixty tires and as we left Stemka turned on the talk again.

"That old goat of a guard is the richest damn employee in that factory," he said. When I showed not the least surprise and asked no questions Stemka regarded me with new interest.

"Jac, did you work as a driver, too?" I nodded, and a light of understanding crossed his grinning face. "Sooooo!" he said, "then you know about the comrade guards and their methods. But with this one they can do nothing more, because he now has so much money that he's become suddenly strict, honest, and even patriotic! But by no interpretation can we say moral. He merely decided to be legal."

We drove to the flea market called Baracholka and parked the truck behind a load of hay where we could watch it, but it could not be seen by the guards. As usual, black marketeers and traders rushed us, trying to get some or all of the tires, gasoline, or even parts of the truck. I watched the bargaining of others, the game that had fascinated me in Stalinabad, Gusar, Djambul—everywhere the drifting flotsam of humanity sought to make a little profit in this supposedly no-profit state.

Two candy salesmen, their goods displayed in trays hanging from their necks, attracted my attention. They looked Polish. After my companion had gone shopping for vodka, I strolled toward them, meanwhile keeping a close watch of the tires. In quick Polish sen-

218

tences I explained my situation, told them I had money, needed papers and advice.

"Stay right here," one said. "Don't, for God's sake, return to the factory. We've got plenty of Poles in Omsk. Some of them don't even know in which direction their country lies. You're sure you have money?" The man looked at me closely.

"Enough," I said, "but I must keep some."

"Of course. My friend is coming tonight. We can discuss the whole problem. Getting papers is not difficult."

Stemka returned shortly with a bottle for the supervisor and one for himself, but how could he guzzle his and still have time to get back and unload? He became hospitable.

"Have a drink, Jac. Your health." He put the bottle to my lips, keeping a finger at the point beyond which one in courtesy does not lower the contents. "Come now, we better get under way."

"Just one more minute, Stemka. Take another pull. I'll be right back." I winked at him, and moved away.

"Right back," he warned, but lifted the bottle again, glad he didn't have to share. I slithered among the swirling shoppers, joined a bartering cluster, and put distance between me and the truck. I kept moving for nearly an hour, then looked toward our parking spot. The truck was gone. Stemka, drunk or sober, had decided to go back without me.

Once more I was a freewheeling man.

26

"SO YOU decided to stay?"

The candy peddler hadn't believed I would take the chance.

"Good boy," he said. "Now let's talk about your situation."

He knocked off for the day—a simple process of closing the tray and flipping it around on his back. I picked up the tripod, assuming the role of helper. Thus I integrated with the market mob.

There was tea with saccharin and a warm welcome at his house, accompanied by a condensed history of his life while we ate. Having traded experiences, we stretched on the floor and slept.

Did one take serious chances thus with strangers? Yes and no. After all, I had not seen this man before that afternoon. A Siberian flea market is not a recommended place to win friends and influence people, but the old rule applied here as everywhere in those times: "It's the war, you know."

My wanderings, escapes, and connivances had developed a sixth sense in me. I could detect a decent fellow as the hawk spots a quarry. Character comes out in periods of trial and hardship, and if one isn't a moocher trying to take advantage, his efforts to establish rapport will usually get response. The artistry is in getting through.

Another safeguard was that we stuck to people whose language and customs were similar. Eastern Europeans, especially Poles and Jews, gravitated toward each other, for all endured the common lot of captivity. We were displaced, at the mercy of a ruthless power waging war, and our survival was strictly up to us.

For that reason we walked and talked together and went promptly to the rescue if a comrade was attacked. By our considerable numbers, and the grapevine established through age-old traditions, we established a bond of mutual security based upon our emergencies and privations.

Above all, we did not mistreat or injure each other. That was more or less an unwritten rule. Call it morality amid the immoral, or religion among the atheists, but it was a retention of principle by which I for one, was able to survive.

My host (he called himself Thad) was up by six o'clock, mixing candy in the lean-to he called his "factory." It was in reality a dirty kitchen containing a copper boiler, a rolling pin and press, a couple of rusty spoons, and a knife. He explained that private enterprise required hours somewhat longer than my eight-hour shifts behind barbed wire.

"But I come and go as I please, and that's the difference, Jac. Who am I to point this out to you?" He laughed, inviting me to sample a new mix of brown sugar with bran. It would do if you must have candy we agreed, both making a face.

"Plenty good for those cheap bastards out there." He motioned toward the market. "What scum!"

The next several days I hung around Thad, making myself useful in his production of sweets while waiting for the purveyor of "guaranteed credentials." This character arrived one evening in wonderful white felt boots and a tall fur cap that without inscription proclaimed: "I'm in the money, boys."

"This gentleman can take care of everything," Thad introduced him.

We sat while I recounted the circumstances for needing new

222

papers, meaning my recent severance of relations with the motor pool.

"A difficult task; yes, a dangerous proposition," the man pronounced the same phrases I had heard from Riga lawyers who knew they had an easy case. "But I think we may manage, providing you can bear the expense?"

"How much?" I asked.

"At least five thousand rubles. You realize, my friend, this can be no one-man operation. I am only an intermediary. There are officials in high authority who pass upon and complete the transaction. When you get papers, I assure you they'll be valid as a gold-ruble note. Incidentally, you don't happen to have a few? I'd prefer them to ordinary currency."

It required no clairvoyance to know this sharpshooter would bargain for his mother's gold tooth. But I had no choice. Having agreed to A, I was committed also to B. Without papers I wouldn't last overnight in Omsk, for my fine-feathered advocate would probably turn me in. I agreed to pay when he delivered signed and sealed documents, but he in turn insisted I first count out the rubles to prove possession. In fact, I counted them twice. Then he gave me a directive: I didn't need to worry about the factory, they wouldn't look for me; but I better get into useful war work. He suggested the local transport agency where a Comrade Lessovski would put me on as driver.

"You will want a duty in some remote village for a time," said Comrade White Boots.

I nodded, thanking him profusely. "I am most grateful," I ended.

"I can't live on thanks," he replied sharply. "I rate sentiment strictly in terms of cash. Appreciation, so much. Friendship, such and so. Gratitude, a little more. Love, a definite price. Take your choice, but pay me."

I had never met such a suave scoundrel.

"Well, why do you stare? My fee is five hundred rubles."

I shook hands on the bargain. There was no alternative. He promised to be back in five days, promptly at 7:00 P.M. And he was. During the interim I got my fill of the sticky candy business and was relieved when his fur cap bobbed into view.

Wasting no time in small talk, he placed the documents upon the table: a Russian identity card without photograph, a membership book in the Union of Polish Patriots.

"Besides these, I have something special for you," White Boots added proudly. "My motto is not the sordid 'as the work so the wages,' but 'as the payment so the service.'"

With that he laid down a written prison release, nicely stamped and indicating I had been discharged the previous week after serving time for a nonpolitical offense.

"What's that for?"

"Can anyone be so naïve? Without this release, how do you explain your whereabouts these many months? This isn't Warsaw; it's Siberia. Remember? Anyway, this additional document won't soil your reputation," he said with a faint smile.

"Bear this in mind, young man: All of Soviet Russia is a massive streetcar. It's filled with people just sitting it out—or waiting their turn to take the ride. So why the reluctance? This release is the best of all alibis. If you're accused of more misdeeds, you have proof you were already in custody. Moreover, I've communicated with Comrade Lessovski, so advise you not to reveal more than necessary when you see him."

The idea of carrying a prison discharge was revolting; it had not before occurred to me that my transfer from the army to a labor camp had been actually a sentence. But I tucked away the packet, paid the 500 rubles, and we uncorked a bottle of vodka. While consuming his share, Comrade White Boots kept reassuring me of the authenticity of the papers, adding that if I would recommend others in need he would gladly kick back 10 per cent. To our host's annoyance he spelled out his address. . . .

Motor transport in Omsk was not for the common man, but reserved for government or military personnel. It was directed from a hive of impressive offices which occupied all of a tall building. When I reached Lessovski's sanctum, I got no attention whatever until a secretary eventually announced me to the director.

It was at once evident that he was the most intelligent and also the most elegant of all my bosses. He even wore a tie, a collector's item in Siberia. When I entered he glanced up briefly, then went back to the local *Izvestia*, sipping a glass of hot tea as he turned the pages. It wasn't very pleasant to be left standing, but he said nothing and I didn't dare. He took his time, too, reading every page. Then he presumed to see me.

"Don't stall around, Comrade," he said. "What do you want?"

"Work," I put it succinctly.

224

"Driver?"

"*Da.*"

"Papers?"

I placed them on his desk. He scanned the prison release.

"Theft?"

"No, Chief. A fight."

"Soooo?" He seemed relieved and glanced again at me.

"We need men for the distant Rajkoms, especially at Tukalinsk in Tobolsk, but they're five hundred kilometers away. Would you drive there, Comrade? There are no trains to those places." He emphasized the last sentence.

"No trains?" I repeated, remembering the solitude of Leninpol. "I'd be glad to go, boss. In fact, at once."

He smiled understandingly. "You won't be the first to drive it, and while the roads are poor from Nasivaevskoe to Tukalinsk the NKVD are most efficient and know all about the passengers that ride the wheat trucks."

"That didn't occur to me, boss."

"Nonsense. It occurs to every Soviet driver. Nevertheless, I order you to Tukalinsk. Agreed?"

I clicked my heels military fashion and said yes.

"*Choroscho,*" he smiled, calling the girl who took the documents from which to register me for work.

When I returned at noon I received a *napravlenie,* or worker's identification plus trolley fare to the motor pool. Then I ran to the flea market to say good-bye to my candy merchant.

Public utilities in Omsk were archaic and overburdened. There was one line for the entire city, from the station to the market place, and all the populace tried to get on at the same time. My stop was near the bridge over the Irtysh, and at the clang of the bell a regular melee began. People fought like wildcats to get aboard, pushing through doors and windows from both sides. Some were dragged back by frustrated straphangers who clutched their coattails, usually starting another brawl. The only ones to profit were pickpockets. They watched contending customers until the jam became impossible, then with razor blades slit the boots of those unable to defend hidden valuables. Many a would-be rider thus lost his money, which most Russians carried in the boot.

The collection of fares was equally intricate. The conductor sat on a bench in one corner, and yelled "Pass it on," as the passengers forwarded the 20-kopek amount. Since twenty kopeks bought nothing more than a streetcar ride in Omsk, everyone was honest and passed it over. Tickets were returned by the same hand-over-head system, accompanied by joshing and giggles. We reached the railway station before half the car had paid.

I had an exhilarating headiness at being once more on my own, with credentials and a job. It was November and the night miserably cold, but I felt warm inside. But this soon cooled off when I couldn't get into the waiting room, which was so crowded that only women and children were admitted. When I told the doorman my wife and two children were inside, he laughed.

"That story has whiskers," he said.

After I had trotted awhile in the open air to keep from freezing, the doorman finally allowed me inside with the others. He hadn't lied. The place was packed. People slept shoulder to shoulder, so that it was impossible to step among them. All lay on top of their baggage, for thievery was rampant.

Only one spot was clear—Red Corner—the public reading room. I went in, wondering whether a literacy test had prevented the mob from filling it. I took a chair near a youth who seemed to be reading with one eye, while the other slept. This enchanted me, so I checked on him twice, finally deciding the open eye was made of glass. This was the one and only time I found a glass eye to anyone's advantage.

Since I was still limited in my Russian, and more interested in sleep than culture, I soon snoozed over my newspaper. But not for long.

"Bum," screamed the attendant, giving me a kick to the delight of his audience, "you came here to sleep, not to read. Is the cultural corner a flophouse, you swine? Out!"

"All ready for Train Ninety-two." The dispatcher's voice saved me further humiliation. The station floor came alive like a disturbed anthill, baggage held ahead of each owner in the manner of an ant pushing grain.

An old Russian was screaming murder. Some skunk had stolen the felt boots from under his head. I knew what that meant. Up here, with the temperature already under zero?

226

Only half the people got on the train, but I was among them. I failed to get into a car, but, with others, pushed past the trainman and sat on the vestibule steps. The wind immediately cut through my threadbare blouse, for I had no greatcoat. The *provodniki* had locked the car doors when we started, and now our fingers began to freeze from hanging on.

Provodniki were female porters and assistant conductors, fairly young and neat in well-tailored uniforms. They also helped in the gentle graft of selling places inside the cars; a practice nobody protested. I beat on the door, but we were about to fall off when the rear car door opened.

"What are you doing out there?" the woman asked.

"Riding along."

"Have you a ticket?"

"Of course. To Nasivaevskoe," I chattered, lips so stiff from the icy wind I could barely frame the words.

"Get in here. It'll cost you fifty rubles, but a cup of tea and sugar goes with it," she said.

My fingers were so numb I couldn't dig out the money, but she flashed the light in my face and said, "You have honest eyes, boy. Warm yourself first." The tea was a pure godsend.

Six hours later we neared the town, and the male conductor, who had holed up with the *provodniki* during the trip, emerged in fine humor. It took all kinds and conditions to get a train across Siberia, I decided.

At the motor pool in Nasivaevskoe I as an assigned driver, had priority No. 1. I climbed into the first truck and five hours later, pausing to drop protesting hitchhikers 5 kilometers outside the village, we reached Tukalinsk. It was a small place, between sweeping fir forests and thick frozen lakes, and had a niche in history as the scene of terrific battles between allied Czechs and Cossacks and the Reds. The first reminder was a military cemetery where lay the early Communist heroes.

Tukalinsk was Siberia at its frostiest. Peasant girls sold milk in frozen blocks, the first such packaging by nature I had seen, but after thawing, it tasted reasonably good.

The truck pulled up to my new place of employment, where to my further surprise chauffeurs were repairing cars outside in the snow.

Every ten minutes they went into the office for hot tea, and to soak up the heat of a huge stove. The stove nearly filled one of two rooms, the other holding our boss, Comrade Konski.

The director, a bigger man even than Nikolai Ptschilinzew in Talas, looked at my documents and then at me.

"Ever work in Siberia, Comrade Feld?" (I had resumed my own name on my new papers.)

"No, but in Central Asia," I replied.

"What do you say to the cold here?"

"I guess if I could stand the heat there, I'll bear the cold here," I said quietly.

"Yes, but we have other things here one should not overlook. The worst happens when it's neither hot nor cold, but the climate always remains in complete charge. For example: We have no roads as you do in Poland, but we drive across the plain which in winter is frozen harder than the best concrete. This makes excellent going unless the purga is blowing, mantling everything with a few meters of snow. In that case, you stay on the truck and wait until we send a tractor to pull you back. If we find you.

"But in the summer we also have problems, for the best road—if we had one—would become impassable in ten minutes. A short hard rain and your wheels are sunk in clay, the car mired while you wait for the sun to dry the ground so you can move.

"Then there is the spring. That is the worst season of all for driving. It provides both rain and snow, so you become more than an expert driver. You become a fatalist and fear no devil, but stretch the tarpaulin over the cab, light the oil stove, and to hell with the elements; just cook yourself some tea and *kasha!*"

Warming to his report on Tukalinsk, Comrade Konski chuckled and continued:

"Whatever you have heard Comrade, just double it for here. The present cold is nothing compared to actual winter. When the moon is full in February and the icy purga whips snow across the swamps, your feet and hands will break off if you don't take care. And the foxes and wolves howl and laugh from the edge of the forest, a warning to keep your truck going if you want to live. Everything is up to the driver—alone!"

I listened to this frightening prospect with respectful calm, and Konski paused. He must have been studying me while he talked.

228

"Do you think you would dare take a truck from here to Omsk, all alone?"

"Dare? Sure, but I don't know if I'd make it."

"Well, at least you give an answer. Who risks something is often successful. I believe you can be made into a real driver.

"Now then. If you want a room, go to Old Lady Prochrova in the cottage next door. She's honest, has nobody, and needs you as much as you will need her. You can crawl through the fence."

My papers in order, I crossed to Mother Prochrova's and received a kindly, "Come in, son." Her cottage, built of rough timbers, contained two rooms, a kitchen, and a stable. In the latter, and the treasure of the house, was Svetlana, the cow. She had been badly spoiled and was more of a pet than a chattel. A pleasant warm breath suffused my chilled body, and the aroma of boiling potatoes came from the large tile stove. I saw the peasant arrangement for sleeping on the rear oven, a centuries-old custom in Russia.

Prochrova was a wonderful housekeeper; the scrubbed floor and paper-covered walls were testaments to her energy. By the oil lamp's light I saw an ikon of the Holy Mother of God, and presently the old lady began telling her life's joys and woes as if we had been acquainted for years instead of minutes. She poured tea, putting saccharin into the pot.

"I'm so glad you've come, Jac. You see, I'm all alone. My Stephan has been at the front for years. Only God knows where he may be." She began to weep, and going to the table drawer brought out his picture. Her work-worn hands were trembling.

"That is Stephan. How we both worked, dragging the planks and timber from the woods to build this home, working from dawn to dark. Now my poor boy is fighting Germans. May the Mother of God protect him!"

The poor woman looked confidently toward the ikon, an expression of simple love softening her wrinkled features. It was the first gentle moment I had experienced in months.

I was transported in thought across thousands of miles, wondering whether my mother was thinking similarly of me. A mother's love is the same wherever one goes, I decided. Rich or poor, it isn't to be measured by human standards. It comes from God, and it must go back to Him, to be given over and over again. . . . What were Stephan and I doing so far from our homes?

229

"Drink, son," Prochrova murmured. "You are probably thinking of your mother, but don't be sad. We are all homeless sheep in God's sight. He decides all things. When Konski sent you here, that was God's guidance, I'm sure. Things have been rather bad with me. I've had to go to the forest to haul wood with my Svetlana. No wonder she gives less and less milk. I also hesitate to beg a drop of oil from the chauffeurs for my lamp. Anyway, I'm happy you are here. I shall take care of you as I would of my Stephan. So lie down on the *petshka* and get some sleep. The heat will do you good."

I was given a quilted worksuit, padded mitts, and an old Zis to repair out in the open. The "garage" was a roof supported by four posts. Why nobody had closed it in and installed a stove, I couldn't guess and didn't ask. One took things as they were, in Siberia.

After a day under the vehicle, when the cold seemed to freeze the wrenches into our flesh, it was wonderful to return to Prochrova's snug *chata,* where often other peasant women gathered to swap stories. Two of them, old Tasis and her girl friend, spun fanciful tales about Gregori Efimovitch Rasputin, the mad monk born in 1871 in the village of Pokrovskoe, not far from Tyumen.

Older inhabitants of this Province of Tobolsk were superstitious still, and as I came to know them I began to understand some of the strange forces at work in Rasputin, too. Their dreams, in that frozen land where there wasn't much to break the solitude, became important manifestations.

Early in the morning, while I still slept on the oven bench, Tasis would hustle in to report her dream and wait anxiously to hear what my landlady made of it. Once, having dreamed of losing her teeth, the old woman left in tears, lamenting loudly. When nothing happened to her, she came back with more dreams.

December came riding the full Siberian winter; the plank walks squeaked under our weight, and the frost-crusted steel froze to our moist hands if we removed our gloves. The dreaded purga howled for days, an Arctic blizzard that stacked snow above the window tops. I shoveled a tunnel from Prochrova's door to the garage.

There were days when it was impossible to go out, when one lay beside the stove without moving, living on potatoes and milk fresh from the cow. I smoked one Machorka after another, and tried reading the stale newspapers that plastered my hostess' walls. They antedated our forced journey through Russia, and told of a world still at peace. Under such sub-zero conditions, I discovered how Siberians start a motor. Finding the oil frozen solid each morning, they would hood the engine with a tarpaulin to hold the heat, place a mixture of oil and gas beneath the crankcase and light it. When the engine's oil began to boil, they went to work with the crank. If, as sometimes happened, the car caught fire and was destroyed, the driver was sure of ten years for sabotage. Despite that gamble nobody ever devised a better way to defrost a motor in that harsh region.

27

CHRISTMAS in Tukalinsk brought a gift from the least likely St. Nicholas: the government. Without mentioning the holiday, Comrade Konski made me Technical Chief for American Vehicles, because nobody knew how to fix them. I was put in charge of other mechanics and given my Bron.

The Bron was certification that one was essential. This for a deportee was something special. Most of us—fugitives, captives, refugees—were definitely expendable, not worth a bowl of *kasha* unless geared to useful production. Although many slaved to their deaths in the grotesque and unwieldy war effort, there was little or no recognition. One was a speck on a tiny cog in the supply machinery.

The custom was to give a group citation for making the quota, at which time the boss was praised and one heard a windy speech. At least Konski spared me that ordeal. As the official arm of the USSR he merely patted my shoulder and pinned on the insignia.

"Jac, you are doing quite well," he said.

Again I felt a strange, satisfied feeling. This had occurred when Comrade Nowitzki read the congratulatory telegram in Leninpol. What was happening? Pride of performance? The response of human beings to reward? Or was it a yearning to be more than a simple, frozen clod in a period of mighty world changes? I didn't know, but it was wonderful to be counted once more with the human race. Downtrodden and a fugitive from a prison factory, I had re-established my self-respect. I felt like a knight receiving the king's accolade.

Mother Prochrova hung up a tarnished ornament that evening and placed a spruce twig under the ikon. She had boiled a vegetable stew and as we ate I told her of my promotion.

"There will be more, Jac. Don't ask how I know, but I know."

Meditating in the darkness, I hoped Prochrova was a prophet. Things had improved since the round trip to Omsk. We had received several beaten-up Chevrolets, part of the "Amerikanski lend-lease" of which I would hear much later. The trucks were turned over to me because I was a foreigner and, the Russians reasoned, I must be familiar with them. And so I was—after a period of trial and error.

Whether because of the promotion or growing confidence, I began to make a conscious effort to serve the state. I wanted to help win the war. Up to then, kicked around by Soviet bureaucracy and treated like starving dogs in the street, we deportees couldn't have cared less which side won. There was for us no victory. Now I had a glimmer of hope.

The fighting was going much better too. The Western allies had freed most of France and advanced toward the Rhine. Italy was almost liberated. But most joyous to hear, the Red Armies were recapturing cities and wide areas that had been under Nazi control. Hitler's dream of capturing Russia had been denied. The Germans did not cross the Volga.

I listened while Prochrova and the women, crossing themselves, prayed feverishly for the return of their men.

"Great, Almighty God, have pity and return my son . . . bring him back home sound of mind and body."

Prochrova's was the voice of Mother Russia, a community of 220 million in which the women worked and prayed, the men fought and died. As the Germans fell back, they were leaving windrows of their own dead beside ours, in the reddening snow. It was a winter of retribution.

But God must have heard the prayers, for with 1945 the end was in sight. On my trips to Omsk I saw posters with different slogans. They no longer clamored "Stop Hitler"; they demanded he be caged. Der Führer was represented as an ape, a crocodile, or a zombi, as he skulked toward Berlin. The exhortation now: "Destroy the dragon in his den!" Such persuasion may have sent a few rushing back to the job, but I wondered.

In March I was ordered back to Omsk. I bade farewell to Prochrova, who had cared for me as her son. It was Easter. The old women were kneeling again when I kissed her wrinkled face, told her Stephan would soon be home, and drove away in the truck. I wondered during the ride if Stephan really would return.

Comrade Lessovski was again having morning tea and paper when I walked into his office, but he was more hospitable.

"Konski wrote that you did a good job," he began. "I suppose you like it up there better than Omsk?"

"It's easier than trying to ride the streetcars here," I joked.

"Well, you won't have to worry about that. I have a mission for you. You will go by train to Gorki to get factory parts for our vehicles. They are for the American cars you've been repairing. So far we've only had allocations on paper. It depends upon your salesmanship how much we get. I think you have a good line of talk. Try it in Gorki."

This was the best news yet. I assured Lessovski it would receive my utmost, honest effort, to which he replied, "I'll be happy if you bring back half of what they've promised."

Then he leaned over to give me a second directive.

"I've promised the traffic controller five liters of genuine Moscow vodka," he said. "He co-operated by reserving a seat for you, and that took some doing. So bring back a nice jugful."

With official passes, several official stamps, and money for my expenses, I found travel as a VIP a definite improvement over previous train treks. I nearly swooned when they served meals on little tables in upholstered compartments. It took five days and nights to reach Gorki, and by that time all of us on the train were on a first-name basis, all comrades in the cause.

Gorki was the Detroit of Russia. Everybody knew about automobiles or worked on them. A few rode in them. From the Moscow station, facing the Square Kanarina, I saw private automobiles in which high-level comrades were going to their tasks. The bazaar was bigger, the streetcars longer and more crowded than in Omsk.

Sight-seeing was not my errand, however. I went past a queue waiting for bread, asked a policeman the way to the G.A.Z.—Gorki Auto Zavod.

"What do you want there?" he countered, probably because of my accent.

"Official business," I snapped, feeling nine feet high. I produced identification, official passes, my requisition orders. He called a colleague.

"Drive along the Chekovskaya, then turn left," the man directed.

Happily the streetcar went near that forest of concrete chimneys. The factory stretched for miles, with the usual guard towers and barbed wire topping its high walls. Trucks emerging were all the same model, I noticed.

It was wonderful what a pass could do. Although I waited to get by several desks, I moved quickly to the head procurement official. Nobody told me his name, but he gave me a hearing.

"Our works in Omsk are at a standstill for lack of parts," I began. "I have come as a personal messenger from Comrade Lessovski, Director. We are anxious to keep the vehicles going, but that now depends upon your understanding our needs," I said.

He didn't reply, but surveyed me with the curiosity of a Russian who wonders why his country has so many dialects. I suppose the Latvian lingo with the Uzbek inflection offended his ears.

"It is a five-day ride on the train, but I must tell you about our conditions," I rattled on, going into detail about the Omsk auto works whose grim interior I knew too well.

"Stop," he said, wearily raising an arm. "I understand."

Whereupon he authorized most of our requisitions.

"They will be in a railway car, ready for transport tomorrow morning," he declared, stamping my papers and scribbling notes on several important-looking pads. Each note received another rousing stamp. I was impressed. There was plainly a lot of power, if you stood high enough on the roster of desks.

Brimming with confidence and exuding importance I returned to

236

the city and went into one of the better hotels, like a well-traveled commissar. The night clerk welcomed me.

"I'll have a single, please." This was accompanied by my credentials and travel orders.

"Exactly, Comrade. You have come a long way?"

I gave him a superior glance. "A long way, yes," I said. This was the customary evasion of names, places, and other information forbidden to snoopers.

"This has a good view of the river," he said, presenting a large key attached to a small wooden shingle. I went up, carrying my bag.

Who was to know that I had never before been a guest in a hotel? I went around the room examining its two windows, washbowl, closet, and even the iron radiator from which—wonder of wonders—actual steam emanated. But most remarkable was a large bed with a spring and mattress, made up with a pillow, linen, and quilt.

Because I was an official messenger the room rental was 10 rubles, including breakfast. I undressed for bed, the first time since 1940.

"Which way to the best vodka shop?" I asked the clerk next morning, having savored to the fullest a formal breakfast in the dining room.

"The Gorki bazaar," he said, naming a first-class store.

It was still a couple of hours before train departure, so I had a look around the square. The shop had several grades of vodka, including one impressive brand claiming to be 110 proof.

"This is definitely the best," the man said. "For field marshals and industrial commissars."

I conveyed a certain skepticism, but looked closely at the label. The salesman continued his pitch.

"This is not made from ordinary potatoes," he said, "it is partly of grain." He whispered the last word, for everyone knew that grain was for making Red Army bread.

"Made in Moscow, I presume?" I held the bottle to the light.

"Absolutely," he assured. "Everyone knows Moscow vodka is the best."

I pretended to hesitate, then asked if he had a proper container.

"A case for the bottle?"

"I cannot be bothered with glass bottles," I snapped.

He turned briskly to another part of the shop, for I had made an impression.

"Just the thing," he said, producing a zinc-plated pitcher with a tight stopper.

I told him to pour in five liters of the Moscow brand. Nothing too good for the boss. Particularly since he was paying.

Eying me in amazement, the man opened five bottles and transferred the vodka to the pitcher, corking it securely. I counted out the rubles, thanked him, and left to tour the market.

To my astonishment, automobile parts were prominently displayed for private sale. Made for Soviet or American cars, they were at black-market quotations. A wily-looking huckster boasted he could sell enough parts to assemble an entire car.

"With a motor?"

"If you have the right credentials," he hedged, and I wondered if White Boots was doing business now in Gorki. It was evident that all crooks weren't confined to Uzbek and Omsk.

"This war must be nearly won," I mused, but not out loud. It seemed beyond belief that here, in the center of Soviet war production, new automobiles could be had on the *marché noir*. But this was none of my affair, so, well pleased with myself and with the vital container cradled to my chest, I proceeded to the station.

There I checked and found the parts ready, crated, and tagged for Omsk. Once more in my compartment, I looked out at Gorki's churches, minarets, and patrician houses, its bustling factories, the Oka winding toward the Volga, and the heroic statue on the mountain. How different from my other passage through this city!

Everything went fine on the return journey, until we arrived in Omsk. There an unpleasant reception awaited.

The station police locked all compartment doors and placed guards outside. Next, they searched the interior, and the passengers, for black-market goods. Any passenger with so much as a yard of calico or kilo of food had to give his name and surrender the merchandise. When my turn came, I showed my luggage and one fellow noticed the vodka.

"So that's the kind you are," he said accusingly. He removed the stopper and took a long, official sniff. I thought he would inhale the 110-proof fumes until his scalp rose.

"It doesn't belong to me," I said quietly.

"Oh, sure, that's what they all say," he sneered. "Maybe *I* brought it back from Gorki, eh? It's damned peculiar that everything in this compartment suddenly belongs to nobody. Perhaps the stuff is from

238

the Moscow Patriarch, for religious ceremonies?" He laughed at his own wit.

"No, no," I hurriedly explained, "it's for my boss."

"In which case your boss is a black marketeer of liquor. Shame on both of you. Come along," he barked, placing me under arrest.

There was nothing to do and with the vodka I was taken to the police station where the captain quizzed me. At the end he said, "Black market," and refused to telephone Lessovski. Then he ordered me out, keeping the pitcher.

"Confiscated," he explained, pushing it under the desk.

Crushed, I went to my room. It was Saturday and nobody was at the office. What could I say to the boss? All my success with the machinery would evaporate because there was no vodka. I spent a depressing Sunday, unable to think of a solution.

On Monday, Comrade Lessovski was furious. During my absence he and the traffic director had talked of nothing but Moscow vodka. Comrade Babilov developed a king-sized thirst and so had Lessovski.

Now they were desolate and dry as the Gobi desert. And both wished I was in the middle thereof.

I had described the station seizure with such clarity that Lessovski didn't doubt. Calling his secretary, he dictated a sharp letter. Then he sent me with it to the police captain. That worthy read it with furrowed brow. He pretended mystification.

"Comrade Jac," he began kindly, "when did you bring this vodka?"

"When? Why, Comrade Natshalink, you yourself tossed me out Saturday and I was forced to leave the pitcher behind."

"My dear Comrade, I throw so many out of here I really cannot remember faces. I have no recollection of yours. Each day I throw out more persons than is permissible in a police station, but the victims are usually delighted. I am among the few in this district who pleases people by throwing them out. But let us get to your case. You say you left a pitcher? What kind was it?"

"A zinc-plated pitcher with a stopper, filled with one-hundred-ten-proof Moscow vodka. The best." I looked at him steadily.

"Would that be it under my desk?"

"It would. And it is," I exclaimed happily. Without a word he passed it to me.

My pleasure was short-circuited by the lightness of the pitcher. Uncorking it, I discovered at most, one liter.

"What is this, Comrade Captain? Someone has drunk the vodka."

"Impossible," Natshalink's surprise seemed real. He put his nose to the pitcher, inhaled and then muttered: "They have all but emptied it, the pigs. What filthy swine, those guards. It was nobody else. A dirty trick!" He repeated this and sat down heavily. I took the pitcher and turned to go.

"Young man," the captain stopped me, "do you really want to return to Babilov and Lessovski with one liter instead of the five?"

"It's better than no vodka at all," I defended.

"Listen," he said. "We can't change the fact those sons-of-bitches have swilled the liquor. As sure as I sit here, I didn't have a drop," he lied like a veteran. "But I think you're mighty stupid to take back only one liter."

"What do you suggest, Comrade Captain?"

"Just this: Let's you and I split this last bit of excellent vodka. Then let's share the cost of five new liters and refill the pitcher. These big shots—they look at a label, but can't tell Omsk from Moscow vodka."

Although I resented paying half the cost, the proposition had definite appeal. I was in no position to quibble. It was also good public relations to insure this man's friendship.

"You have yourself a bargain, Comrade Natshalink," I said, and in perfect agreement we divided the last liter, pouring his share into an empty container that just happened to be under the same desk. Then, with our pooled funds, I went to the nearest shop and purchased five liters of Omsk.

Lessovski and Babilov were waiting impatiently.

"Got it," I announced with feigned triumph. "They're scared stiff of you, Comrade Lessovski. It wasn't even opened!"

Eagerly, and with ceremony, the exalted bosses allowed themselves a test slug, drinking from a small jigger. I didn't breathe.

Lessovski's eyes sparkled; Babilov's face mooned appreciation.

"Marvelous," they spoke in unison. "There is simply no comparison between Omsk and Moscow vodka. Thank you, Comrade Jac. You got the best!"

Thereafter, all things considered, I rated my Moscow vodka deal the apex of operations.

Director Lessovski kept me in Omsk as Garage Superintendent and put several coal trucks under my control. Among the places to which we took coal was the Omsk shoe factory, a plant with a reputation for making its quota every quarter, 100 per cent. This had been publicized in *Izvestia* until all patriots admired its manager and crew. Having become acquainted with the director, I arranged to swap extra coal for a pair of shoes, but he stalled delivery until I insisted he keep the bargain.

"You may not like them, but I'll send the shoes," he finally agreed.

The messenger arrived with canvas-strap clods with wooden soles, made for prisoners and concentration camp inmates. Only then did I understand the quota performance.

My living quarters and life in Omsk were no better and no worse than for anyone engaged in war work behind Stalin's front. I rented a sleeping corner with a family, and moved in with my wooden suitcase and knapsack. It was a pre-Revolution apartment building, the walls covered with newspapers under which faded remnants of gorgeous patterns remained. I slept near a window, a screen separating me from the landlord, his wife, and their child.

But sleeping was a steeplechase routine; we constantly disturbed each other: the baby had to wet, the pot would be fetched, the mother would stumble over the chair, and if I wanted to read, the landlord turned out the light so he could snooze. Everyone snored, and next door a character played a phonograph to all hours. We didn't dare open the window for fear the child would catch cold, and altogether I thought one rested better in the prison-camp dorms.

Each morning I had to carry out my screen, otherwise "it's dark in here as the forest," the landlady complained. Because she never aired my bed, I retaliated by sweeping only my corner of the room. She would counter by sprinkling her part of the floor from a bottle of water, whining, "Not so much dust, Jac. The baby is sleeping."

However, I could take it. You can take almost anything after a deportation train, sleeping in heaps in railway stations, or nestling in roofed dugouts like woodchucks. I didn't brood over the fact that there were cities with apartment houses containing suites of two rooms and more, with bath and kitchen exclusive to one family.

There was also a sports club next door with an illuminated sign that enraged me. It said, "Life is getting better, simpler, and richer—Lenin."

That one night in Gorki had planted seeds of discontent. Anyway, I decided Vladimir Lenin was the biggest liar of them all.

241

28

IF THE WORLD'S political scientists wonder what keeps
Soviet Russia going, I have the answer in one word: vodka.

Vodka is the fuel, the lubrication, the spark, and the internal
combustion that moves Russia's millions, and I speak as a mechanic
who kept wartime motors running at 130 degrees above and 60
below zero. If there had been no vodka to keep me going, I couldn't
have made it.

Without vodka Russian activity would grind to a standstill and the
economy would congeal. This colorless but complete stimulant has
more wallop, less taste, and greater penetrating qualities than the
highest-octane liquor distilled in monastic cloisters and stolen by invading hordes. Napoleon had his own brandy and Adolf Hitler provided schnapps, but both lost to the Russian winter, backstopped
by the fermented juice of potato.

A warming ingredient for body and spirit, vodka substitutes for a

243

thousand Soviet needs and shortages, thus compensating for the endless frustrations which among other peoples cause nervous disorders. In Russia when one is inclined to worry the prescription is vodka. It fills a social void, illuminates the political darkness, takes the chill from physical interiors at every level. Patent-medicine peddlers don't go broke in the USSR because they never get started. Vodka is a cure-all, a magic fluid of many uses.

It's good inside and outside, can be used as liniment or antiseptic, lighter fuel, paint remover, furniture cleaner, and for the common man contains the medicinal qualities of antibiotics and barbiturates. I suspect it's used in the secret Soviet rocket fuels.

Ask a Russian if he's cold, he will smile and say, "I have a blanket on the inside." Vodka.

Vodka is made, sold, and controlled by the Soviet state, and some Russians declare their government "floats on vodka." Costing only a ruble per liter to produce, it sells according to the purse and taste of the customers in sixteen Socialist republics, sometimes for as much as 50 rubles the liter. It is much more the national drink than wine is of France or beer of Austria and Germany.

Characteristically, there are few laws regulating the sale or distribution of vodka, except the party policy called *"nye kulturny."* This discourages underage drinking, public misbehavior, delinquency in minors and loose-lipped garrulity in their elders, which sometimes reaches to high places. But the old-fashioned guzzling of vodka is a recognized national custom without which, climate being what it is, the peasants would emulate the bears and hibernate.

Russian vodka has an oily consistency, not to be found in the paler imitations elsewhere. Moreover, it seems to have more of a tranquilizing effect upon the imbiber. Where other spirits are apt to produce a bright, hilarious, even pugnacious change in the consumer, vodka develops a philosophic strain, a pensive and reconciled attitude emerging under rather trying conditions.

The world may be in sorry shape, but under the veil of vodka its downtrodden inhabitants take a tolerant view of it. The situation may not seem especially better than before, but at the same time it doesn't loom so hopeless. Vodka helps one to adjust mentally.

Foreigners visiting the Soviet Union often complain of gastric troubles, gall-bladder upset, and biliousness. Russians nod knowingly. "Not enough vodka," they say, and they mean no jest.

244

Vodka is an additive like ethyl in gasoline. It provides a slow glow. Since Russian cooking contains plenty of mutton fat, vodka cuts the grease and sluices the alimentary canal. It is considered indispensable when eating *shaslik* or negotiating an international treaty.

There is an old saying that if you spill your vodka—which often happens in the bottoms-up tradition of the Russians—"your house will resound with song and laughter."

During my Omsk experience, there was plenty of opportunity to investigate some of these legends about vodka. I could add a few more, but one gets the idea from a few incidents. Personally, I believe that except for vodka I would not have survived; it's as simple as that.

There were two motion-picture theaters in Omsk, both on the banks of the Irtysh. "The Simple" offered only a film; "The Artists' Cinema," on the other hand, showed the same film but with a jazz orchestra, better seats, and higher prices. With a bottle of vodka to keep one company, this provided a pleasant evening.

The first time I went to "The Artists' " there was a double feature and the place was jammed. It was advertised as "a picture on American workingmen's conditions," and titled *Golden Times*. In reality it was Charlie Chaplin in *The Gold Rush*.

Party propagandists had distorted Chaplin's humor to portray the deplorable existence of the little man in America, in this case a sourdough so hard up and neglected that he ate his shoes. We were supposed to believe the *Kultur* leader's version of this plot, so naturally the vodka had to be extra-high proof.

"The comrade would better omit that explanation," the Poles laughed, "or else the government should forbid our black market in chocolate and tinned rations shipped to us by the Americans." It seemed poor gratitude toward allies whose lend-lease trucks and jeeps now filled the Omsk garage. The Soviets kept the vehicles' origin a secret from most, but we knew.

There were sometimes other variations in the social-recreational spectrum of the province, such as the occasion of my official request for rations and quarters, Comrade Olga Feodorovna, in charge. Women had not played a romantic role in my adventures up to then, and Olga was at best an unexpected break in celibate journeying. Lessovski sent me to her.

As the head bookkeeper at the Sojustrans, Olga Feodorovna had

245

an office with five co-workers on the second floor. She was nearest the entrance and during the half hour's wait, I studied her. Women in Siberia as a rule look much older than they are. I was frankly trying to estimate her age. The Omsk climate is not kind to the skin with the winds and blizzard providing "facials" unlike those other countries dispense in salons.

"So . . . you wish to eat meat also?" she laughed. "I won't let you starve. It may be more complicated than Tukalinsk where the villagers can supply themselves, but you shall have the proper stamps.

"Go down to the commissary; you will get dehydrated meat and margarine, but no butter, no sugar, and no soap. To make up for that, think of the many friends you'll have here!"

She gave me a warm smile, and said, "Return later, and pick up the books when I have them ready."

"When will that be, Olga Feodorovna? After office hours?" I was suddenly afraid of my own boldness.

"Yes, if you wish. Perhaps you will tell me something about Europe then. Anyway, I have a lot of work to do now."

I bowed respectfully, still wondering how many years Olga might have behind those inviting eyes.

When I returned a few hours later, she was still at the books. The door slammed behind me and Olga jumped to her feet, startled.

"One knocks here, before entering, Comrade," she said severely. "Particularly, if one expects to get meat stamps. But everything is ready." Handing over the envelope, she rolled two cigarettes, one for me. "Good appetite," she said.

Suddenly I felt self-conscious. "Comrade Feodorovna, if you don't mind, I would be pleased to accompany you home, because. . . ."

"Because what, young man? I live here. I am home."

She reached back with one foot and pushed the door open. "This is my apartment, and behind it a kitchen. All private, only for me."

I stared in unbelief. This girl, or woman—I wasn't yet sure—had an apartment to herself? Right next to the food office? How convenient, and by whose arrangement? Such thoughts flashed into mind, a sort of automatic caution I had developed.

"Will you come in?"

I walked around the partition into a small room with a scullery. The furniture was functional. The couch-bed, or to be exact a large mat-

246

tress supported by two wooden blocks, had a lump at one end and a deep hole in the middle, but was covered with a flowered spread. There was a nicely carved wooden chest and a tile stove with a comfortable chair before it. In one corner stood a closet faced with a full-length mirror, a luxury I had not seen thus far in Siberia. There was also a small table with a record player, a rocking chair beside it.

"Very cozy, especially for Omsk," I said, unable to hide my surprise.

"Make yourself at home. Sit by the fire," Olga encouraged. "I'll brew some tea and warm a bun for us. But for good guests"—she glanced coyly in my direction—"there is something special."

She pulled open the mirrored closet, and brought forth a bottle of vodka and another of cherry brandy. With a light laugh, she stood both on the table, put her hands on her hips and stepped back to survey them.

"As a starter, vodka or the liqueur? Or maybe both together?" she teased.

"Which does Comrade Head Bookkeeper drink?" I continued my caution.

"You shall see immediately, Comrade Garage Chief," she replied, pouring each of us half a water glass of vodka and brandy mixed. Then, "Na sdrovje," she toasted, and we drained the two glasses.

What a woman! I thought, the liquor burning clear down to my heels. She drinks like Joe Stalin.

Olga Feodorovna sensed my admiration, and must have decided I rated guest handling.

"Now I'll bring tea and some food, so turn on the music and if you get impatient, have a vodka," she said.

I threw two birch logs in the stove, started the music, and poured out a drink. It's still the best medicine for impatience. The first drink had taken hold, a rippling warmth flooded my veins, and I tossed my coat in a corner. How quickly a little comfort, some leisure time, and the feminine touch can banish the day's toil and troubles.

Olga came in balancing the buns on a tray, but had a little trouble balancing herself as the vodka-cherry took its course.

"Comrade Jac, why do you throw the coat there?" she pointed vaguely.

"Because I'm hot, Olga Feodorovna."

"Then it's time we had something to cool off," she said, handing me another drink. Hot or cold, drinking another vodka is a ritual I don't decline. We bent elbows in unison, down to the last drop.

"Put on the Argentine tango," Olga urged, pushing the buns aside. "It's my favorite, a gift from Comrade Konski. I guess perhaps you don't make presents?"

"Give me time to get settled with the company and I'll pile gifts on you like St. Nicholas," I bubbled, feeling no pain whatever.

We went through the tango twice, at least that was the impression I had, although I was now hotter than a kolchos motor with a dry radiator going uphill in Uzbek.

"You must take dancing seriously," Olga prattled as she removed blouse and skirt and danced in her bra and panties. It really was warm in that small apartment with the wood fire in the stove and the liquid fire inside us.

"Equal rights for men and women," she announced gaily. "You must take off your shirt, too." I did not need to be urged.

The strip tease ended there, but through the vodka haze I was aware of her frilly underwear. The lace fascinated me, for I had seen the same pattern somewhere else. After the fourth tango, I remembered.

"Olga, my compliments on your decoration. That is the kind of lace my grandmother had on her curtains in Mitau," I exclaimed in all sincerity, raising my glass.

"Do you like it? It's imported. Very difficult to get. And how about the ribbons?" She twiddled the bow at her waist.

Suddenly everything seemed funny. The lace was funny, my boots were funny, even the buns were droll. We laughed at the mere wag of a finger, and as the bottle's contents went down and temperatures went up, I felt positive Comrade Olga was dancing with three guests simultaneously. I could see them in the big mirror.

I have no clear recollection of how or when I got back to my own room, but my head ached until noon the next day.

248

29

SUCH interludes were few and far between in Omsk, or anywhere else behind the Soviet lines. There were plenty of women, but they didn't have much glamour. For the most part it was work, quotas, regulations, reports, and more orders. Love, sex, and gentility had tough going in Siberia.

Our meals were the main items of interest, and they varied little. Now that I was a part of the production machinery, with official rations, I enjoyed meat occasionally and the everlasting *kasha* was interspersed with soups and stews. I lived no better but no worse than others in Omsk, and by that I mean infinite numbers and nationalities that now made up its labor pool.

Several times a month I went to the Polish Patriots' Club, a clearing house for news of home, refugees, and rumors. The latter were in abundance, unconfirmed, and exaggerated with hope now that the war went in our favor.

Many of my friends had received letters from their home towns, most of them death notices or grim and bare statements that all were missing.

It is not pleasant to be in such a community, for each visit to the club was like playing Russian roulette. Who would be next to get bad news? The grapevine had established a system of oral and written reports and these were relayed to various Polish and Jewish clubs throughout the USSR.

Shocked at the tragic news, although such confirmation of fears had been expected for years, some would drink heavily to forget; others withdraw from their comrades. A listlessness set in; nothing really interested them. It was as though they had kept alive and hopeful in vain.

"What do we do now?"

Whatever the answer, there was one irrefutable fact: We were driftwood in a sea of despairing humans for whom there were no immediate objectives.

I had become acquainted with a cheerful young fellow named Mischka. He suggested that since Poland was one big graveyard and the Baltic republics no longer existed, it might be well to look for a new country. Palestine interested him, and for lack of something else to discuss we began to plan postwar travels. Mischka was among those who had already learned that his relatives had all been slain in the Nazi invasion. Naturally, he had no further interest in going home.

My own feelings had changed since coming to Siberia. In the first two years I had held resolutely to the goal of seeing Mitau and my family once more, but now I knew Latvia would never be the same. It seemed improbable that my parents, if they were still alive, would have remained there. But where could they have gone? Perhaps on another deportation, as I had?

The last days of April brought a succession of sensations and celebrations. The Red Army was driving into Berlin. The Red flag was flying over the Reichstag building. Then came the one welcome death notice: Adolf Hitler's.

The tyrant who started the global slaughter had left the stage amid less clamor than one expected. Omsk, at least, took his obituary in stride. Maybe there were too many other things demanding attention, such as the May Day programs throughout Russia.

May Day had not been very happy since 1940. The Nazi attack that year had put a blight on the normal calendar of events. May Day of 1945 would compensate, we were told.

Every Party headquarters, school, military camp, and industrial complex was ordered to make ready. If you could walk, you must parade. There were a number of preliminary drinking sessions, naturally. How otherwise would one train for such a May Day?

The faithful were called in from the outer fringes. Konski and the better drivers and mechanics showed up from Tukalinsk. From the tank and vehicle repair center, where the clock never stopped on work, bosses allowed time out for trusted comrades to parade. Konski and the boys got in early, and having fetched their vodka along, got a flying start in wassail. They did not participate in the procession but settled down in the Auto Center where, Comrade Lessovski promised, there would be feasting "beyond description" and "enough vodka to swim in."

There was, of course, a formal speaking program and it brought a surprise to us Poles. We did not expect anyone except Red Army soldiers and fliers to get credit, but when Russia alone was called the winner of the war it made us wonder. There was no room for questions, however, after the commissars finished denouncing the "monopolistic capitalists and makers of war" in repetitious and increasing violence.

It was still a week to V-E Day, although we didn't know exactly when it would come, and this unfriendly oratory against our allies across the Elbe seemed in poor taste. With Mischka, I went to the Center where some of the crew, well along in the festivities, shouted halloos.

Comrade Lessovski began a short exhortation, but soon quit extolling the virtues of May Day to praise the work of the drivers and repairmen. Instead of the usual lauding of Stalin and Soviet rulers, he interjected several *prosits,* the international code for "bottoms up." This kept vodka flowing and everyone in good humor. Lessovski added a coarse joke or two, and then we set about serious drinking.

A group of musicians had appeared, several riding in on the mechanics' shoulders, while space was cleared in the middle of the hall. Then the *kamaruschka* began.

The free-for-all dance in Russia is something to behold—from a safe distance. In many cases the men dance by themselves. Given a head start at the vodka bar, the *kamaruschka* evolves a pattern of organized chaos that, like the battles royal of medieval days, proceeds to a survival of the fittest. The rhythm of the Russian dance is fairly fast, and when the accordions and balalaikas are tuned to vodka the cadence quickly generates frenzy.

Men jumped up and down in heavy boots, tossing benches aside to make room for individual exercises. The dancing Russian requires no partner, and if he has one she had better hang on. I saw a couple of mechanics hurl their women under the tables when the terpsichorean r.p.m. exceeded female limits, and there they remained, bleary-eyed but safer than if left to the centrifugal hazards of the dance. A couple of husky peasant mamas were toddling by themselves.

Older persons backed against the wall, beating time with cupped palms. Any reserve between boss and employee dissolved in alcoholic miasma; I saw Lessovski spinning madly beside coal haulers and floor sweepers.

"Go it, Grischka!" others yelled as one of our crack mechanics hurled his new cap on the floor and began to pirouette about it. A graceful fellow, Grischka's solo flight attracted a growing audience, and his outflung arms flailed faster and wilder. Urged on by whooping comrades, the perspiring mechanic spun to a dizzy climax in which he leaped high and came down with both feet on the cap, crushing it into a gray pancake.

I was warming to the occasion myself, eddying in the crowd that was now shoulder to shoulder. It was as hot as the Stalinabad plain.

Konski, flushed and breathing hard, pushed toward me. "I'm not good at this dancing," he shouted. "I wait for the waltz." He swayed from side to side and I made another turn of the floor before spotting him again.

"Jac—e-e-e-e!" Konski was hollering and waving a letter at me. "There you are, Brother Jac. Maybe from your girl, hah?" He laughed thickly as dancers swirled him around and I clutched the envelope. It was postmarked Riga.

So there it was, at last. The long-awaited, long-hoped-for letter from home. Amid such a mob and at such a bizarre moment, the answer to an inquiry I had sent from Tukalinsk to the "address table," the Soviet clearing house for scattered families.

Now that I actually had it I was reluctant to read it.

"Let Kantika dance!" the people were shouting. "Dance, dance and play until the roof comes down. It's a holiday!" Another mechanic began to spin.

I groped toward a dim and quiet corner, alone beyond the dancers. My heart was throbbing, but not from vodka. Not now. I could see that the letter was from nobody I knew; it was an official communication from the Latvian Soviet authorities. Shaking, I ripped it open and scanned the few lines on a provincial letterhead. Then I read them again more slowly:

We have no record of your relatives. They were last reported in the Riga ghetto. We regret to have to inform you of this.

(Signed)   Rajkom Riga
Department of Missing Persons

The world seemed to collapse inside me. All my dreams, all my determination to get back and see my parents and home—gone. Banished by four lines of typewritten intelligence. My brain buzzed. So the papers and the radio reports had not lied. It had happened.

It was common knowledge that Riga's ghetto had been created and then overrun by the Germans in 1940, the inhabitants expunged to the last person. Scores of my companions had received the same news. Now it had come to me.

This sheet of paper made one thing certain: I was utterly alone in the world.

"Just once more, just once more again. . . ." The band was playing a Russian folk song and the dancers were whirling madly.

"Your health, Jac!" The chauffeurs shouted, but I barely heard. In my ears was the solemn booming of a Mitau church bell. A bell that rang for births, for marriages, for deaths. And now, far away, it tolled in memory of my dear ones.

I walked slowly toward the dancers and the drunkards. Several mechanics had already collapsed and lay senseless on the floor. Others stepped over and around them, but they cared not. They had their fling and now reclined, perfectly relaxed.

"Maybe they had the right idea," I thought, moving toward a table.

There was plenty of vodka left, but I called for a new bottle and drained a tall glassful as my comrades stared. Such drinking, and at so late an hour.

"This Jac is a devil. He drinks like a hole in the desert but gives us not a drop," they chided. Grischka, disheveled and grimy, contributed a philosophic: "We thought you Poles couldn't drink. What a mistake!"

"Oh, but we can, Grischka, especially when we have reason."

I looked at him a moment and then at the letter before me. He understood.

I sat there drinking for a long time, as one by one my companions slumped in slumber or staggered into the spring night. The dance was over, the guests gone. It seemed that I was falling, falling . . . and I couldn't stop.

Mischka found me on the floor with the others, a large lump on my head. The morning sun was already high. The place was a shambles; drunks strewn everywhere. Mischka shook me into wakefulness and I felt in my tunic for the letter. It was there, crumpled but intact. It had been no dream, then. Mischka read it and pressed my hand.

Then, like a big brother, he raised me up, hooked my arm around his shoulder, and helped me into the clean morning air.

30

WAR is like a glacier that crushes all before it. Having passed, it leaves a massive and long-lasting imprint upon the land and its inhabitants. This the people rarely realize, as each day brings its own crisis, and it comes as a great disappointment when, having lived through it, they cannot resume prewar habits and forget the whole evil experience.

The fact is that only the beginnings and endings of wars are much remembered; in between is but a time of weary submission to events beyond individual control.

Everyone recalls where he was and what he did when the conflict opened. Those who survive will also describe precisely the time, place, and the part they played in the rejoicing at war's end. The rest is a blur of fear, suffering, mixed luck, and contrivance—like a man fleeing a falling wall who, having escaped, looks back at the settling dust and debris.

May 7, 1945!

It was a brilliant morning and the skies seemed to smile at the good news. Omsk, hours ahead of Paris time, had word of the German surrender before Colonel-General Jodl signed the documents at Rheims. Thousands of newspaper extras proclaimed peace with the rising sun: Victory, ours at last!

All schools and factories, the surrounding kolchos and markets closed at once. More accurately, they never opened. Children joined grownups for impromptu parades, the second time in a week. On this occasion there were no prepared programs, for which all were grateful, and so attendance was greater and more spontaneous than for May Day. Nobody needed oratory to bring tears of relief and shouts of happiness. Even in my sorrow, I smiled for my Polish friends.

"Our husbands and sons can come home!" the women cried, having nothing more to go on than faith. It was touching to hear. Especially since troop trains continued to roll through the station, bound for the Far East where the war still went on against Japan, and the Soviet expected to join.

"Now we can have new shoes," an old man said, contemplating his rag-wrapped feet.

"Peace will bring us 'Golden Times,' " his friend agreed, quoting from The Artists' Cinema.

"Long live our Leader," a commissar cheered, with scattered approval.

"Thank you, God," a one-legged veteran muttered, scowling after the commissar.

Squads of soldiers marched through the streets, firing rifles into the air. Before noon many a flask was drained.

To the Polish Patriots assembled that evening in their club, the speechmaker's promise: "We shall return all men to their fatherland," seemed emptier than the vodka bottles strewn about.

"Jac," said Mischka, "if anybody wants to hear of suffering and sacrifice, let him interview us."

I agreed but couldn't answer as somebody started another discourse on "binding up Russia's wounds."

"They should think of the wounds inside men that can't be healed," one of the deportees said. "Who actually has a home or family in Poland? In Latvia, Lithuania, or Estonia?"

"I certainly don't," said another. "Two days after our deportation old Mrs. Stinkwicz, the hypocritical she devil, moved into my apartment with her family. I know she went to church every day, and I'll bet she prayed I wouldn't return."

There were more embittered asides, as the day closed with another feast at which rhetoric gave way to heaping platters of mutton, rice, and potatoes. For once rations were adequate for appetites, and the celebration lasted into the night. Meanwhile the Poles became strangely formal, using only their own language and clustering together as if a message had been passed. I stuffed a few rolls in my pockets and went home.

A few weeks passed with no important changes in the life of Omsk. The work went as always. Quotas were assigned and increased when met. Food was just as expensive, clothing and commodities as scarce as ever. Munitions factories continued full speed, as if victory in Europe had only been a practice period. People conscripted for work weren't sent home at all. The only things altered were the slogans:

"Who Wants Peace, Must Prepare for War!"

The promised Polish Republic remained theoretical, and none of us troubled to discuss its indefinite future.

The public bazaar assumed a more prosperous appearance, however, but not from the expected output of civilian goods. A trickle of veterans had begun to arrive from the front, bringing with them all manner of "souvenirs." Each man seemed to have liberated something from Germany, until we wondered how they packed it all so far.

There were plenty of Leica cameras and assorted photographic equipment, offered cheap, but since there was no film they roused little interest. Also for sale were several pianos, bathtubs, and radio sets the service men had lugged across Eastern Europe. People admired a samovar a soldier had transported on his back, a large gas-heated model which the Russian declared would warm water without coal or wood.

"Turn this valve," he explained, but neglected to say it must first be attached to a gas line. When a *kolchosnik* bought it, the soldier confided that the "faucet" was out of order and promised to repair it when he was rested.

I purchased an American army overcoat, mainly because of its handsome buttons. The G-Ivan was generous in his praise of American equipment, and particularly of the tasty rations they had. He

257

said, "I would love to spend just one day among those chocolate-eaters."

One June Sabbath the boss sent me to an outlying kolchos for a load of hay. I started late so as not to spoil the entire day, but upon arriving at the Progress Collective found the village deserted.

Driving through the single street, I overtook several peasants in holiday attire, hurrying toward the local cemetery.

"Where's the Sawchos, father?" I accosted an old chap who lagged.

"At the cemetery with everyone else," he snorted. "Why shouldn't he have fun, too?"

This puzzled me and I yelled another question. "What amusements does your graveyard provide, Comrade?"

"It's not the graves, but the mardi gras," he puffed. "Every spring it's staged there. Come, you'll see."

I gave the old boy a lift and presently we beheld, in a meadow surrounding the cemetery on whose walls the audience sat smoking Machorkas, a rural Russian shindig. It was just beginning: In a jumble of mixed fabrics, homespun and gay, a group of well-oiled males and giddy females had gathered for a prize competition of costumes and masks.

"Forget the hay, driver. You're just in time. The load won't run away," said the kolchos boss, escorting me to a front seat on the grass. It was pleasant in the sun, the place redolent of bruised clover and millet, with the girls washed up for the occasion and their hair done in braids. One or two looked not too bad, and after a couple of pulls at the Sawchos' bottle they appeared even better.

The boss, well illuminated by this time, was explaining: "Every year the villagers dream up and painstakingly make new costumes and masks, keeping them secret all the while. Then, on the appointed day, they are judged for three prizes."

The decision was in the hands of a dignified committee composed of the director of the itinerant movie, a local farmer, and the kolchos administrator.

At a signal the noise and merriment subsided, bottles were put away, everyone sat on the ground, and the show was on.

"Bring them before us." The chief judge required no megaphone as he blared the invitation.

From behind the cemetery wall a motley array appeared, spear-headed by three men, each playing a musical instrument with which he had obviously little acquaintance. The first carried an enormous and battered tuba, its bell gleaming golden in the sunlight as the "oomp, ooomp, ooomp!" provided background for the wailing clarinet. A third little man clashed two cymbals fiercely, in reasonable time with the others.

"Bravo, the best in Omsk is no better," yelled a half-crocked farmer, falling backward onto a grave.

This sally set off peals of laughter, and no frowning by the committee could restrain it. Then came the first competitor, a fellow dressed as a tree and calling himself "Spring." It was a most original and inexpensive costume, for the man had squeezed himself into a hollow birch trunk. Only his feet protruded. He minced toward the judges, peering through a slit in the bark, atop which for a crown he wore a small wagon wheel. A stork's nest was anchored on the wheel, and to the enjoyment of all, a stuffed stork with a movable bill (operated by a string from inside the costume) surmounted the getup.

"Klak, klak," the stork greeted as the ambulatory birch passed the judges. The crowd applauded.

Next came a towering apparition wearing knight's armor made from hundreds of corks sewn together, all coated with silver paint. This obviously had taken months to assemble, the only difficulty being that the knight had run out of corks and finished in everyday breeches which, however, he also had dipped in the paint. Dried, it now crackled and looked somewhat like Crusaders' mail, a wooden sword adding certain identification.

A woman in flowered dress and red shawl, and carrying a basket of fruit, was accompanied by a large wolfhound, who registered disapproval of the program by barking disagreeably at the stork. The dog, plainly resenting the stuffed bird, was more of an attraction than his mistress.

A fireman in a cardboard helmet came on; next the inevitable clown in a figured costume, and finally a peasant dressed as a pirate. The last was impromptu—a pair of wooden carved pistols and a breadknife thrust into his belt, a black bandage over one eye.

The audience was professionally critical and I gathered that originality rather than effort would decide the winner. The contestants formed a semicircle as the chief judge called on them for a bow.

"Comrades, we present Mask Number One, 'Spring.' "

As the birch tree inclined stiffly, the stork klak-klaked and the wolfhound lunged toward it. But the fireman snatched the leash and the clown fetched him a kick, so the dog bided his time. The spectators whooped at these diversions, being more interested in action than art.

"Silence, Comrades. Next is the Giant Posharski," cried the learned judge.

At this the knight stepped forth, drew and raised his sword in traditional salute, its hilt pressed to his forehead.

"Hey, Posharski, where's your beard?" a heckler yelled.

"Yes, what happened to the bush?" another jeered. "What a fake knight, without a beard!"

"Besides, he had a beard, and what a beard," a chorus of kolchos companions chimed in. "We have a picture of it at the club."

The knight glared and seemed about to crack the varlet's skulls when the chairman again interposed.

"Listen," he cautioned, "we want no harassing of the contestants. Posharski had a beard when younger, but he is now a senior giant— or knight," he corrected himself. The chairman was hazy on his heraldry.

"It's a lie," the audience chanted, "a lie, a lie, a lie. He lacks a beard, not we!"

At this they began whistling through their fingers, age-old signal of contempt, while Posharski's face grew redder.

When the motherly soul with the red shawl stepped up, the chairman said, "Little Red Riding Hood en route to Grandma, with her friend the wolf."

"Ha, ha! She looks more like Babushka herself," they guffawed, and a heartless wench suggested she let the dog go and appear as a witch.

"Fireman Petja," the chairman continued.

"Yes, the one whose own house burned down!"

So it went. The humor was heavy, personal insults profuse, deportment strictly from the barn.

It was a tough audience, but this was only a prelude. It took the committee half an hour to reach a decision, during which the beardless knight kept acting more bellicose. He took practice swipes at the clover, as if planning to behead someone if he didn't win.

"Comrades," the Comrade Chairman pompously arose to make the big announcement, "we unanimously award first prize of three hundred rubles to 'Spring'—the mask of the tree and the stork. Second prize of one hundred and fifty rubles goes to Posharski, the——"

"Robbers! Cheaters!" cried the knight, stamping the pasture and interrupting applause for the popular choice. "This is rank favoritism. Is that justice? My wife and I worked every night for months, piercing these damned corks with a hot needle. And now what do we get?" He snorted the answer. "A lummox crawls into a rotten tree and wins the prize. Phui!"

"Phui, is it?" the chairman turned to him sternly. "Let me advise you, Comrade: take it easy. With a beard, you would have won. But you don't even know that a knight must have a beard. Your lack of knowledge has cost you first prize."

"Beard or no beard," Posharski screamed, "I'll show this damned 'Spring' not to cheat someone of the reward!"

With that he swung the sword, slicing off both legs of the stork. As it tumbled to the grass, the wolfhound grabbed it in one leap, ripping it to bits amid shouts of the onlookers. At the same time the cart wheel came off "Spring's" head, landing on his bare feet, and his yelps added to the tumult.

With a muffled roar from inside the log, Comrade Birch now fell upon the berserk knight, and there ensued the greatest combat between trees and swordsmen since the Forest of Dunsinane attacked Macbeth's castle. The two contestants tore up the meadow, rolling over and over, while the crowd cheered and encouraged, having the time of their lives all for free.

When it became evident that the knight was getting nowhere against the birch tree, the boss rekindled Roland's ire by suggesting he fight someone more his size. This resulted in a second battle, the Sawchos bending to the knight's splintered sword while "Spring," somewhat tattered but now unencumbered by his disguise, joined in the spectators' laughter.

Indulgent farmers eventually separated the principals, but Comrade Sawchos had a black eye, the knight was ready for major repairs, the dog had galloped cross-country with the stuffed remnant of stork, and never did so much hilarity resound from a Russian graveyard.

"What a fool, I, to get smacked by that Posharski," the boss muttered as we went for the hay. "But anyway, Comrade, you saw a lively party, yes?"

"Yes, and you can say it again," I replied, for it was my funniest experience of the war. I loaded the hay and drove away, grinning all the way to Omsk. . . .

The fighting was over but the war dragged on. Life behind the lines continued as though the anti-Nazi campaign still raged over Europe, but with troops now heading in the opposite direction. We, the labor conscripts, kept producing for the Soviet front.

There was little or no change in routine: more quotas, the same pressures, the drab food, the same low pay. I was no longer approached about or involved in shady business, for Omsk was thoroughly controlled by the Party and police and whatever kickbacks and private enterprise may have existed were well above my low-echelon office.

There was a new element in the local economy, however. The returning veterans brought more and more loot from occupied areas of Central Europe, flooding the free markets. Most of the stuff was not adaptable to life in Omsk, unfortunately, as the city was still far behind in civic facilities. Except for clothing, a few watches and jack-knives, it was useful only as junk. So prices gradually slumped in the bazaars, and latecomers from Austria, Czechoslovakia, and Germany were disgusted at the poor returns on the articles they had lugged so far.

"The Soviets are getting a lesson in the laws of supply and demand," Mischka philosophized.

So the summer passed, with temperature pleasanter than on the sizzling plains of Uzbek and Kazakhstan, and soon early autumn hinted at another Siberian winter. I shuddered at the thought, wondering if this was going to be my life's work and permanent residence.

The months since I learned of my family's liquidation had served to weave a set of new ambitions and objectives. I had lost all desire to return to Mitau and considered now what the rest of the world might offer, although my only experience was with the depressing contrast I had survived.

"There is only one thing of which I'm sure," I told my companion Mischka. "I don't want any part of the Soviet Union. I have had my fill of this life, where, even if you like it, conditions require that to live decently you become a thief."

"I know what you mean, but from now on you had better keep such opinions to yourself, Jac. Even a friend cannot be trusted—if he is caught."

Mischka had a penetrating mind. I remembered that advice many times afterward. But with all his freedom-loving soul he agreed with what I had said.

The next day brought another step in our ultimate destiny. Both of us were summoned to headquarters by the NKVD. You do not delay in responding to such notices in Siberia.

When I arrived at the tall building in midcity, I was relieved to see other Poles also waiting. At the office we were greeted with cordial words and pleasant smiles and given a form to sign. So there could be no traps or misunderstandings the papers were in both Russian and Polish. Shortly after we received visas to Poland, prepared by sweetly smiling, well-mannered girls in the transients' department. Again, the official message was in both languages.

"Mischa Jac Feld, resident of Danzig," I read aloud to Mischka, as we walked alone outside. "That's the same fellow who was sent here as a criminal when he wouldn't take the Red Army oath and volunteer. Of course, he doesn't happen to be from Danzig."

"I have never received such polite handling from any policeman," Mischka mused. "I wonder what it means?"

"I have no idea, but I doubt if it means anything good. Still, I never thought we could fool them so completely," I replied in a cautious whisper. We were strolling along an open street, but one could never be sure in Soviet Russia. The stumps and fenceposts had ears—built in by espionage agents.

As the year 1945 drew to a close, we discovered why the girls were showing more interest in deportees. A matrimony campaign was being subtly pushed among Russian women, many of whom had looked over the casualty lists, received the bad news from the government, or counted their limited chances for a husband in a country where men were outnumbered by four or five to one. There was a regular dowry-and-courtship service if one had a few rubles to finance it, but this was only for selective persons. The really eager maiden and the truly lonely youth needed no such encouragement in the business of boy meets girl.

For my part, I had no trouble postponing such romantic affairs. Olga's attentions had become something of a luxury. My supply of money was limited and prospects for another quick coup were not good. To be sure, a Russian woman marrying a Pole was permitted to leave Russia immediately with him, and what sane female would refuse? But this would mean a traveling companion who might complicate one's exit. I decided on Kipling's rule: "He travels the fastest who travels alone."

Having no problems of the heart, Mischka and I went cheerfully to the New Year's Eve party where we expected to see evidence of this rapprochement of the sexes. To our surprise the authorities had provided an extra large hall, and the program became in effect a farewell party for the Poles.

Dressed in their best, which was shabby from years of wear and patching, the captive guests were on good behavior, providing their hosts a flashback to traditional Polish manners. Surprised Russian women were deluged with courtly bows and hand kisses, with the occasional presentation of an imitation flower corsage. Some of the boys from the club acted like kulak lords.

"And maybe they are," whispered Mischka. "Who can tell in this omelet of nationals?"

The Soviet representative of Omsk offered his arm to the Polish chairman's lady, and festivities began with a Chopin waltz. Everyone joined in sedate and graceful dancing; the drinking was dignified and in moderation. Everything was restrained and orderly.

The Russian and Polish anthems were played at midnight, with everyone standing at attention.

"Snovim Godom, Snovim Chastjem." We wished a Happy New Year all around. Way back in Omsk, we didn't recognize the preliminaries to promoting a puppet state.

"Drink, my comrades, to new happiness and a better life," the master of ceremonies proclaimed from a raised platform. This was an invitation to more serious intake of vodka, and within ten minutes the hall porter, having had a good start while others danced, collapsed and was carried out.

Time is of secondary importance in Soviet Russia. It has not even that high a priority in Siberia, and in Omsk it seemed to mean only perpetual postponements. We had been cleared by the NKVD, we had our Polish visas, and we had had our farewell party, but we still went to the same jobs and worked for the USSR. I began reading the papers, hoping to detect some change in our status, but all I read was praise for the approaching "democratic elections." New representatives from the Omsk district were being sent to the Soviet Council in Moscow.

It seemed a worthy subject for investigation, so I asked Sergei, chief drivers' instructor at the motor pool, to explain the Soviet franchise. He had a reputation for being informed, and was willing to share his wisdom. He was eating a herring sandwich when I found him.

"What are these elections I hear so much about?"

Sergei gave me a pitying glance.

"Dumbhead. Have you no eyes to see? Pictures posted everywhere of the candidates, and you ask about the elections. They are the nominees, and it is they who will be elected," he said.

"So many? Do you have that many political parties?" I pretended to be genuinely interested.

"Don't be stupid, Jac. You know there exists only one Party for us, and that's the Bolsheviki, but every section of the town can run its candidate, provided, of course, he's approved and of the Party. The one with the most votes goes to Moscow."

"Fine, Sergei. But do you call that a democratic election? It seems to me more of a popularity contest."

"Jac, I've always thought the Poles were fairly smart, but you must use your head for balancing sacks. Listen, in Soviet Russia anyone can be elected from any part of town, regardless of rank or position. Of course he must be of the Bolsheviki, but that is understood. If he isn't he doesn't become a candidate, that's all.

"Now then, in Poland the workers are not allowed to vote at all, much less run for office, and the other political parties try to squash the Communists. Is that your idea of democracy?" He assumed a lofty and sarcastic attitude.

I realized it was no time to suggest that the exact reverse was true; that all of our political parties had candidates and everyone voted in prewar Poland, exactly as in the Baltic States the Russians had also seized. But I compromised and "agreed" that his description was a revealing report on democracy. "You are quite right, Sergei, my friend. I can see it plainly now, clear as the water in a Siberian coal mine!"

I thanked him, and he was delighted with my Soviet-inspired metaphor. Sergei had not inspected the water in a Siberian mine.

The election was set for Sunday, but all day Saturday officials prepared. Large red curtains and stacks of propaganda leaflets were distributed to the voting places, along with heavy urns to receive the ballots. Early in the day people began to crowd around the booths, munching sausage sandwiches, although voting was a full day away. In the evening a big rally was held by the Party workers in a school building, where Comrade Kutschereva, a leading woman candidate, was introduced.

Unfortunately there was another of these serio-comic interruptions that spice most public gatherings beyond the Urals. At the height of the chairman's panegyric for Kutschereva, an enraged old man rushed toward the platform shouting and gesticulating violently.

"Thieves, robbers, beasts," he yelled, shaking a fist while staring beyond the speaker toward the schoolhouse wall.

"Stop your foul talk and let us hear your complaint," the chairman said. "What causes this uncultured behavior?"

"What causes it? The dirty thieves who took the school's clock while you've been talking. Look behind you, Comrade Speaker."

Sure enough, against the grimy wall the outline of a large clock loomed in the dust and the clock itself was missing.

"It was there half an hour ago, before this crowd entered. Now it has disappeared, and I, who am responsible for all property here, will be dragged to jail although everyone should have seen the one who took it."

The man had scarcely finished when police collared him and took him cursing and protesting to the lockup.

The next evening, after the totals were in, Comrade Kutschereva, as widely predicted, was winner in a landslide of a seat with the Soviet Council in Moscow.

31

"*EVERYTHING* loaded? You have more junk than when you started this tour of Russia."

Mischka had a sly way of alluding to things that was sometimes disconcerting. It prompted the landlady to remark, "Yes, he now has eight cases, a complete dowry. But when he came all he had was one bag and a knapsack."

We were taking leave of Omsk, and to judge by the parting comment one would have thought we were successful capitalists, proceeding to brighter bonanzas.

It was March 15, 1946. We had three months less than five years' captive service in Soviet Russia's war effort. The eight suitcases represented one man's worldly goods after those years of uninterrupted hard labor. At that, I had about eight times what my companions possessed, for I had been among the luckiest.

I had found friends among the unfriendly: Chardiroff, the Mennonite Klaus, Nowitzki, Ptschilinzew, Anushka and Timka, and finally Lessovski and Konski. Could I complain when I considered how others had slaved and made no money? I had been close to extinction several times, but always something or someone turned up.

While packing, I had reviewed my experiences amid the excitement which gripped all deportees preparing for home. Many of us had lost hope and now we met and checked the reports, reassuring each other it was true.

"The fact is we must leave. It's Moscow's order. We've accomplished what they wanted—emergency labor to release Russians for the front—and now we're surplus. Who wants Poles and Balts in the heart of the Soviet Union?"

Mischka as usual expressed the fact. He had been through the mill and learned the hard way. We had swapped adventures and freshened memories "to tell our grandchildren," as he said.

For some reason, the Russians wanted to perform little services for us at parting. They were sincerely sorry to see us go. Perhaps we had worn better than we thought, and in return we had to admit that it had been safer behind Stalin's front than facing German tanks.

"If I had remained in Mitau, I'd be dead now," I once told Mischka during a vodka session. We were both quite drunk and therefore confidential. He had pretended not to hear and it angered me. I told him to stop drinking and listen, but he laughed.

"Jac, the more I drink the better I understand what you're trying to say," he demurred.

Now all at once I realized what Mischka meant. My story was his story. It was every deportee's story.

We had performed our duty in the war, although against our will. Nevertheless, we Jewish nationals of conquered territories like Poland and the Baltic republics owed our lives to the fact that we had been sent away. Those left behind had been exterminated by the Nazis. So in the ultimate balance Soviet brutality actually had enabled us to escape that and since then we had slaved our way to survival.

Renee was among the Russian friends who came to help. He was in the garage and had an old flivver on which we piled our cases. A lift to the railway station was his parting favor. There was a lot of noise and handshaking, and my cantankerous landlady went so far as to peck my cheek in a farewell kiss. Toward the end she had been sweeping out my corner of the room.

268

The NKVD gave friendly assistance as we entrained for the outward journey. It was the same string of freight cars with benches and stoves, with this difference: Chalked on each car were the words *"Dla Zydow,"* (for Jews). The last car, however, was inscribed: "For Poles," which, after all the years spent combating discrimination by the Nazis, seemed a bit out of order.

I watched the "elite" of our labor gangs step aboard, and wondered at the grotesqueness of human vanity. Here amid a few Polish pictures and placards, including the familiar silver eagles of a dead-and-gone regime, the recent slaves from Soviet camps were resuming superior poses. These "patricians," who had endured the same indignities as we, now were speaking pure Polish while holding themselves apart in their gaudily adorned, but rickety and ridiculous, special car.

There was the customary confusion and noise, the same mixed crowds waving good-bye, the same haughty overseers locking the doors, and the familiar old signal—one long, one short blast of the whistle—and we slowly moved out of the Omsk station. There were also last-minute instructions and farewells to those deportees who had to wait for the next train. The passengers settled down quickly.

"I'm so damn happy I can't believe we're going," I whispered to Mischka. But how much more joyful I would have been had the train been taking me to home and family!

"Me too," Mischka said. "I've pinched myself, and it's true. This train definitely is going out of Soviet Russia."

We laughed, shook hands for the twentieth time, and opened the first food parcel. The government had given rations, and it was also possible to buy extras like hot soup or stew in the stations. How different from the ride in 1940!

The first large town was Petropavlovsk, where I had nearly become a Soviet soldier. On the platform I saw the sad, searching eyes of my countrymen still trying to spot a friend or relative as the trains went by. When the train passed Tokushi I recognized the rough training terrain on which with other *soldateska* I had repeatedly flung myself to avoid the oncoming "tanks."

We were off on another long ride through Russia, but this time we enjoyed it, for freedom waited at the other end. Or so we believed.

The homeward route was almost due west across the Ishim and Tobol rivers with their lengthy bridges, and after several days we reached the flaming city of Magnitogorsk. Everyone knew of this mighty manufacturing center where belching furnaces stood shoulder to shoulder like puffing Molochs supplying the war god Mars, and every head was out of the windows as we pulled into this arsenal of the Soviet Union.

There was a pause to take on fuel, water, and, most welcome, fresh rations. We had finished ours from Omsk, but this journey was no shambles like the deportation. To the best of their abilities the Red authorities made our departure easy.

At the end of the second week's travel, we came to areas overrun by the Germans during the war. The first big place was Kursk, still a wreck from enemy shells and bombs.

"A masterpiece of destruction," I said, scarcely able to comprehend now that I saw it.

"There will be worse, I'm sure," Mischka gloomily predicted.

The trees in what once were forests stood bare, blackened by fire, dead. Villages near the city were also destroyed. Nobody moved in the rubbled streets. In fact, nobody could move in most of them. Streets and buildings jumbled, a continuous heap of masonry and debris.

Empty windows yawned from gaunt ruins like the toothless mouths of witches. Huddled against a hill, a German tank pointed its cold gun like Death's finger, toward the sky. Farther on, a whole column of wrecked tanks lay as still and useless as the bodies of those who had brought them there. A troop of German prisoners removed bricks from the streets, the same quiet streets on which their bombardments had rained.

Next day we came to Orel, due north on the way toward Moscow. It was no different from Kursk, and in some respects worse. The closer we drew to Poland, the more complete the destruction. Many of the Poles had become silent and depressed by this time, sensing what it would be when they reached the border. We were crossing White Russia's soil, and the winter was almost gone. Melting snow had left large ponds in fields and beside the roads. Nature was awakening after its long sleep, but the towns we passed were not going to have a rebirth that spring.

I studied the terrain as we clattered along. Wonderful black Russian soil, it cared not who tilled it. It produced the grain, the potatoes, the fodder for the cattle and sheep that fed Russia's people. All that soil asked was someone to work it. Never had it begrudged or denied

270

a living—the bread, the minerals, the fuel that man requires for civilized existence—yet contending men had desecrated and despoiled it in a struggle that obliterated everything except the good, productive soil.

We looked back at the hills, the forests, the steppes, and the mighty rivers with contrary emotions. The train was nearing the border, but each of its passengers was leaving a tiny bit of something back there in Russia.

The train slowed and stopped, heads out of the windows again. There!

"Hi, Polski?"

The border policeman with rifle and eagle insignia was obviously Polish and a symbol the deportees had waited six years to see.

"Isn't the uniform splendid?" said a tailor with an eye to national lines.

"The shoes—genuine Polish workmanship." This from a cobbler who had been making footwear from discarded inner tubes.

"He marches so proudly," a peasant girl remarked. She was one of the few I had seen who lived through the captivity.

A youngster leaned out to admire the uniform and almost fell to the platform. Meanwhile the superior Poles played their national anthem and sang, having organized a band during the ride. It was a pathetic show of patriotism by slaves returning to a country conquered and divided by both vanquished and victor. Nor could any at that time foresee the subjugated role that lay ahead for Poland.

The music stirred few, and reality soon returned to the meditative passengers. The fact was we were from widely spaced places in this country we called "home," but our true home had been eliminated or destroyed. Jewish youths could expect no family welcome, no return to customs, traditions, or the warmth of familiar scenes from which Soviet police had torn them in 1940.

"So we come back to a country which isn't ours. Where do we fit in?" Mischka summed it up.

It was all quiet when we reached Przemysl, the first important city beyond the border. To our amazement it stood unscathed. The forces of conflict, as if remembering its suffering in the first Great War, had bypassed this Galician juncture on the age-old route of invasion. We were allowed to go sight-seeing during the hour in which the train was resupplied.

271

It was Easter Sunday and the first time I had felt any Sabbath spirit since leaving Latvia. Strangely, the city reminded me of my boyhood. I could hear the subdued summons of a church bell, just as in Mitau when Trinity's great chimes called to me the day before the Russians arrived. Odd, how a long-unheard note carries one across the years!

Deep in thought, I strolled toward the church. I forgot the surroundings and train to which I must soon return, for immediately upon turning a corner I seemed to step into yesterday. Here were gentlemen in fine clothing, high hats, and carrying canes, each escorting his silk-clad lady to devotions. They walked past me into the churchyard, the men doffing hats and exchanging stilted greetings—exactly as they had before shells and bombs reduced gentility to a memory.

It had been so long since I had beheld people going to church unmarked by war's privations that I stood gaping, a foreign bumpkin in felt boots and ugly fur-lined jacket. It didn't occur to me that I must be as incongruous and surprising to them.

Presently a coterie of uniformed officers appeared, on their arms young matrons attractively gowned in remnants of prewar fashion. Their laughter subsided when they saw me, and my reverie was as quickly shattered.

"Attention! March step. Eyes right—to the surviving Jew!"

The ranking young Pole snapped the command with a smirk and his companions promptly moved into single file. Then with an exaggerated goose step, they strutted past in mock review.

It was over in a moment, and they broke into loud laughter, clasping arms with the women to hurry inside the church. Trembling and deeply hurt, I hurried back to the train. The Sabbath spirit was gone. The town looked ugly now, and the unpainted cars with their unkempt, unwashed, unwanted passengers seemed a place of refuge.

I didn't tell anyone what had happened, but my soul seemed to shrivel and I slumped in a corner, brooding. Was this to be our reception in the world beyond Soviet Russia? Had we offended, by surviving hard work and misery? For the first time I felt a twinge of apprehension, a touch of fear that all the victory and release could not erase.

The ration master had a surprise when the train moved out of Przemysl. Each car received a carton of matzos marked "Gutkin,

272

made in USA." Somewhere across the seas, our people knew that some of us had lived.

The remainder of the ride was uneventful. One by one the cars emptied into towns and cities the fighting had shattered. It was a sorry home-coming for Polish Jews. There were no welcoming committees or waiting friends. The last car with its elite had already been vacated, but Mischka and I rode on to the end. It was now weeks since we departed Omsk. But why not ride? We had no home anywhere; we didn't even know enough Polish to explain why.

"Last stop, Breslau!"

What a dismal destination. The old capital of Silesia lay in rubble like its sister cities, the railway station half destroyed and black-market operators swarming through the remainder selling American cigarettes.

"Camels or Chesterfields?" a youth asked when I paid the exorbitant price.

"Either. It must be better than Machorka."

Better? It was pure delight. Mischka and I inhaled as if the smoke dripped honey, agreeing that never had anything tasted so good.

"Can one eat smoke? This is better than breakfast," he said.

A pair of young women approached, inquiring: "Who needs quarters for the night? A place to sleep, Comrades." Their expressions suggested more accommodation than a place to rest. We hurried off to explore the terminus of freedom's journey.

Breslau had suffered terribly, but already it had recovered some of its commerce. Temporary stores were full of merchandise, so inviting we stared at it with open mouths.

"We're acting like the Russians when they invaded the Baltics," Mischka reproved.

Four of us rented a cart and pushed our baggage before us as a Polish official led the way to transients' quarters. They were in Victoria Street and rather dilapidated even for Breslau. We didn't unpack the bags, but flopped on the floor and slept. It had been an exhausting ride across Russia and Poland.

"All ready? We have work for you," the man said next morning. He was an officious sort, walking stiffly in front as if he had been a drill master.

"What kind of work?"

"You'll see. It won't hurt you," the Pole replied.

A large warehouse around the corner contained housefurnishings for our quarters. There were literally hundreds of beds, couches, cushions, eiderdowns, and blankets. There was no end of kitchen utensils and beautiful porcelain, crystals, portraits, carved sideboards, chiffoniers, and tables.

"Help yourselves," the man invited, "it's all yours."

"But whose stuff was this?"

"The damned Germans, masters of the world. Whose else?"

"That too?" I picked up a candlestick engraved with the Star of David.

"That also, Peter Pan. So God's justice comes full cycle. They stole everything from you, including your homes and happiness. Now you return to claim some of it back, and they are leaving Breslau as beggars." The official had obviously made this speech often.

It was a logical rationalization, but it gave me a queer feeling to touch the uprooted articles that once had adorned quiet households.

My eye picked out some toys: a rocking horse without a head, a doll's crib; a child's bonnet near a framed photograph of a mustached grandpa from the Kaiser Wilhelm era. Instinctively I was repelled by such evidence of persecution; no doubt most of the owners had had no actual part in any German looting.

"It was always that way, wasn't it? The innocent suffer for what the wicked perpetrate," Mischka said.

Burdened with all manner of furnishings, we returned to the apartment to establish ourselves in comfort. I took no pride in the whole business, and decided I would soon be moving again. A long column of civilians—men, women, and a number of undernourished children —blocked our way at a street intersection. All had numerals on their backs, and each clutched a few personal belongings. Their heads were bent, and the women and children wept.

"The *Herrenvolk,*" Mischka said. "They are leaving us."

"But not voluntarily," I observed.

Polish soldiers marched on either side of the ragtag column. They carried rifles, but that wasn't the worst. As the Germans were herded along, Polish citizens reviled and cursed them at every step. Some of the abuse was harsh even to ears accustomed to Kirghiz and Kazakh commentaries. It didn't become the Poles. Nor did it do honor to Eastern Europe to reverse the role of revenge and injustice.

At intervals someone would step forward and try to strike the de-

274

parting Germans. A few kicked them. Some threw stones. It wasn't a pretty exit and I, who had seen its forerunner in Latvia under the Reds, was sick at the sight.

Mischka again had a phrase for it.

"Jac," he said, "this is where we came in."

32

"*POLAND* is not for us," I said to Mischka a few days later.

"No, but what do you suggest?"

"Let's go anywhere, as long as it's away from here. I hate this place. Did you hear what happened last week in Lydia? Seventy Jews murdered by Poles."

"By guerrilla fighters who got weapons from Hitler's supplies. Some were caught and hanged, I hear." Mischka took it in stride.

"It's not only the collaborators. Some of the officer martinets think because they're free of the Nazis they can keep robbing and killing Jews as before. These are little pogroms, Mischka. They will get worse. For you and me. . . ."

I had been suppressing my inner tumult since the churchyard incident in Przemysl. That was the beginning of a readjustment. We, who had also served, were not welcome in repartitioned Poland where they were now ousting Germans and moving into their properties and provinces. It was a political version of musical chairs on the grand scale. We were left out. The invaders came, conquered, and commandeered, and the people shifted, according to who won or lost.

Mischka knew how I felt and motioned for silence. The apartment assigned us was crowded, and one never knew who listened for the benefit of others. We were all strangers, from many corners of Eastern Europe and with divergent ideas and aspirations. Discretion had high priority.

No matter how we placed the beds, our room looked like a hospital ward. Maybe the white enamel frames and bare walls made it so. I was getting the jitters under such conditions and with curious and hostile eyes always upon me.

At night we slept uneasily, having equipped ourselves with knives and some old swords found in the heaps of household goods. They must have come from a museum, but I sharpened one so it would slice off an attacker's head. If Poles who couldn't get over their bloody ideas came after me I would at least give them a battle. Although Hitler had been gone nearly a year, the poison he spread was still in the air, fouling the minds of many who mingled with the liberated.

"We can't stay in Breslau," Mischka finished my sentence. "When we report to the Polish police they'll discover you are not a Pole and order you back."

"Back where?"

"The Soviet province of Latvia? Maybe Omsk again?" He shrugged, and a chill went clear through me.

We decided to leave at once. When we reached the Polish border we would seek an escape route.

My limited Polish vocabulary, the fact that I had pseudo Polish nationality, plus the periodic questioning by Polish authorities left no alternative for me. Sooner or later they'd discover I was an ersatz national. Mischka fell in with my plan; we secretly packed one suitcase each and mapped a course. We would go first to Lodz which lay northeast in old Poland, then double back toward the German port of Stettin. We left enough stuff in the room to avoid suspicion.

On a Tuesday evening we waited for the train. Poles from everywhere were flooding west to resettle in the newly awarded province of Silesia. Thousands of them had been evicted by the Russians in 1940 and more had left war-ravaged villages and cities in and around Warsaw. Each peasant had been promised his own farm, one of the false hopes that spurred the migration.

As I looked about, there were few happy faces. Some were already retracing their steps, cursing the Polish-Russian administration that failed to promulgate announced programs. The "farms" were a mirage; there was only a desolate, unorganized waiting time.

The cars were jammed and we stood up all the way to Lodz. It was a worrisome trip through dark forests; every time the locomotive slowed or whistled, passengers would bless themselves against attacks by the AK—patriots' army.

"With your luck we won't be stopped," Mischka said.

We reached Lodz late but without trouble.

This was another surprising city. It had escaped all damage. European-style stores were crammed with goods. One would suppose nothing had happened in the seven years since Hitler struck. Mischka, deep in thought, nearly walked in front of a car and I grabbed him just in time.

"This is my home town," he announced. "I never would have guessed it was still like this."

We began to make calls where Mischka's friends had lived. Every house had been taken by a stranger. The Jewish occupant had disappeared.

"They left no address," was the invariable reply.

But we could see the astonishment in many a Polish face. At the place where Mischka had once lived the new landlord, courtesy of the Nazis, could scarcely believe that the former tenant would reappear.

"Such a coincidence! That you . . ." One of them didn't complete the sentence. He meant, of course, what bad luck that this particular Jew, Mischka, had remained alive to return and trouble him.

But Mischka and I had other plans. We didn't want to stay in Lodz or any part of Poland. This was no place to begin again.

Waiting for accommodations to Stettin, I fell into conversation with a young fellow from Latvia. We became excited when it developed we had mutual acquaintances. He was from Riga, and had made a serious mistake in his travels.

"I went back," he said slowly. "It's worse than here. Nothing but Russians. Communist bureaucrats. Completely changed."

"Did you know Mitau?" I asked, hesitating.

"Mitau? Mitau. . . ." He stared at me wonderingly. "Your town?"

"My home, yes."

"Don't ever go back," he spoke abruptly.

"You saw it?" I grasped his arm.

"Can you take it? . . . Then listen. You remember Trinity church and the island? The ruins are all that remain. The church steeple is badly damaged, and the city water tower still stands. But the place was fought over for weeks. The Germans took it and lost it, retook and relost it several times. When the tanks had passed over, Mitau lay flat—completely ruined. You can stand on one side of the stream and look across the site, as over a meadow. Everything is burned or knocked down." He paused and put both hands on my shoulders. "My friend, don't ever go back," he repeated.

While in Lodz we heard of a Jewish committee helping refugees to Palestine where a new homeland was in the making. The radio sputtered with reports of revolt against the British mandate, attracting young fellows without family to new adventure. We agreed to look into this when we got to Stettin.

It was an eight-hour ride, but this time we traveled in style. Although it was a local train that stopped at every hamlet, we rode on cushions in a compartment, as regular passengers. Mischka answered for me at the check points, handling the credentials so control authorities would ask few questions. We couldn't afford to gamble on my clumsy Polish.

Stettin like Breslau was a battered German city which had not yet changed to Polish dress. Street signs and inscriptions were still German and the trolley cars contained the same old placards. At the Jewish committee headquarters, I was glad to see several friends from Uzbekistan and Leninpol. They were coming out of all Soviet areas, from the Black Sea to the Baltic, from Siberia and the Asian steppes.

"Our homes are gone, but now we have a new homeland," the registration official explained. "Would you like to join the volunteers?"

"For Palestine?" I wasn't sure what he meant.

"Of course, Palestine. Where else?"

The suggestion had an evangelistic quality that stirred me. Resentments I had harbored since arriving in Poland weighed heavily against

280

further wandering and flight. I detected a new, unifying spirit in this offer and asked what would be required.

"Military service, for a time. Strict training and preparation."

Mischka tugged my sleeve. "Let's think this over," he cautioned. "We can come back tomorrow."

How strange that those who had survived the Nazi liquidations, the Soviet deportations and forced labor, the unnumbered hazards of wartime and its disruption of human affairs—all these would now be welded together ready to fight for a free and independent country of their own.

More important, the privations and toughening experiences of slave labor made rugged candidates of these youths. A fully operating underground was passing them along by truck over secret but dangerous routes via Berlin. Everything was handled through the committees, at no cost to the individual.

"It looks good to me," I suggested to my companion that evening.

"You must be crazy, Jac. What's happened to your judgment? I had enough of soldiering at that dismal Siberian camp. Dying for a potential fatherland isn't my idea of new freedom," Mischka emphatically declared. "What do we know about Palestine, anyway?"

"It's better than no country at all, or one that treats us as they do here. I'm not going back to Russia," I argued.

"You've forgotten the battlefield cemeteries we saw along the railway, haven't you? Those heroes are rotten in their graves by now. And who remembers a single name? Who will think of them any more, and it's only a year since it ended? Except for the pious orations at a few ceremonies once a year, the living don't care a damn who died for the fatherland!" Mischka was shouting now. He worked himself into a bitter mood whenever military activity was mentioned. He truly hated war and everything connected with it.

"Your mind is made up?" I hardly needed to ask.

"And so is yours. We want none of this folly. Otherwise we go separate ways." He laid down the ultimatum.

There was nothing I could say. Without Mischka I would be lost in Poland. The police would turn me over to Soviet authorities. As a Latvian I would take the long ride back. Under no conditions must that happen.

"I'm with you, my friend," I said, and we shook hands.

281

We soon discovered there was a private underground, better described as a border-running firm that charged a fee. But it took time and connections, also a good sum of cash. We found it difficult to make the necessary contacts, as together we roamed Stettin.

One day we met the least likely intermediary, an elderly holy man who seemed to have time on his hands. Despite his robe, cap, and beard, he knew the proper party.

"Let us go to a restaurant and talk," he invited himself, indicating the expenses were ours. His fee would be 300 zlotys, and a liaison would take us to the boss. Then the old scoundrel lifted his eyes toward the sky and prayed. It was thoroughly out of place and prompted one of Mischka's tempers.

"Look here, Uncle. Do we pay this other bird, too? And maybe he wants to take us to someone else?"

"Oh, no. He works directly for the boss. Mine is the only preliminary fee," the holy man explained.

We paid the 300 zlotys. We were to meet the following day in the park.

"What do you think of the holy thief?" Mischka demanded after he left. "I say he's a crook and the beard also is false."

But next day our holy operator was there as promised, the liaison with him. We were conducted to an undemolished house in midcity; two quick raps opened the door.

A Mr. Mogilewski took us to a private office. He came directly to the point: "Do you men have money?" We nodded.

"To Berlin?" More nods.

"Much baggage?" We said no, very little.

"Aren't you carrying bacon or Ami cigarettes?"

"Why?" we naïvely inquired.

"Why? To make money, you fools. But don't come around with a couple of suitcases after the arrangements are made. Understand?"

We understood.

The man's daughter, beautifully attired in a new nylon gown, entered and whispered to the pudgy racketeer. He suddenly was in a hurry.

"Are you boys ready?" he asked.

"Ready," we replied together.

"Well, pay me then. That's the first move here, gentlemen. It will be thirty thousand zlotys."

282

Mischka and I nearly fell off the chairs. We stared at Mogilewski, who glared back. "What's the matter with you? The usual price is forty thousand zlotys, but you aren't clumsy kids so I'll make a reduction for less risk. . . . Chaim"—he ordered the holy one—"see if there's room for two more."

"But Mr. Mogilewski," Mischka began, "we're just out of Siberia and don't have that kind of money. Together we have only five thousand zlotys and we'll give you every bit, if you'll take us along."

"Five instead of thirty thousand? Who puts up the other twenty-five?" He turned angrily upon Chaim. "What sort do you drag in to me? These aren't customers, they're displaced beggars."

Chaim reading his prayer book, said nothing.

"All right, twenty thousand zlotys, or you can walk it," Mogilewski growled.

We shook our heads as he held out his palm.

Chaim, our 300 zlotys hidden away, rocked back and forth in prayer. We rose sorrowfully and without a word walked from the house of the holy and greedy patriots. Poland was getting worse every day.

The possibility of getting to Berlin receded as our funds went for food and living expenses, but just as I was ready to join the underground organization we happened upon a youth who gave us guidance.

"There are several small German freighters that run between here and Berlin," he told us. "They bring freight but return empty. I know a captain who'll take you for two thousand zlotys."

We jumped at the opportunity. Until that moment neither Mischka nor I had known that water transport from Stettin to Berlin had resumed.

The freighter *Leningrad* formerly bore a German name and Nazi flag. But that was before the Thousand Year Reich disintegrated. The youth led us down a steep stairway to the quai, where a broad view of the harbor revealed the converted German ship towering above smaller coal freighters anchored together. All were hauling reparations from Berlin to Soviet ports. That explained the one-way cargoes.

Our young friend entered one of the small launches at the wharf and returned with a seafaring chap in a dirty cap. His name was Wilhelm, and he walked us down the dock to confer, stuffing the cap in his pocket lest Russians identify him.

"It's easy as smoking a cigarette," he assured us. "Once aboard the freighter you're as good as in Berlin. You'd have to be especially unlucky to get caught."

"But the control authorities?" I demurred.

"Our KP-Twenty carries nothing but reparations for Russia. Our papers are in order, the Reds are friendly, you have nothing to fear," Wilhelm said firmly. The inference, of course, was that the Russians didn't bother the ship's racket.

We agreed on 4,000 zlotys for the two of us, and that at one o'clock in the morning Mischka and I would slip aboard. During the evening we bought a few odd items and stuffed them in our suitcases, cheerfully cursing the greedy Mogilewski and his gang while getting ready. We also bought a fine farewell-to-Poland dinner.

Wilhelm was waiting impatiently, his motor running when we went down the ladder.

"Let's go, let's go," he rasped, and in fifteen minutes we were on his vessel, in a cabin next to the coal bunker. We curled up in the bunks, whispering in the dark about our good break. A melancholy Stettin clock struck two, but the slap of water against the hull was a lullaby for me. I awoke to a faint tremor as the propellor turned and heard Wilhelm aloft call, "Stay below, we're starting."

Mischka and I watched through the porthole as the *Leningrad* slowly began its journey up the Oder toward Berlin.

Captain Wilhelm was on the bridge when we came on deck about noon.

"A fine day, boys. No Russians in sight. When we reach the locks at Hohen-Saaten you can stay on deck in the sun all the time."

We steamed all afternoon and evening without seeing more than fields, forests, and an occasional river village along the shores. It was a slow and restful voyage.

Next morning, while I spelled a fireman at breakfast, two Russian patrol boats sped up. Inspectors came aboard, but Wilhelm had cautioned us to stay below and to busy ourselves like crew members. Mischka hid in a corner, but the Russians only scanned the skipper's papers, asked about contraband cigarettes, took a couple from the pack he offered, and without glancing below left the ship.

"See what I mean?" Wilhelm gloated. "They asked if I had American cigarettes and liquor, so I said no. The fact is, our coal bunker is half filled with cartons."

We passed the Hohen-Saaten locks which seemed to hoist the

freighter as if on a bridge, an astonishing technique. When Mischka saw the guarding Russian troops, he hurried below again. Thereafter we were in German waters exclusively and met no more patrols. That evening the fireman played his harmonica while the captain's wife fried a bacon supper and we looked forward to our arrival next day.

There was a large British banner of welcome beyond the Berlin-Spandau channel, and little sailing boats rocked on the swell. I breathed deeply of the cool spring air.

"Well, we won't get to where we're aiming for a long time, but at least we're in Berlin," Mischka observed.

"In the British sector," I added. "No Russians at the moment."

"Yes, and that's a damned lucky thing. You and I would be just what they'd like to intercept and put back to work," he said.

We pulled up in late afternoon near the Spandau Bridge, the anchor chains rattling through the port.

Captain Wilhelm approached. "Well, boys, congratulations. We've made it, and you're at the end of a long passage—Omsk to Berlin. There's nothing like travel to improve the mind," he grinned.

We shook his hand gratefully and said good-bye. He was a German and our late enemy, but he proved the fairest and friendliest fellow I'd met since leaving the Soviet Union. But for him we might both have been sent back.

Clutching our suitcases, we climbed up the canal bank and were in a suburban region of Berlin. There was no war damage immediately at hand, and several British military vehicles were moving along the road.

"Well, Jac, Berlin's a big place. Where now?" Mischka put it up to me.

"A place to sleep. But first I'm going to see if my mother's old friend is still here. I know where she used to live."

"Were you here before, then?"

"Yes, in nineteen thirty-two," I replied.

Mischka looked at me in pity.

"Of course she's been waiting for you all this time," he snorted. "But let's go. You're a lucky bird, and you have the optimism of Daniel in the lion's den."

"Have you a better suggestion?" I countered.

Mischka smiled, and we picked up our cases.

"Taxi," he hailed. It was our first order as free men.

33

"*DO YOU* know Oranienburger Strasse?"

The taxi driver looked as sad as his vehicle, a dented relic with a large yellow disc painted on the door. It was larger than the yellow blotch the Nazis required Jews to wear on the left breast. But he knew the street.

"I will drive you to the tramcar which you take to the zoo, gentlemen. Then to the Friederich Strasse station."

Since we were as short of marks as the taxi was of gasoline, this was mutually agreeable. Everywhere people were digging in ruined buildings, hauling stuff on wheelbarrows and hand carts. The trolley was as crowded as in Omsk, and people turned it into a freight car. Some had large bundles of wood; others had potatoes in khaki sacks, buckets, or knapsacks. Young girls laughed too loudly with the British soldiers who blew smoke teasingly in their faces. The frauleins employed a language composed one part each of English, German, and Russian.

"Hallo, Johnny. *Komm heraus,* we are *da,* comrade."

There was continuous chatter, complaint, witticisms, and flirtation until the majority got off at the zoo.

"Amis, amis," an elderly German was muttering as the crowd swept him with us into the street. Did he mean Americans or the French word for friend?

At the top of Kant Strasse the utter wreckage moved Mischka to comment.

"What a monument to Hitler!" he said. "This is the world domination he went after. Look at that bathtub dangling from the fifth floor—sliced in two by the blast. I'd give ten years of my life to see him hanging in its place."

"The whole area has been flattened. What bombings this place must have taken." I didn't say, but wondered how many bodies were still under the rubble, for little of the wreckage had been sifted.

It was late afternoon when at last we arrived in front of 39 Oranienburger Strasse. Incredibly, it stood intact!

The little café next door, its gay green and white awning bleached white, remained as if nothing had happened since I lived there with my parents. Only the "hotel" sign had been replaced by a gleaming white disc. More of the reversal of fortunes, expressed in symbols.

"Well?" I turned triumphantly to Mischka.

"So, Jac, you've found your pension. But its concierge of those days? I still say the squirrels have overlooked you."

Mischka was joggling my *kasha.* That is to say, he was upsetting my equilibrium.

I flared back. "At least wait until we've had a look." I led the way up the short outside steps. An elderly woman looked at us, surprised.

"Does Frau Powejanski live here?"

"Frau Who, please?"

I repeated our former landlady's name.

"Gentlemen, we were bombed out and only recently billeted here. We have no acquaintance in this part of Berlin, but let's ask the neighbors. One of them has been here for twenty years."

She led us into the very room above the café in which as a child I had resided with my parents, fifteen years before. The good, solid furniture was gone, but the piano, too heavy to move, remained. I raised the cover, passing my fingers over the dusty keys. They were out of tune and twanged a protest, an old dog's snarl at being disturbed.

"Do you play?" the woman inquired.

"I did—once," I said.

"Ah, music, I love it. A little music and some strong coffee at evening, that's my delight. Do you by chance have coffee to sell?"

I stared at her, unbelieving.

"Where would I get coffee, lady? I'm just back from Siberia. Don't fool with us longer; where is Frau Powejanski?"

"Now, now boys," she soothed, "I realize you're searching for an old friend, but actually you want to sell coffee." She smirked confidently, and my anger spilled over.

"Look here!" I snapped. "I want to know what happened to my mother's good friend. That's all."

"I'm sorry if I've made a mistake," the woman stammered. "Do you mean the woman who formerly operated this pension?"

"Yes, yes, her!"

"I don't think you'll learn anything about her now. She was picked up in nineteen forty-one, has never been seen or heard of since. They wanted to take me, too, saying I was part Jewess, but my German husband was able to prevent it. We had a terrible time, though."

"Could we rent a room for the night?" Mischka broke in, bored with the chatter now that his prediction was confirmed. "We're mighty tired and don't know our way around Berlin."

"Yes, it's quite a distance to the International Relief Organization's camp, in Schlachtensee. I'm glad to accommodate friends of dear Frau Powejanski. You must stay with us tonight."

The tensions had relaxed. But another thin hope evaporated as I followed Mischka into the small, neat bedroom.

After a makeshift Continental breakfast with ersatz coffee, we went to a nearby barbershop to have our hair trimmed. We looked exactly what we were: two guys from Omsk. There was no use pretending. Even in battered, smelly, and jumpy Berlin, we were outcasts—despite the money in our pockets.

"We frighten these charming old ladies," I warned Mischka, breaking down his resistance to tonsorial treatment.

The barber also had a story for us. He claimed a certain kinship

289

by marriage, being a sort of Jew-in-law because his daughter's husband had been expunged during the open season of '41.

Those were working days in Berlin, and conditions no respecter of sex or age. Old and young, male and female, toiled in the ruined buildings, clearing away the debris. Piercing locomotive whistles warned pedestrians as temporary, narrow-gauge tracks for rubble cars wriggled among mountains of bombage—a new word bred by high explosive and damage.

"Look at it, Mischka. Those broken walls and tottery remnants are telling us, who sweated it out behind Stalin's lines, what it was like here, within Hitler's *festung*. They must have bombed this city day and night, without stopping, to smash it this way."

Mischka walked in silence, eyes appraising shrewdly the passing soldiers and civilians who scrutinized us in turn.

"Do you realize how many people were killed here? I am convinced, Mischka, we'll see the day when nations will have to forego the luxury of wars. One more might be necessary first, though."

"Are you completely daffy?" Mischka broke in. "Why don't you quiet down? One minute you're pessimistic about the Golden Age, the next you're ready to endure more war to eliminate what we're seeing. Jac, if you'll take my advice you'll look where you're stepping, keep clear of suspicious characters, and button up your lips!"

"All right," I muttered, but he couldn't prevent my thinking. Mischka was in a rut. He lived for today, one day at a time. He had no imagination. A real clunk, but a lovable and loyal clunk. I patted his shoulder, and we grinned an understanding.

War, as an American general once said, is hell, and Berlin proved it a thousandfold. Furthermore, I concluded, when a war is over the first forgotten are those who fought and died. Who lives best afterward? Not the veterans. Not even the generals who are retired.

No, indeed. The best of everything goes to the noncombatants, to those who smelled no powder and heard no shots in anger. In short, the ones who ran or stayed away have lived to see a brighter day. It's not heroic, but it's true. Even those picking rubble were better off than those beneath it. Who stops to inquire what courage and fortitude these people displayed? Of course, they have plenty to tell. But they have no audience, now it's over. A poor man and a dead man are worth the same the world over, except the poor man has to keep trying. I tried to put aside these depressing thoughts as we left the trolley at Schlachtensee.

"Let's rest a week or two, and find how things go here," Mischka suggested in his practical way, so we headed toward the IRO camp at No. 307 Potsdamer Chausee, about 500 yards from the Soviet sector.

"Keep walking, it's *gerade aus*," a man in US uniform told us in response to an inquiry. He was one of the camp officials who, like all postwar relief workers, wore the olive-drab costume with insignia and shoulder patch. He had the Yankee habit of mixing his English and German.

Several of our Siberian sufferers were already there, fattened up and looking no worse for six years' hibernation.

"Welcome to our lodge, Jac. And you, Mischka! Where's the blue-bird you've been chasing? Catch it yet?"

Mischka's pursuit of happiness despite our gloomy prospects had become the deportees' jest. He grinned tolerantly and said, "Somebody's feeding you better than *kasha*. Fat bacon, I'd say."

"Go in and sign up. You'll like it better than Uzbekistan," they said laughingly. "By the way, Jac, they've got plenty of towels here."

Thus we joshed each other about the bitter days.

Before us, sprawled along a two-lane highway, was the former German Supreme Military Command Post. But now a mighty banner—the Stars and Stripes of the United States—waved above it. As American Military Police in white helmets, white gloves, and smart uniforms dashed by on motorcycles, Mischka and I read the great sign in front of this place: UNRRA Camp 597. Our first glimpse of the United Nations in operation. Up to then its existence had been only an unverified rumor.

Uniformed guards opened and closed a heavy door through which glided sleek, new automobiles larger and more powerful than anything I had worked on in Russia. My jaw sagged at their power, silence, and over-all splendor.

"Come on, we're here," Mischka reminded.

We presented ourselves to the guard.

"Just arrived?"

"Yes, off the boat."

"Report at once to the police bureau."

The next fifteen minutes were crisp, cordial, but quickly over and we were enrolled as refugees from the Eastern areas. The only question was whether we were shuttling between Berlin and Stettin in unlawful trade. Convinced that we spoke the truth and were not involved in shady deals, they gave us temporary identification cards, a woolen American blanket and pillow, and a room in Block 50, our new dormitory. Crossing the plaza I stopped a moment to listen to the news of Palestine coming over the loud-speakers.

"Come on, come on," Mischka muttered.

The living quarters were like a first-class hotel, and our room surpassed all expectations. We had linen and mattresses on army cots, nightstands, reading lamps and literature, hot and cold water, and three full-course meals every day. Furthermore, there were bells to call us to the dining room—as if we might forget! After life in the Soviet Union we walked around dazed, as though someone had pushed us across the dividing line into Paradise.

During the first week we heard many things about UNRRA and the generosity of the American people who, through their government, were supplying everything we ate and used, including warm new clothing. The name of Franklin D. Roosevelt, the American President who died before the war in Europe ended, was praised repeatedly. I did not hear such things of Josef Stalin; on the contrary, the reports were that at Potsdam he had acted unpleasantly toward his Allies.

Common sense told Mischka and me that this delightful interlude could not last. As new refugees flowed in, the rehabilitated moved out. Thousands continued toward Palestine, where the new Jewish homeland was definitely rising.

"It's time we went on our own," Mischka said one morning. "We can't stay in a camp indefinitely. We have our lives to live."

So it was that after two weeks we signed on as chauffeurs and began transporting refugees to new homes. I drove an American Studebaker. As we learned our way around Berlin, we found that in a city of poverty and misery those with sharp wits could make more than a day's pay—with this understanding: He who did so lived dangerously.

"We're accustomed to chances, why soften now?" I challenged my friend, but he was curiously reluctant.

"Jac, this is a military occupation. The Four Powers get along like cats and dogs. If you start operations, be sure you have an escape."

292

"Don't you forget it, my friend," I shrugged.

That conversation was to return to me many times.

Meanwhile the weeks became months and 1946 drew to a close. The chauffeuring provided a variety of opportunities to make a little on the side, but there was one ever-present menace: Mischka and I were still Soviet subjects and armed Soviet soldiers literally swarmed in Berlin.

That was the rub. Our temporary identifications had no standing with Soviet troops and plain-clothes henchmen, and the latter had become the scourge of Berlin. They pounced upon sight-seeing Poles or Balts, demanding to see documents. Those from Latvia, Estonia, and Lithuania were bundled into jeeps or cars and hustled into the Red Zone. They were not seen again at the IRO camp. US protests piled one on another. Displaced persons? A dime a thousand.

But we were not the only ones to clash with Stalin's thugs. Berlin had become the vortex of Europe's human flood. Among the millions of displaced, all desperate to escape the postwar shambles and start fresh in life, there were some extremely tough characters. The incidence of violence increased, and it involved both soldiers and civilians.

Red Army prowlers, carrying pistols and looting at will, had made a hunting ground of the Reich capital. Attacking American GI's when off duty, they stole their frauleins in the parks, grabbed them on the streets and out of vehicles. Robbery, rape, and murder were common in the early days of the Occupation. Fraternizing was against Allied rules, but those who wrote the order had forgotten the human equation. Ill-feeling neared the danger point.

Then the US Command acted. General Eisenhower sent in the 82nd Airborne Division, a hardened combat outfit. In baggy pants and high-top boots they patroled jittery Berlin. A story circulated after the first couple of nights. Red marauders had gone out as usual, but this time on their dates the American troopers carried carbines. They didn't haggle with the attackers. There was no protocol, only the quick blast of .30-caliber rifles and automatics. Next morning the bodies were trucked to the sector barrier.

"Here, bury your dead," the paratroop sergeants told Russian sentries, and tossed the bodies from the tailgates.

"Not ours," the Soviet examiners shrugged, "they must be guerrillas in our uniform. This sometimes happens. Bad fellows. A mistake."

293

But they buried them. The word spread. In a couple of days the raiding ceased. But there were many incidents, and the snatching of those wanted by the NKVD continued.

Spies swarmed in underground cafés and night spots. It was foolhardy to venture beyond the Brandenburg Gate. The excitement got into one's blood, nevertheless, so that Mischka and I found it more adventurous to roam around the city than to wait for something to happen at the IRO camp.

The inclination toward Palestine increased. There was a growing sentiment among the young to start their own country, free of all that oppressed them elsewhere. Moreover, there was plenty of encouragement. Money was no problem; if you were willing to serve, the doors to the Middle East opened quickly.

"Sometimes it seems a wonderful idea," Mischka said. "Then again, we would be crazy to gamble our lives after the last six years."

"But the British won't fight us for long," I said.

"There may be others. Do you know anything about Palestine?" Mischka was solemn again. He had been reading a lot after I went to bed. But I could detect a change in him. The Polish experience, especially in Lodz, had rankled.

"It would be a change to have our own government," he said when the light was out and the book put away. "It will be a republic, of course. I wonder if we could all agree?"

"Why would we disagree, Mischka? We all want freedom, don't we?"

"Yes, but who agrees what freedom is? There are always two ends and a middle, unless we are going around in a happy circle and I don't think you find that in politics. But at least we all have a common denominator of suffering. These fellows who go to Palestine . . . does anyone ask whether their late fathers were rich or poor, educated or illiterate, socially important or not? Not that I have heard. All that is required is physical fitness and the desire to fight for a homeland."

The last phrase suddenly took on meaning. I had heard it over and over as my stateless colleagues discussed the future but had paid little attention, although some spoke with astonishing intensity. I had rarely seen enthusiasm in refugees anywhere, but here in Berlin, these men, eddying bits and pieces from war's rapids, entered this new whirlpool of events with fervor.

294

"Yes, that could be the reason we got here—to lead the way to better things."

The remark coming from me must have amused Mischka, for he studied me, and one of his rare smiles flickered briefly. "You too, my friend?"

"Sometimes." I stubbed out my cigarette, its half inch unconsumed in our new opulence. . . . God, but it was wonderful to have a decent smoke. I exhaled in satisfaction and relief such as I had not felt since jumping that night train out of Gusar. (That was ages ago, Jac, and you should be dead many times since. So now, what are your plans?)

"A great many sign up every morning," Mischka continued. "One never knows his fellow beings until calls like this. Do you know, Jac, I saw three of our trainee comrades from Siberia in yesterday's Palestine consignment? They missed the Red Army's glories because of their Polish allegiance; remember? None of us yearned for that fighting, but this is different. Yes, definitely different."

"What you're trying to sell yourself, Mischka, is a logical reason for enlisting. But can war ever be logical for the individual? And after what we have seen . . . how many rascals remember the hero dead, even at this early date?"

We had another smoke and, like amateur von Clausewitzes, discussed the extension of political action into war. We had the additional evidence of two World Wars which the old Prussian missed.

"If, as he argued, it's a logical development, then certainly our cause in Palestine is worthy. And we, without countries, families, or roots elsewhere, are prime candidates for the mission," I said, proud of this vestigial recollection of history. Mischka clapped his hands like an approving professor, an irony we both appreciated.

Whatever we might think, the fact was that thousands of young, patriotic Jews were moving through Berlin in a tide reminiscent of the Poles who were transferred from Soviet Russia to the Western front. I recalled the trainloads shuttling toward the Middle East and how, in the first weeks beyond the Volga, I had been moving vaguely in the same direction. Then someone had closed the escape route. General Anders had sufficient volunteers. The trains shuttled back whence they started.

"There will be no damming of this flow," Mischka promised.

"How many Jews can Palestine hold?" I wondered.

"A great many more than are there now. First the fighting troops, then pioneers to settle and make the land produce—oh, they'll explain all that while you're in line. There is literature, too."

"What about weapons? Who produces the guns?"

Mischka gave me a tolerant glance.

"With all the stuff taken from the Nazis? And millions of arms left around by the Americans? They tell me the Americans have more weapons still unpacked than they used on the Western front. If it's like cigarettes and chocolate there is no end of it. With enough tobacco, chocolate, and vodka—and these surplus arms—we could make a pretty good liberation in Palestine," he concluded.

We lay in the darkness, thinking. It was the first time, I had to concede, that something besides my personal desire had loomed as an objective. Perhaps I had not considered a future in the few days of a reasonably safe present. Until our arrival in Berlin, nothing had mattered except the day in progress. "Get through until tomorrow's sunrise, then look to sunset" was a Russian adage, but captive Jews knew its reality. I went to sleep with a blurred and completely inaccurate idea of Palestine, a homeland beckoning to me, a young man who felt he had no need of a new cause.

Next morning I hung around while the interrogation of candidates went on. Since most of them had been through years of hard experience there was no question of physical fitness. A few said they had relatives in some far country, but they wanted to join the forces in Palestine.

"They have made their own lives, now it is our turn," one tall, willowy youth said. "Can I have a machine gun?"

"Yes, a fifty-caliber if you wish." The recruiter motioned him into the next queue. "That's the spirit."

By 9:30 there must have been 200 waiting Jews, and I had seen none turned away.

Answering the first call at the motor pool, I felt again the pull of the phrase, ". . . a homeland. Homeland. Homeland."

Driving along the ruined Tiergarten, I could not know that the same phrase would recur to me a decade and a half later. That it would have full and exciting interpretation through the years. That I would learn at last how deep one's roots go, and that this sentiment, first experienced in this rubbled, reduced city of retribution,

296

would in the future cast illumination upon hazy, groping days when new adventure, new life, and new purpose again beckoned.

The weeks slid by. We were marking time, and it was evident that a subtle decision was taking form in our minds. We could not remain indefinitely in Berlin, and we lacked relatives and sponsors anywhere else. Mischka could return to Poland. But I was a Soviet citizen through absorption of Latvia by the Russian Government. I did not want to return to the misery I had so recently escaped.

One evening I decided to go to one of the smoky *kellars* where dancing, loud music, and vodka were mixed on the program. Mischka, deep in his book, said I was infected with what the GI's called "itchy dogs."

"Funny, these Americans. They call their feet dogs," he commented, but went on reading.

I got a taxi with two other refugees and we drove to the Kurfürstendammer, now brightening up under American restoration. It was a welcome change from Omsk and The Artists' Cinema. Besides, there were girls. The place was full of them.

I was on my second vodka and angling for a dancing partner when I glimpsed a familiar face at a side table. The young woman was also staring at me, and in a few strides I reached her.

"Sinoshka! You, here?"

"And you, Jac? You look so well. A long way from Mitau, no?"

She was still attractive although a little plump, but her poise had not deserted. The deportation years had brought premature lines, but Sina's eyes still asked saucy questions. I decided she was prettier than in my dreams at Leninpol. Besides, the little girl of Mitau had grown up.

"What happened?"

I looked at her companion, a stoutish chap who rose slowly and extended a hand.

"My husband, Josef," she said. "We came here from Poland, after the fighting. You must visit us soon, and we can exchange stories."

"Yes, we must be going now. There is no transport after ten." Josef paid the bill and I wrote down their address. Sina also seemed anxious to get away.

The next afternoon I looked her up. The address was that of a small house along the border of the British and Russian sectors, and

I parked the Studebaker down the block. A German and his daughter shared these quarters. Josef had a civilian job, reorganizing the food supply.

"It's in the Soviet area," Sina said. I began to understand how she had come to Berlin.

"And Ben?" I asked gently.

"Killed by the Germans. His father, too. Poor old Botshka. Ben hid and the Russians missed him for deportation. But when the silly old father stood in the street defying the German panzers, they ran him down, and then shot Ben. Mitau was a battlefield for weeks, Jac."

"How did you get away?"

"Some of us had become nurses with the Red Army. We retreated all the way to Leningrad. I was there for the siege and it was terrible, Jac. A half million starved to death. The Americans sent food across Lake Ladoga's ice and that saved us."

When the Russians pushed the Nazis back Sina's medical unit reached East Poland where she worked in a base hospital until the war ended. Josef had been a patient, being a Pole in the Red Army. They were married when he was ordered to Berlin.

"What are your plans, Jac?"

"Palestine, maybe." I didn't venture more, for now it was my turn to feel uneasy. Josef would, of course, know I was a Soviet subject.

"You work for the Americans. A lucky thing," Sina said, as the German girl at that moment entered the house. Sina introduced her, explaining that Maria was a secretary in the American headquarters. She didn't have to say how that had happened: one look at Maria was enough. I had never seen anyone more beautiful.

"I take passengers there frequently," I said, with a view to impressing both women. Yes, these were no longer teenage girls, and if they had been, the war's experiences would have hastened the maturity so evident in each. Maria was certainly the sort of girl one would wish to see again. And often, I decided.

Sina had excused herself, but returned shortly with a small tray on which were glasses and a pitcher.

"We have nothing better than plain red wine," she said. "We really should drink to something." She filled three glasses.

"To being alive," I said.

"Yes. To life. . . ." Sina joined me.

Maria closed her eyes and after a moment raised the glass.

298

"To a good life, in peace," she said in German. We drank, quickly.

I couldn't explain why, but suddenly I wanted to know more of Maria's story, and what had befallen her family in this blasted Berlin. Sina, perceiving my interest, rose and said, "Well, I have to make some kind of supper now. Josef has the appetite of a wolf."

"Yes, I've overstayed already. I'm due at the camp before five o'clock," I added, preferring time to think before any further encounter with her husband. But how to arrange a meeting with this fascinating Maria?

"What building is your American boss in?" I sparred for time.

"The former Wehrmacht headquarters. But it's next to impossible for a civilian to get in. We meet our friends in the canteen, two doors away."

"I know the place. Perhaps . . ."

"Say, you two are getting on very well," Sina laughed from the doorway. "Why don't you just make a date now and save time?"

Same old Sina, I thought, but why not be practical?

"We must have a chance to exchange experiences," I ventured, "for it interests me that anyone could have been in this city and come out alive. Would you want to tell me about it?"

"I might. If you care to listen. . . ."

"On Friday I usually drive to the American military headquarters. That's day after tomorrow. We could have an ice-cream soda in the canteen. About twelve o'clock, yes?"

"Yes," said Maria in a whisper, and then was gone.

Sina looked at me, extending her hand.

"Wherever you've been, whatever you've done, it has changed you, Jac. That is the first time I ever saw you take an interest in a female. Good luck."

We parted with assurances that we would meet soon, possibly for a meal in some black-market hole-in-the-rubble. My mind was already weighing possibilities for taking Maria on such an evening. I was also conscious that in all my reluctant travels, no member of the other sex had had such a startling effect on me.

What's the matter with you, Jac? Is life not already well complicated? Steady . . . steady. . . .

But Maria's face and her whispered yes to my impulsive canteen invitation pushed out more rational thoughts. I drove toward the refugee camp automatically, feeling much higher above the street than the low-slung seat of the car. I had closed one book, but in so doing had another one, more exciting, been opened? Yes, I must see more of this girl.

Mischka had gone to the movies when I returned. I glanced at the book he had left open on the table, surprised to discover it was a Bible. My eye caught the first three verses of the 40th Psalm:

I waited patiently for the Lord; and he inclined unto me, and heard my cry.
He brought me up also out of an horrible pit, out of the miry clay, and set my feet upon a rock, and established my goings.
And he hath put a new song in my mouth. . . .

Yes, I thought, it has surely been that way with us. The afternoon's report on Sina, on Ben, on Mitau bore that out. We, the deported, had been lifted out of a horrible pit. Now our goings might also be established.

Mischka apparently felt the same.

34

IT WAS the night before the New Year, a great holiday among our people who, although refugees, strictly observed the Day of Atonement. Camp 597 had never been so solemn.

But other things agitated Mischka. He had been restless all week, but the last two days he seemed especially upset. He would not leave me out of his sight.

"We have been spotted," he said as we walked together after dinner. "There are spies and informers here among us."

"In this camp? Soviet spies?" I was incredulous.

"Yes, and all they need is to hear our accents. Yours particularly. You are easy," Mischka muttered. And after a pause: "Rotten traitors, who work for Soviet money. One is from Leipzig, a German Communist."

"On whom do they inform?"

301

"Anyone who has Soviet citizenship, or belongs to an area now controlled by Moscow."

He looked at me and we didn't speak for several minutes.

I finally broke the silence. "When do we have to move?"

We had reached the camp gate, and as I spoke an altercation broke out inside the enclousure. Three German police had arrested a Jewish youth in a stolen Mercedes and were trying to drag him to jail. Naturally our fellows went to the rescue, belaboring the police. While the fight was on I disconnected the police car's ignition. When they tried to escape they couldn't start. US Military Police intervened just in time. The Germans were being pummeled on the ground.

Only when order was restored did we discover that the accused actually had taken the car. He had been doing a thriving business in such "liberations." The director changed his accommodation that night to the camp detention cell.

Mischka noticed a load of Russian plain-clothes men observing the melee, and his apprehensions doubled.

We discussed our chances after reaching the room.

"It would be a serious thing if they picked you up," Mischka pointed out. "I am Polish, so the worst they can do is send me back to Lodz. I wouldn't like it, but Poland isn't Siberia. But Jac, if they look you up . . ."

"I know. I know."

Through my mind ran thoughts of Chardiroff, Nowitzki, Lessovski, and the deals I had helped them put over. Did the NKVD have definite word on me? Or would I be no different from the other luckless drifters they grabbed and returned for slave labor?

"If they have my record, or somebody who was with me has squealed, we should move quickly," I said. "What I know about their production methods wouldn't look good in print."

"What about the rest of us? We've seen sovietism from the lowest workingman's level," Mischka snarled. "I've had a bellyful of communism and its lying crooks."

We both were expressing the fundamental truth about the system behind Stalin's lines. In war or in peace, its over-all deprivation of the worker had sown the seeds of corruption. In order to exist—to gain bare subsistence—honest and patriotic men were forced to steal and to lie. It had become an accepted part of the whole economic system.

"I can't take any more," I concluded.

302

"Then let's make plans," Mischka began. "Tomorrow I'm going on sick list. It's a holiday and our best chance. Maybe the secret police won't be out. I'll hide in the back of your car until we get to the US Military Police compound. I've made up my mind for us both, Jac."

"To Palestine? Or America?"

"Never mind. Just say I'm getting out of Berlin. What about you?"

"I'm staying," I said. "I must talk this over with a very special person."

"Business?" Mischka was skeptical.

"Partly."

"A girl?"

"Do you remember once I told you about a girl named Sina? She's here, and I've been to her home."

"Home? Surely not her family from Mitau."

"No, of course not. She's married and lives here."

"Where do you come in, then?"

"I've met someone else, through her. A girl named Maria. Mischka, we've been missing a lot in life. These girls, now. They aren't all the kind you see on the street and in cafés. This one is lovely. Beautiful, but intelligent with it. A blonde from over in ——."

"The Soviet side?"

I shook my head negatively and Mischka relaxed.

"I see," he said. "Or *maybe* I'll be seeing you—someday."

Explaining that I would be comparatively safe as the driver of an American military car, I tried to raise Mischka's spirits. Berlin was a good place to start for anywhere, I argued.

"If anything ever goes wrong, I've told the Ami MP's to hold the gate open," I told him. "Otherwise, I'll drive through it."

"You may have to," he replied. "They've had some practice the last few days. A dozen like us this week changed from here to American custody. It's the only escape route. This city is surrounded by Soviet troops. But we could get an American plane out of Berlin, where they can't stop us."

He spoke so earnestly that I wondered if he held back something. Then I saw his suitcase was packed. And mine was brought out of the closet.

"Mischka, what's it about?"

"All right, I'll tell you. I spoke to our American friend here in

303

camp. He gets counterintelligence reports. The Red agents have a list of names. Jac, yours is one of them. I asked what to do.

" 'Get out of Berlin. It's too hot for both of you,' he said. I'm going to take his advice. If you're smart, you will, too."

We each smoked a cigarette and turned in, but it was hard to sleep after Mischka's warning. I lay thinking for a long time.

If I had not met Sina I wouldn't have seen Maria. I had been with her only a few times, but I already knew I couldn't leave without some plan to return. But my number would be up then, as much as now. A little more time in Berlin, a few more weeks, and perhaps. . . . The place wasn't so bad to live in, once you became accustomed to the wreckage. I could hear Mischka's regular breathing and knew he slept. Never had I stayed awake unable to solve a problem as on this night. . . .

My first trip ticket was for 10:00 A.M. When I reported at the motor pool I noticed the blanket had fallen from the car's rear seat. It moved slightly as I looked in; I knew Mischka was there. My mind was not yet made up. But I must take my friend to the compound.

After a quick turn off the Potsdamer, to make it look like a local run in case a car was waiting, I doubled back two blocks beyond. Half a mile along the Chaussee a curtained vehicle pulled from the curb and began to follow.

"We have company," I spoke over the back seat, increasing speed. The curtained car kept up.

It was midmorning but traffic was light. The holiday, I supposed. No Amis in sight. I couldn't lose the pursuing vehicle, so slowed down. He also slowed. I knew how they worked. Another car would be waiting up ahead, and at a prearranged signal they would close from front and rear.

"German driver, two passengers," I relayed to Mischka.

"I hear you," the words were muffled. "How far to go?"

"Ten blocks. We can't speed."

I jockeyed for six more blocks; we were in a repaired stretch of the city where traffic lights were operating. I got through three of them. Then suddenly, and against the red, the accomplice moved in. He cut squarely in front, struck the left front wheel and fender to block me completely. We were 200 yards from the American compound. There was no time left.

304

"Here they come. Jump for it," I yelled. Mischka dived out head first.

The trailing car was on top of us, three men bounding for the doors. I jumped out the right side into the street, running in a crouch. Mischka rolled toward the sidewalk—but on the wrong side. Before he could rise two men swung at him with clubs as I ran for life toward the compound.

"Jac, this way!"

Was it Mischka? Or a trick to slow me down?

I kept running and the pursuing footsteps faded. I could hear shouts and curses, but no shots. A motor roared. I whirled inside the stockade gate and looked back. My damaged vehicle was still at the intersection. The accomplice had backed clear and disappeared. The other one had my pal, and then two men were pummeling something in the back of the kidnap car. It careened in a U-turn, speeding toward the Russian sector.

I looked after my best friend, the man who helped me get through Poland and into Berlin. Without him, I would never have made it. Now, trying to capture me, they had seized him instead. Had he anticipated what would happen? Was that why he hid, so they would grab him by mistake if it came to a fight? As a Pole he might talk himself free again, but I could not. And Mischka knew it.

Something was lying on the sidewalk where they struck him down. A small boy approaching picked it up and came to where I waited. It was the round fur cap that Mischka had worn since Siberia. "My lucky bonnet," he had called it.

"You lose this, Mister?"

I took it with shaking hands. It was smeared with fresh blood.

The American flag flapped noisy welcome above the entrance. My odyssey was ended. People were crowding around the disabled car. MP's were coming toward me.

Motionless and stunned, I stood safely inside the gate, my tears falling on Mischka's cap.